Cerro Prieto (Mexicali) ▲

San Felipe ▼

The moving finger writes,
and having writ

Moves on; nor all your
piety nor wit

Shall lure it back to cancel
half a line

Nor all your tears wash
out a word of it.

Stanza 71
The Rubaiyat of
Omar Khayyam

CAMP AND CAMINO IN LOWER CALIFORNIA

A RECORD OF THE ADVENTURES
OF THE AUTHOR WHILE EXPLORING
PENINSULAR CALIFORNIA, MEXICO

BY

ARTHUR WALBRIDGE NORTH

AUTHOR OF
"THE MOTHER OF CALIFORNIA"

WITH A FOREWORD BY
ADMIRAL ROBLEY D. EVANS
U. S. N.

The Rio Grande Press, Inc.

GLORIETA, NEW MEXICO · 87535

© 1977
The Rio Grande Press, Inc.,
Glorieta, N. M. 87535

First edition from which this edition was
reproduced was supplied by
INTERNATIONAL BOOKFINDERS, Inc.
P. O. Box 1
Pacifica Palisades, Calif. 90272

NEW MATERIAL

1. New Publisher's Preface.
2. New Scholarly Introduction, by W. Michael Mathes, Ph.D.
   (a) 72 contemporary but
       germane color photographs taken by Dr. Mathes,
       printed on 38 color plates.
   (b) List of other publications
       by author North, researched
       by Dr. Mathes.

Library of Congress Cataloging in Publication Data

North, Arthur Walbridge.
   Camp and camino in Lower California.

   (A Rio Grande classic)
   Reprint of the 1910 ed. published by Baker &
Taylor Co., New York, with new pref., introd., list
of the author's publications, and col. photos.
   Bibliography: p.
   Includes index.
   1. Baja California--Description and travel.
2. North, Arthur Walbridge. I. Title.
F1246.N85 1977   917.2'2   76-30795
ISBN 0-87380-122-9

A RIO GRANDE CLASSIC
First published in 1910

First printing 1977

The Rio Grande Press, Inc.

GLORIETA, NEW MEXICO · 87535

Publisher's Preface

On a map, Baja California looks like an afterthought of The Great Creator, a crooked dogleg of spiny land mass which – as W. Michael Mathes says in his Introduction following these words – has ever excited the curiosity and imagination of travelers. No less for us; we have always wanted to explore the peninsula ourselves. Once upon a time some years ago, before the trans-Baja blacktop was completed, we intended to take our car on the ferry from Mazatlan to La Paz, but by mistake we timed our journey during the hurricane season. We got no closer to La Paz than the Mazatlan dock (and the dock also at Topolobampo); at both places we looked out on a dark sea piling high with wind-driven spume-laden breakers. Even the big ferry sought the safety of a harbor anchorage, so instead of the lower Baja we split to Guadalajara where it was a lot cooler but like all big cities, sort of dull.

We have seen the Baja on a clear day from the headlands of Kino Bay and the Seri village of Desemboque. If we hadn't been such arrant cowards, we would have (we could have) crossed *Estrecho Infiernillo* and gazed upon Baja from Tiburon Island, firmly and permanently anchored just offshore and north of Kino Bay. Ever since we saw the movie *Jaws* we have been scared stiff of water; it frightens us to take a shower, even. That "infernal strait" between the mainland and the island is only a few miles wide, but it is said to

1

be home sweet home to at least a gillion hungry sharks. We may be a tired old man to our friends, but we are convinced we would be a tasty morsel to those mad marine monsters; according to the movie, sharks will eat anything.

So we have never gotten to Baja, but we have read a great deal about it. One of the most delightful of the many travel books about the peninsula is this one, written six years before we were born. It ties in pretty well with several other of our books that deal with rambles in northwestern Mexico and the Baja − *Travels in the Interior of Mexico, 1825-1828*, by Lieut. Robert William Hale Hardy (1829) and *In the Land of the Cave and Cliff Dwellers; Northwestern Mexico*, by Lieut. Frederick Schwatka (1893) being our latest (there are others). Until we can actually go in person, we will have to travel by way of books like these.

We invited Dr. W. Michael Mathes, Professor of History at the University of San Francisco, to write an introduction to this book for us. He not only did that, ever so promptly and ever so well, he loaned us the 72 color photos we have added to our edition. There are 32 pages of color, each with two photographs, and with four more on each of the front and back endpapers, making altogether 72 contemporary photos with some of them corresponding to the pictures taken before 1910 by author North. Dr. Mathes took these beautiful shots himself, revealing an unerring eye for composition and a total familiarity with his camera.

Mike is a native Californian who has actually lived on the peninsula since the mid-1940's. He has traveled from Tijuana to Cabo San Lucas on dirt road and highway thirty-two times since 1948. He holds a Ph.D. in History from the University of New Mexico. He is Director, Archívo Histórico de Baja California Sur Pablo L. Martínez, La Paz; and Commissioner, Commission of the Californias for the State of Baja California Sur. Thus, who could be better qualified than Dr. Mike Mathes to write something for us? He did it with grace, felicity and eloquence; we greatly appreciate his willing cooperation.

We should pause here to thank our always good friend and bibliographic colleague, the President of International Bookfinders, Inc., Mr. Dick Mohr, for supplying us with the first edition we used to reproduce this edition. We have never asked him to find a book for us which he did not promptly and efficiently locate. He's the eighth or ninth or maybe tenth, wonder of the modern world and without his help we often would be helpless, virtually.

For those who are curious about the quatrain from the *Rubaiyat of Omar Khayyam* on the very first page of this book, well, there it

2

is, an immutable truth nicely said. We put it in all of our books now. It does not have a lot of relevance here, but it does in other titles. What it means, in simplest terms, is that what is done is done; what has happened, has happened; what has been written, has been written. History simply can't be changed because we do not like what has been done, or what has happened, or what has been written. For a better explanation of what we mean, we invite the reader's attention to the late George Orwell's *1984*, wherein he describes an enormous bureaucracy set up to change everything that has happened in the past to conform to what the bureaucrats today want it to be. This book of pristine prophecy got a lot of laughs when it was first published in 1949; nobody's laughing now, though.

This is our 115th beautiful Rio Grande Classic — one of our magnificent reprints of distinguished Western Americana.

Robert B. McCoy

La Casa Escuela
Glorieta, New Mexico 87535
December 1976

Introduction

The thousand-mile long peninsula of Baja California has held a unique and mysterious fascination for all who have read of it and visited it; it has evoked emotions reflecting deep adoration or intense hatred of its rugged, varied terrain and extremes of climate, but never has it produced indifference. Born of the legendary Isle of Calafia in the *Sergas de Esplandián* (Medina del Campo: Garci Ordóñez de Montalvo, 1510) and first settled by the *conquistador* Fernando Cortés, Baja California has, for over four centuries, retained its legendary status as the guardian of great treasures of pearls and gold, Amazons, rich mines and lost missions, despite extensive exploration since 1535 by men on ships, foot, muleback, automobiles, off-road vehicles, motorcycles, airplanes, dirigibles and helicopters. This intense fascination with the Peninsula has, furthermore, created an inordinate desire among its visitors to write of their experiences of travel, and of visitors and non-visitors to research and record its history, geography, ethnology, natural history and geology, thus creating an abundance of both excellent and poor literature relative to the region disproportionate to its physical extension and span of history.

Explorers, soldiers, missionaries, governors, scientists, miners and potential investors comprised the majority of travelers in Baja

California prior to the twentieth century. Of those who traversed the majority of the Peninsula for the purposes of exploration and settlement, Sebastián Vizcaíno (1596; 1602-1603), Nicolás de Cardona (1615), Francisco de Ortega (1632; 1633-1634; 1636), and Pedro Porter y Casanate (1644; 1648), by sea, and Esteban Rodríguez Lorenzo (1719), Father Clemente Guillén S.J. (1719), Father Fernado Consag S.J. (1751; 1753), Father Wenceslaus Linck S.J. (1766), Gasper de Portolá (1769), Fray Junípero Serra O.F.M. (1769), Fray Juan Crespí O.F.M. (1769), Fray Francisco Palóu O.F.M. (1773), and José Loaquín de Arrillaga (1796), by land, have left excellent descriptive journals. Scientists and potential investors such as José Longinos Martínez (1792), Robert William Hale Hardy (1826), J. Ross Browne and William M. Gabb (1866-1867), W.E. Bryant, Gustav Eisen and F.S. Brandegree (1890-1894), Edmund Heller (1903), E. W. Nelson and E. A. Goldman (1905-1906), John Steinbeck and Edward F. Ricketts (1940), and Maximino Martínez (1944), likewise combined descriptive narrative with technical data to provide highly readable travelogues of Baja California. All of these writers, however, traveled the Peninsula or its seas for specific reasons and as a part of their professional employment or labors, rather than as free-lance, casual observers or curious tourists drawn by the mysterious and forbidding reputation of the region.

Although preceded by James H. Bull in 1843-1844 (Doyce B. Nunis, Jr., ed. *Journey of James H. Bull, Baja California, October 1843 to January 1844*. Los Angeles: Dawson's Book Shop, 1965.), Arthur Walbridge North may well be considered to be the first tourist to travel the peninsula of Baja California, for unlike Bull who despised the region, North was enamored of it and wrote extensively and favorably of it. Born 26 October 1874 at Marysville, California, North was educated at Apricot School in Winters, Oakland High School, and the University of California where he was graduated in 1895, and where he was active in developing athletic competition between eastern and western universities, managing the first track team to visit the eastern seabord. From 1895 to 1897, North served as a bailiff in the California Supreme Court, and, from 1897 to 1898, as a member of the State Legislature during which time he introduced legislation establishing state scholarships to the University of California for superior students. Having read law from 1895 to 1899, he was admitted to the California State Bar in the latter year, and established the firm of North and Lovejoy in Woodland, California.

A product of the era in which *mens sana in corpore sano* was extolled by such leaders as Cecil Rhodes and Theodore Roosevelt, Arthur Walbridge North was drawn to the outdoors. An avid hiker, camper and hunter, he spent long periods in the Sierra Nevada throughout his youth as well as during the decade following his graduation from the University of California. North's father, George North, a descendent of Thomas North who settled in Dorchester, Massachusetts in 1670, had traveled from New England to the gold fields of California via the isthmus of Panama in the 1850's and had settled in Marysville where, as a hardware merchant, in 1853 he had resisted the request of William Walker to join his ill-fated filibustering expedition to form the Republic of Sonora and Baja California, a fact made known to his son. Thus, with his curiosity of the Peninsula aroused and as an highly experienced outdoorsman, in early 1905 the younger North left his law practice to visit the Colorado Desert, Calexico, Yuma and Mexicali, and later to travel by burro, camping and hunting, throughout the length and breadth of Baja California from December, 1905 to May, 1906, and from July to September, 1906.

Prior to this expedition, North had researched the available literature on the Peninsula and, upon his return, expressed his knowledge and love for the region through eight articles (1905-1908), principally in *Sunset* magazine, and one book, *The Mother of California* (1907). This latter work, notwithstanding its many often glaring errors in language and fact, its romantic tone, and its perpetuation of legend and rumors of wealth, is a pioneering effort in the production of a short history of Baja California. North, with great feelings for the land, its historical figures, residents and native peoples, provided a highly readable descriptive narrative of the history, geography, *flora* and *fauna*, economics, politics, ethnology, population centers, customs and lifestyles of the region. His reportage on the operations of El Boleo at Santa Rosalía, the value of salt at Laguna Ojo de Liebre, pearl fishing, mining, and contemporary development is of great value to historians, as are the thirty photographs showing the towns, missions and people as they were at the beginning of the century. Also of importance is a discussion of the strategic value of Bahía Magdalena as a port in the era of coal-burning ships and on the eve of the opening of the Panama Canal, the possibilities of acquisition of Baja California by the United States, and the division of the Californias into three entities. The bibliography, citing the works of such authors as Baegert, Venegas, Clavijero, Palóu, Lassépas, Browne and Nordhoff, reflects the scholarly, serious interest held by North in the Peninsula.

Upon his return to California, North removed to Salt Lake City, Utah in 1909 where he served as attorney for the Union Pacific Railroad Company until 1913. During those years he traveled throughout Glacier and Yellowstone National Parks, the Uintah Range and Green River region, the canyon country of southern Utah, and visited his ancestral home of Walton, Delaware County, New York; in 1912 he married Irene Goss in Washington, D.C. Also while in Salt Lake City, in 1909-1910, North wrote his reminiscences of travel and adventure in Baja California which was published in the latter year as *Camp and Camino in Lower California.*

Camp and Camino reflects the many-faceted North: traveler, outdoorsman, ecologist, hunter, social observer, patriot, romantic, athlete and lawyer, as well as amateur naturalist, ethnologist and historian. In the latter fields it perpetuates many of the errors of *The Mother of California*, but in the former areas it excels. Descriptions of the Caminos Reales, modes of travel, people, dress, customs, foods, countryside, climate and ardors of the trip, all little changed since North's time, are excellent and may be appreciated by the contemporary reader. Similarly, the descriptions of mission ruins, towns, Indians, and wildlife, all greatly changed or non-existent since 1906, are well detailed and thus are of great value to the historian, ethnologist and naturalist. The twenty-nine original photographs illustrate a bygone era, and, in many instances, the ravages of time and man upon the monuments to early settlement. North's fascination with, and love of, the Peninsula, its peoples, legends, *flora* and *fauna* is evident throughout, as is his concern for its future. The foreword by Admiral Robert Dunglison ("Fighting Bob") Evans, who, as the commander of the United States Atlantic Fleet, led its sixteen ships into Bahía Magdalena on 12 March 1908, demonstrates the esteem given North's work by his contemporaries.

Following the publication of *Camp and Camino*, and possibly as a result of the memories that it evoked, in 1913 North retired from active legal practice to his family's farm in Walton, New York. Apart from service as an infantry captain in the United States Army during World War I, he devoted the remainder of his life to writing and lecturing on the virtues of travel and the great outdoors, and to traveling in Canada, Mexico, South America, Europe, North Africa, New Zealand and the southwest Pacific, northern Norway, Sweden and Finland, the Middle East, and to canoeing the length of the Danube, Tajo and Duero Rivers. He was active as a member of the Royal Geographic Society of London, American Farm Bureau Federation, Explorers Club of New York City, Masonic Lodge, Episcopal Church, and American Legion. An outdoorsman to the last, Arthur Walbridge North lost his life in a canoeing accident on the Genesee River near Letchworth Park, New York on 25 April 1943.

Camp and Camino, long out of print and reprinted herein for the first time, is a classic in the travel literature of Baja California. It is a pioneer work, and has served as a basis and model for later travel writers who, as did North, demonstrated the deep affection they held for the Peninsula. Walter Nordhoff, writing under the pseudonym of Antonio de Fierro Blanco, based much of his description in *The Journey of the Flame* (Cambridge, Massachusetts: Houghton Mifflin, 1933), the great novel of Baja California history, upon North's work. *Camp and Camino* further set the tone of the work of Erle Stanley Gardner who traveled the Peninsula between 1947 and 1970 by car, off-road vehicle, motorcycle, helicopter, dirigible and airplane, publishing with William Morrow, New York, *The Land of Shorter Shadows* (1948), *Hunting the Desert Whale* (1960), *Hovering over Baja* (1961), *The Hidden Heart of Baja* (1962), *Off the Beaten Track in Baja* (1967), *Mexico's Magic Square* (1968), and *Host with the Big Hat* (1969), and of Fernado Jordán (1948-1950) whose work, *El Otro México* (La Paz: Gobierno del Estado de Baja California Sur, 1976) is the first Spanish language travelogue of the region. Guidebook-travelogues have also been produced by Peter Gerhard and Howard E. Gulick *(Lower California Guidebook*. Glendale, California: Arthur H. Clark, 1956, 1958, 1962, 1967, 1970.), and by Walt Wheelock and Howard E. Gulick *(Baja California Guidebook*. Glendale, California: Arthur H. Clark, 1975.) following the descriptive style of North. Not only the historical-travelogue style of North's writings, but his mode of travel, muleback, has been followed by Jesús Castro Agúndez in *El Estado de Baja California Sur* (Mexico: Sep-Setentas, 1975) and Harry W. Crosby in *The King's Highway in Baja California* (La Jolla: Copley Books, 1975). The continued fascination in Baja California is evidenced by the many publications dealing with the area as exemplified by the, at present thirty seven volume, *Baja California Travels Series* (Los Angeles: Dawson's Book Shop, 1965 –) edited by Glen Dawson and Edwin Carpenter; and, the subject of transpeninsular travel and routes in *Paralelo 28°* by

Enrique Cárdenas de la Peña (México: Secretaría de Obras Públicas, 1976).

Although a paved highway, completed in December, 1973, now covers the length of the Peninsula from Tijuana to Cabo San Lucas, permitting the traversing of the region in the comfort of a modern passenger car with the luxury of fine hotels conveniently located, the reprinting of *Camp and Camino* is most timely. Through this work, many of the places described by North that are today bypassed or non-existent are made known, and the new traveler may gain a greater appreciation for the grandeur that is Baja California, while those of us who knew the land before the highway was built may be reminded of times past — open spaces, camps, solitude, the *camino* and the *rancheros'* welcome *café de talega*.

W. Michael Mathes

Archivo Histórico de Baja
California Sur Pablo L.
Martínez, La Paz
University of San Francisco
November, 1976

Other Publications by
Arthur W. North

"The Cut-Off; being a narration of the adventures, along the Hastings cut-off into the Great Salt Lake Basin, of the Reed-Donner party in 1846 and the Mormon pioneers in 1847," *Sunset*, 27 (December, 1915), 1095-1104.

The First Grandmother of Walton: Margaret Furman North, Revolutionary War patriot and interpid pioneer. n.p., 1926.

The Founders and the Founding of Walton, New York; being an intimate historical sketch of the making of an American settlement in the critical period immediately preceeding the adoption of the Federal Constitution. Walton, New York: Walton Reporter Co., 1924.

"Francesca of Mexicali, a story of the southwestern borderland," *Sunset*, 15 (September, 1905), 420-425.

The Glow of the Campfire, revealing through the mellow light of radiant impressions, a symposium of the Yosemite lovers and their intercollegiate friends at "Northwold", in the Catskills of New York, on June 21, 1924. Transcribed by the many with just a little lacing together left for Arthur North and Archie Rice. Walton, New York: 1924.

Handbook and History of the Delaware County, N.Y. Organization of the American Legion; being an intimate sketch of the erection and development of one of the earliest county units of the Legion. Walton, New York: 1925.

"Hunting the Bighorn," *Sunset*, 19 (October, 1907), 523-532.
La Madre California. Translated by Rafael Sousa. Mexicali:
1924.

"Magdalena Bay," *Sunset*, 20 (March, 1908), 411-420.

"Map of the Sierra of San Pedro Mártir," *Bulletin of the
American Geographical Society*, 39 (December, 1907), 769.

"The Mother of California," *Sunset*, 18 (1906-1907), 33-41
145-155, 177-188.

*The Mother of California; being an historical sketch of the
little known land of Baja California, from the days of Cortez to
the present time, depicting the ancient missions therein
established, the mines there found, and the physical, social and
political aspects of the country; together with an extensive
bibliography relative to the same.* San Francisco and New
York: Paul Elder and Company, 1908.

"Native Tribes of Lower California," *American Anthropologist*,
New Series, 10 (April, 1908), 236-250.

"Resources of Lower California," *Monthly Bulletin of the International Bureau of American Republics*, 25 (December, 1907),
1374-1376.

"The Uncharted Sierra of San Pedro Mártir," *Bulletin of the
American Geographical Society*, 39 (September, 1907),
544-554.

*Walton World War History; being a brief account of the
participation, in that struggle, of residents of the town and
village of Walton, Delaware County, New York.* Walton, New
York: Reporter Press, 1922.

List of New Color
Photographs by
W. Michael Mathes

Scene on El Camino Real

CAMP AND CAMINO IN LOWER CALIFORNIA

A RECORD OF THE ADVENTURES
OF THE AUTHOR WHILE EXPLORING
PENINSULAR CALIFORNIA, MEXICO

BY

ARTHUR WALBRIDGE NORTH

AUTHOR OF
"THE MOTHER OF CALIFORNIA"

WITH A FOREWORD BY
ADMIRAL ROBLEY D. EVANS
U. S. N.

NEW YORK
THE BAKER & TAYLOR COMPANY
1910

THE PREMIER PRESS
NEW YORK

In memory of the loving hospitality of that peaceful Catskill home wherein these pages were written, I inscribe this volume to my kinswoman, Miss Sarah North, of Walton, and to the memory of her sister, the late Miss Margaret North.　　　　*A.W.N.*

FOREWORD

When a man is in the midst of dangers himself he has small chance for books; but let him once be deprived of personal excitement and then even to read of the adventures of others becomes a most satisfying diversion. I have enjoyed looking over the manuscript of this work of Mr. North's. Indeed, every man with an ounce of red blood in his veins or any fondness for a dash of excitement or a whiff of fresh air will obtain a whole lot of pleasure by reading it. In following the author along El Camino Real and about the old Spanish missions, I have had glimpses of a fascinating life—a wholesome out-door living—that have driven other things from my mind, while his experiences with maurauding Indians and in pursuit of big game make one anxious to share the excitement with him.

But it has not been merely because of the fascination, the humorous situations and the interesting characters that I have enjoyed the perusal of these pages; they have deeper interest. Years ago, on first entering Magdalena Bay, I was impressed with the magnificence of that superb harbor; in March, 1908, anchoring there with the fleet, I realized more than ever its prospective importance. But I could merely look at the grim shores from the deck of the *Connecticut* and wonder, as I had done before, what might lie inland. In these pages, however, one learns—and it is a knowledge worth having—of the whole territory in an intimate and agreeable fashion, the author having ventured across and up and down the entire California Peninsula: it is, therefore, a pleasure for me to link, by this introduction, my Lower California associations with Mr. North's adventures in the romantic "Land of Magdalena Bay."

R. D. Evans,
Rear Admiral U. S. N.

Lake Mohonk, New York.

AUTHOR'S PREFACE

If when writing the closing chapter of this volume I could have looked ahead, reading in the future that a year and a half must intervene before final revision, such prospective delay would have been almost incomprehensible to me. And yet you who peruse these pages may smilingly understand how their author might turn abruptly from conventional life, seeking anew the fascination of the frontier.

"Yes, they're wanting me, they're haunting me, the awful
   lonely places;
They're whining and they're whispering as if each had a
   soul.
And now they're all a-crying and it's no use me denying,
The spell of them is on me and I'm helpless as a child.
My heart is aching, aching, but I hear them sleeping, waking;
It's the Lure of little Voices; it's the mandate of the Wild.
There's a whisper in the night wind, there's a star agleam to
   guide us,
And the wild is calling . . . . let us go."
                                              —*Service.*

How can a wanderer withstand such pleadings!

Now that I write again the year and a half seem good. Neither a shoulder doubly fractured in the Rockies, nor a lesser accident in the Arizona canyons count in the summing

9

up.   Life is invariably good; provided the trail to the wilderness lies open.   And if these pages can bring to their readers—particularly to those who craving the charm of the wilds and the thrill of adventure yet may not wander from fireside or desk—a share in the keen delight, the rare exhilaration of the succeeding months of out-door living therein outlined, then to the writer this work, though delayed, was well worth the doing.

ARTHUR W. NORTH.

Salt Lake City,
  March 1, 1910.

CONTENTS

PART II. THE WIDENING OF THE TRAIL.

PART III. LA FRONTERA AGAIN

ILLUSTRATIONS

13

▲   Mission San Miguel de la Frontera

Ensenada   ▼

▲ Santa Catarina

Santa Catarina ▼

PART I

TERRA INCOGNITA

Camp and Camino in Lower California

CHAPTER I

A MISSION AND SOME INDIANS

IT was the last day of the year 1905. With sweater, hunting shirt, coat and slicker drawn close about me, I bent forward before the raw wind that came shrieking down from the snowy peaks of San Pedro Mártir Sierra. With chattering teeth, I thrust my aching fingers deep into my pockets. The reins hung loose over the iron pommel of my stock saddle: my mule could keep the trail or not, I was too cold to care.

And this was hot, barren, desert Baja or Lower California, land of palms and deserts and snakes, *terra incognita* where once missions flourished, the territory over whose broiling sands I had often traveled *en route* to equally hot, barren, craggy mountains where the exciting prospect of mountain sheep ever awaited me! A territory in which I had found the heat making night the preferable time for travel!

Certainly there must be a mistake. But no, before me was the ever necessary canteen tied short to the saddle pommel. Yet no sound of jolting water was to be heard. The canteen contained a solid mass of ice! Each biting gust of the wind seemed sharper than the one preceding. I beat my elbows against my ribs and pressed my knees close against my mule in the hope of obtaining some warmth. And this was Lower California weather! Heavens, I thought, what does any one know of this ancient, deserted, next-door neighbor of California!

Two young American friends of mine were riding somewhere near with Juan, a Mexican ranchero, and two pack mules. It required no questioning to determine their state of frigidity. Even the mules looked at me accusingly. We were perhaps a hundred miles east of the Mexican pueblo of Ensenada and about sixty miles southwest of the mouth of the Colorado River. We had come through a mountainous region which opened into a grease-wood covered stretch of land that strongly reminded me of the Coconino Basin near the Grand Cañon of the Colorado.

Suddenly Cabeza de Vaca stopped abruptly and looked to the east. Cabeza is a powerful, fine-looking, buck-skin mule; stumbling is a frailty of which his zebra-striped legs have no knowledge. His name he acquired by gift from me, his temporary master. It is certainly a fitting name, for Alvarez Nunez, Cabeza de Vaca, was one of the greatest of Spanish wanderers, and this clean-limbed buck-skin is expected to carry me over a couple of thousand miles of rugged exploration. I followed Cabeza's glance and saw a black horse, a bay colt and a black dog strung out in line following an Indian along a trail that promised soon to unite with ours. My spurs urged on my steed and we joined the dark company. The Indian proved to be a Catarina Yuma, an ex-chief of the tribe, as I was to learn later. He was on his way to his home, a mile farther to the southeast. From this information, gleaned through my poor Spanish, I knew that we were near the old Dominican Mission of Santa Catarina de los Yumas—and, also, near the *rancheria* of the worst of the Peninsula Indians.

I studied the man. He was doubtless in his fifties, a wiry,

pleasant-faced, copper-hued hunter. On his shoulder he
carried a muzzle-loading shot-gun, an ancient weapon. He
wore a broad-brimmed sombrero of felt, a grey *serapa,* or
blanket, drawn close about his shoulders, and a thread-bare
pair of faded overalls. Although raw-hide *guarachas* or
sandals protected the soles of his feet from thorns, his feet
and ankles were left uncovered and exposed to the cold.
He would neither speak in nor respond to English, which
fact is, however, no proof that an Indian does not understand that language. In response to a question in Spanish
from Juan, he stated that his father had lived at the mission in the days of the *Frailes,* or Friars, and that the holy
men were hard taskmasters, frequently tying the Indians to
trees and giving them twenty-five lashes on the back in punishment for refusal to work. A true statement, perhaps,
though I could see no trees.

Our party advanced in the wake of the Indian and his
animals. Juan, though an exceptionally well informed resident of the country, could give us little information concerning either the mission or the Indians we were approaching. The former, he believed, had been the scene of much
trouble; of course there was a rich ledge of ore somewhere
near it, for all the missions were near good mines—only
it is usually impossible to locate the ledges. A dozen years
ago, he said, at the time of his last visit to the mission, he
had found the metal handles of an ancient Spanish chest
and had seen an excavation in the mission ruins where a
lucky Sonora man, on the previous day, had found a chest
of buried treasure; all the missions had buried treasure—
only it is usually impossible to locate the hiding places. Of
the history of the mission he knew nothing; during the excitement over the gold placers at Alamo, near by, many
strangers had visited Santa Catarina, but even they had
seemed ignorant of mission records and traditions. The

Indians? They had always been bad Indians, *ladrones* (robbers), and even worse; it would not be well for us to remain long near their *rancheria*.

Coming down over the brow of a hill, we entered a lonely valley, set away in the grim mountains which rose in rougher and higher ridges beyond and to the southeast of us. Of ruins we could see nothing. Barking dogs, however, drew our attention to several Indian shacks at the further side of the valley and to one, more striking than the others, crowning the crest of a small circular knoll immediately below us. To this latter shack our guide directed his steps. We turned to the left; a furlong brought us to the mission ruins, lying on a slight eminence overlooking the valley. There was little enough to see: mere earthen outlines rising from a foot to a yard above the surface, tracings of what once, however, had been a considerable adobe fort with bastions at the corners and apartments built against the walls and opening into the central square or *patio*. The anger and cupidity of predatory Indians and the force of the elements had doubtless begun the destruction and the avarice of treasure hunters had thoroughly completed it. Disappointed, we rode down to our new friend's shack.

Several Catarina Yumas came out to meet us: the men armed with bows and arrows and muzzle-loading shot-guns, the women bedaubed with red and blue paint. In spite of this uncouth ornamentation, one of the young girls, Anita by name, was decidedly pretty. She was the grand-daughter of our friend and, with him, was about to pose before my camera when an interfering old squaw rushed out of the shack and protested, nor would offers of tobacco and sugar pacify her. So bidding the Yumas good-bye, for the day was well advanced, we rode away and made camp by a water-hole a full league down the valley, a sufficient distance to satisfy Juan, who had his doubts of the Indians. From the different shacks we saw, I should judge there were as many as seventy or eighty of the tribe, women and children included.

That evening, before the camp-fire, my mind wandered over such history concerning the Mission of Santa Catarina de los Yumas as I had at various times picked up from Lower California records and mission chronicles and in odd corners. While old "Mad Anthony" Wayne was thrashing the rebellious Indians out in the region that later became the President-producing State of Ohio, Governor Arrilliga, then Spanish ruler of Baja California, was exploring this country, that is still a wilderness, in search of a place where he could establish a mission and a *presidio* to serve as a base for more extended operations. Immediately thereafter the Dominican Frailes, Tomás Valdellon and José Llorente, founded the desired mission, giving it the name of Santa Catarina de los Yumas. This was in 1797. At that time there were fifteen hundred Indians about Santa Catarina; they were never peaceful. Even the gentle process of shipping some of the fiercer families to the south and substituting neophytes from other missions was of no avail. Again and again the Indians revolted against the control of the missionaries. Finally, in about 1840, they killed or drove away the last Fraile and set fire to so much of the mission as would burn. Santa Catarina was the last of the long list of clerical foundations established in Lower California.

To an American the most interesting feature of this mission lies in the fact that here, in 1827, came James O. Pattie, the first if not the only American to visit this portion of the Peninsula and leave any record of his journey. Pattie was a Kentuckian; in company with his father and several other American frontiersmen, he had trapped beaver along the Colorado River, then wandered inland from the head of the Gulf of California, enduring frightful hardships; finally, the party chanced upon Santa Catarina Mission, though the discovery did not end their troubles. Close in the wake of the Patties came the fur traders, linking *El Camino Real* with the Sierra trail of the Hudson Bay trappers.

While pictures of the past unfolded before my mind, my two friends, crowded warmly near me, slumbered deeply and Juan, in a mass of blankets, was fast asleep under a protecting clump of brush close by; and the fire had burned low. The sharp night air recalled me to the present, and hastily piling wood on the coals, I plunged into the blankets and fell asleep. But the coyote chorus had made sleep difficult for a week past and this particular night it seemed as though the puppies from forty kennels had surrounded our camp with the firm intention of testing their lungs; for coyote "yipping" resembles the whimpering of many puppies rather than the efforts of a serious minded dog. What with this disturbing chorus, the extreme cold, and my vain efforts to keep a fire burning, the long hours brought me slight repose. At midnight, I plainly heard the rush of many hurrying feet to the neighboring water-hole, the whinneying of horses and the half-suppressed oaths of vaqueros. At daylight, to our consternation we found that all our animals, save a lone riding mule tied close to camp, were gone.

With one man guarding camp, the rest of us made search for the strays. I was five miles to the east, trying to hold my carbine in numb fingers, when the snow came down blindingly. At the same time I discovered that the tracks, which I had been following, belonged to a bunch of strange mules. With the snow in my eyes and brush and cacti hindering my advance, it was no play finding camp, but when

I staggered in, chilled and bleeding, I learned from my companions that all the animals had been located, except Cabeza. The poor creatures, fresh from the lowlands, had kept moving throughout the night, despite their hobbles, in frenzied effort to avoid freezing.

Late in the afternoon we secured the lost one. After stampeding our animals in the night the Catarinas had cut out Cabeza from the bunch, obliterated his tracks by hauling brush over them, led him a distance through a brook and finally driven him, with three of their own, to a brushy hiding place in the rear of one of their shacks, where they carefully tied him; one of the Indians, armed with an old .44 caliber rifle, had mounted guard while the others took turns watching our movements. But Juan, versed in the lore of trails, was not long deceived by these artifices, and, following close in his wake, we took Cabeza and asked no questions. Whether the Indians were bent on theft, or were scheming to hold the mule until we should offer five *pesos* (dollars) for their assistance in finding him, were questions we did not try to decide. After all, there was some sense in lugging about the mighty six-shooters which we had strapped on after leaving Ensenada—and I am quite sure that the old Frailes knew what they were about when they tied the Catarinas to trees,—even if the "trees" were thorny shrubs,—and walloped 'em. A few lusty wallops these days would be improving.

That night we spent in the same camp, though the falling snow had changed its appearance. The following day the earth was well covered; Juan, who was half sick, grumbled his Mexican dislike of the cold; one of my friends suggested sending to the High Sierras of Upper California for snow skis and the other rallied me about bringing them into *tropical* Lower California. The maguay plants, the chollas, ocotillas, tunas and all the rest of the cacti family seemed to eye us from their untropical drapery with resentful expressions. We broke camp in the early morning light and took a southeasterly course. In order to keep active our circulations, we soon found it necessary to dismount and proceed on foot. The jack rabbits, also, considered it advisable to keep on the move. In sixteen minutes along a single stretch of mesa land, I counted twenty-six of these long-eared fellows. At Alamitos (Little Cottonwoods), a small water-hole, the ice was so thick that our thirsty mules were at a loss as to how to obtain a drink until one of them, a jaunty little animal, suddenly smashed in the ice before her with quick stamps of her forefeet, a shrewd procedure which the others promptly imitated. That evening I found that quail which we had killed during the forenoon were frozen stiff so that they broke apart like brittle wood. However, we were far from the *ladrones,* and in consequence slept peacefully, despite the cold.

Though this proved merely my introduction to the Catarina Yumas, intervening adventures must be narrated before I relate my subsequent experiences at their rancheria.

CHAPTER II

MOUNTAIN SHEEP.*

LATE one afternoon, a week after our New Year's Day experience with the Yumas, Juan and the youngest of our party were high up among the mountain peaks while Lawrence, my other compatriot, and I were riding along the sandy floor of an immense *arroyo*. In places the surface glistened in unbroken whiteness, then again pale desert pines, thorny mesquit and verdant *palo verde* rose from the sandy bed, making fair gathering places for great flocks both of the valley quail and their dove-colored desert cousins. But our eyes gave small heed to these immediate surroundings; they were raised to the lofty red and copper colored ridges that rose sheer above either side of the floor of the arroyo. Lawrence was mounted on Pedro Ximenez. Cabeza de Vaca bore me along and we gave our steeds their heads. We were desperately anxious for the sight of mountain sheep and our attention was not to be wasted on anything else.

Students of natural history, wise hunters, and close observers of museum specimens will smile when I state that the southern big horn or mountain sheep has no wool and is not white. Nevertheless, I make the direct statement for the benefit of those not coming under any of the above classes, for I have not forgotten how, on my first hunt for mountain sheep, I searched the surrounding cliffs for a woolly white animal with big curling horns, and how, when

* Reproduced, in part, from the *Sunset Magazine* of October, 1907.

I finally saw a light dun-colored creature, I would have allowed it to escape as a deer that was in too steep a place to bother with had not its immense curling horns suddenly come into view. And why not? Do not all ordinary, respectable sheep have wool? And aren't they white?

For several hours we had ridden along with no sight of our quarry. Once, I exclaimed at sight of what seemed to be a man standing on a jagged peak, a half mile above us, but the "man" shufflled uneasily, then spreading out a pair of giant wings floated majestically away, advising our astonished eyes that we were in the land of the mighty condor. Other than this we had advanced with no incident or sound save the dull steady break of the sand beneath the small feet of our mules. Cabeza kept me in the lead, perhaps fifty steps or more, and I, forgetting even to scan the cliffs, was feeling compunction because my companion had ventured hundreds of miles, at my suggestion, in the hope of killing a big horn, and a week's hard hunting had not even given him a sight of one.

"Look, look! On the ridge to the left."

I looked, and slid over the right side of my saddle, hauling my carbine from its saddle scabbard as I went and jerking loose Cabeza's hair picket-rope. My meditations were ended. Silhouetted against the sky-line, a mountain sheep was ambling peaceably along the distant ridge.

As my companion's sharp eyes had discovered the game, I waited until his big .40-.82 had said the first word; then I turned loose with my .30-.30. Mr. Ram paused and gazed in questioning attitude down at us, then calmly continued his business of going somewhere. As though angered at such uncomplimentary composure our rifles barked sharply in unison, but our target seemed in nowise disturbed thereat. *Where* were our bullets striking? I wondered, taking a long aim and figuring the distance at something

Upper entrance to Arroyo Grande

less than four hundred yards. I blazed away and heard the .40-.82 at my left sending out its message. Again the ram paused, gazing fixedly into the distance before him. Such unconcern! Suddenly the outlined figure, the curling horns, the back-line and the design of the legs—for all the world like pen and ink strokes against the sky, struck me as ridiculously like one of Gellett Burgess's "goups" and I burst out laughing. Were we shooting at an animated "goup"?

At this stage Lawrence swore, I believe. Don't blame him either, if he did, for his big rifle, sighted for five hundred yards, had thrown up the loose earth ten feet below the big-horn. With the rising of the slight puff of dust, the sky-line swallowed up our target and the whole experience might have been a dream except for two neat little piles of empty rifle cartridges, fifteen in all, for which we were responsible.

We rode on strangely cheered and expectant—and rallying ourselves.

An hour later my companion's voice again aroused me; this time it was hoarse with excitement.

"G-glor-ry," he cried, "look to the right!"

I looked, and as long as hunting blood flows in my veins I shall not forget the thrilling sight I saw. There, on a spur of the main ridge, assembled side by side, were three— four—seven big mountain sheep, their great ram heads inclined slightly sidewise as they curiously studied us.

"On, quick, to that mesquit ahead! Don't stop, don't let them know that we see them," I continued, turning half in the saddle so that my voice would carry, in an undertone, to my companion a hundred steps back of me.

A slowly passing moment brought us to cover in the middle of the arroyo. In an instant I was stretched on the sand, behind the mesquit, carbine in hand. Then Lawrence crouched by me. There was neither laughing nor swearing now: wondering admiration, tense excitement, cold steadiness, too, if you please. Appreciation of the moment came to us both: rarely is it given one to watch, face to face, the mountain sheep in his wild home. There they stood; they had seen us, they were disturbed, yet they remained immovable, statuesque, seven great rams.

"Oh, Lord! Look at that giant to the right."

"Yes, and see the middle fellow," I gasped back.

"See 'em all," responded Lawrence.

I glanced down my rifle barrel. The light was failing and I could just see the great rams over my white bead.

"The middle one is mine," I muttered, "you can take your whopper at the right."

We stretched out at ease on the sand and with left forearms raised, gripped firmly our rifle barrels and looked through their rear sights.

"I can hardly see," whispered my companion doubtfully, "and if we miss, they'll slide over that ridge at the first shot and be off. Suppose we camp here until morning and then creep 'round that ridge and bag 'em?"

The light was beastly dim and there was good sense in my phlegmatic companion's suggestion. Left to myself, doubtless I would have blazed away and missed. Full fifteen minutes the sheep stood motionless before us, a noble sight for anyone, sportsman or not; great independent creatures limned against the shadowy sky-line, watching, doubting. Then suddenly their leader, the big ram at the right, gave his command and with the precision of a cavalry squadron, all wheeled about, in their retreat showing their white rumps and crowding together like an alarmed flock of domestic sheep.

Seven big mountain sheep just over the ridge from us. Seven big rams to sleep with just a ridge between them and

▲ Mission Santo Tomás de Aquino

San Telmo ▼

▲ Sierra San Pedro Mártir

Sierra San Pedro Mártir ▼

View from the North Slope of San Pedro, Mártir Sierra, toward Colentura Arroyo, where Walker led his Filibusters

our rifles, and in the morning— Quietly we unsaddled and tied our mules to a palo verde; in great content they began nibbling the brittle branches. Silently we each ate a piece of hard-tack.

"Lawrence, I shall not kill over two of them. I'm no butcher."

"Two are all I want."

We stretched on the sand and pulled our saddle blankets over us. It was only 6:15 P.M., but there was nothing to do.

"Say, do you know that William Walker led his filibusters down this arroyo on his way to Sonora in 1854?"

"Seven big rams—"

"And do you know," I continued perseveringly, "that there are ancient hieroglyphics near here made by some prehistoric people?"

"Seven big rams and a giant at the right—"

We found sleep, eventually. I dreamed that I was the seventh son of a seventh son and was driving seven mountain rams into a corral built in the White House grounds. Then it was the gray half light of morning and two coyotes, sitting on their haunches a few yards distant, were quietly surveying us. I poked Lawrence and he murmured, sleepily,

"Well, well, seven big rams and a giant—"

But search as we might we never again saw those seven big rams. However, that evening at camp we partook of mountain sheep. Juan and the youngest member of our party, had had their overnight experiences, too. Said the succesful one:

"Juan was tracking and I was admiring the world when I saw a whole barn-yard of sheep—fifteen! Say, I counted them straight, too. I pulled up my rifle, forgot about my rear sights, aimed at the whole bunch and missed 'em all—

and kept on missing about seven times.   Then we turned off in another direction and by-and-by we saw another barnyard full and I got this ram.   Juan and I cooked and ate a piece right away.   It's a cross between a juicy mutton chop and a fine thick porterhouse steak.   Have a hunk—you fellows look blue."

A Cavalcade of Easter worshippers

CHAPTER III

ON the 22nd day of January, 1906, just a month after our entry into Mexico, I regretfully bade my American friends good-bye. The rounds of business in northern civilization demanded their attention; the southern wilderness claimed mine. Accordingly, the sheep hunt concluded, we parted at the little mining pueblo of Alamo, ten miles west of Santa Catarina Mission.

As they spurred northward, the faithful Juan riding in the lead, the chill of utter isolation fell upon me: there, passing from sight, were all my companions and even the familiar mules, excepting the smallest in the train, the usually impassive Pedro Ximenes. Tied to a post, the poor brute was now braying disconsolately. Lonely and depressed, I at once turned my attention exclusively to the work before me, the wisest course for anyone in such a frame of mind. Obviously, pack animals and a muleteer were my first requirements. Accordingly, I proceeded to make general inquiry for three burros and a man, for with burros rather than valuable mules I trusted to escape the avaricious attention of such as might not be possessed of a law-abiding appreciation of the rights of property. As the news spread that the *Americano* was desirous of purchasing for cash three large burros and engaging a *mozo* to journey with him down the length of the Peninsula, Alamo rippled with excitement. Every Mexican in the pueblo at once offered me some wonderful animal at a more wonderful figure, and

several expressed a willingness to receive wages from me.
Finally an array of burros and burro men assembled about
the inevitable plaza and with an American parson, an English "remittance man," and an Italian merchant, acting as
judges at what the Englishman facetiously called my "burro
show," I picked out a fine young gray burro, shortly christ-
ened Cortez, and a sharp-eyed brown wood-carrier. This
latter chap I made my bell burro and named Coronado.
My judges had pointed out the strong points of these burros; let him who would be possessed of a good burro keep
them in mind, viz.: no obvious tendencies toward balking,
backs covered by unbroken hides and thick hair, good teeth,
sturdy shoulders, stocky build, and long hoofs—for, burros
being unshod, the short-hoofed fellows soon become tender-
footed.

Meantime, and in short order, I engaged successively an
Italian and three Mexicans to serve as my mozo. The
Italian and two of the Mexicans grew faint-hearted at the
prospective dangers of the trip and the third Mexican was
restrained from departing by his creditors. Then the
American parson of my "burro show," a Texan of some
thirty years of age, came to my rescue. He gave his name
as "Ben" and stated that he would be glad to enter my service for three months. By way of references he explained
that while he had passed his early life as a clergyman in
Texas, for the past seven years he had been a muleteer in
Chihuahua and Sonora. As there was no question about
his being "up" on burros, I engaged him on the spot, though
the prospect of having a parson in steady service seemed a
trifle novel. I did not pry into his reasons for leaving his
pastorate, such questions not being polite near the Border.

In fact, in the midst of my search for a man, a tall Irish-
man took me aside and, in an undertone, said that he would
be glad to make the trip, provided the wages be raised

somewhat. "Quite easy for you, sir," he parenthesized; and then, with a look of cunning appreciation, continued, "It's the ridge trail that I can show you, and down that we can slip widout maten' a sowl. Sure," and here he gave a wink, "you've heard of Brown, the Los Angeles cashier! Well, 'twas me that took him safely trou to the port of Santa Rosali', where he got a ship, an' I can pull you trou over the same route." Respectfully declining this kindly offer, I took up with my parson. By the way in which he hustled about and secured for me two pack-saddles with accompanying harness and *alforcas* (raw-hide panniers), I am convinced that "Ben's" parishioners must have taken pride in his energy. To me it was a great delight after the dilatory manner of the natives. One stout, ragged looking Mexican whom I endeavored to engage to make a harness for one of my pack-saddles, calmly gave his half-rolled cigarette an added twist, leaned back against his adobe and soberly remarked that he "didn't have the time." Unquestionably, the Mexican eight-hour law provides that every able-bodied man shall *desist* from labor eight hours in the middle of every day!

"Ben" was very anxious to be upon the trail. So was I. At his suggestion, in place of delaying until I could secure a third burro for him to ride, we postponed that matter until a convenient burro ranch came in our way. Accordingly, leaving Alamo at noon of the 22nd, we climbed into the chemise-clad mountains at the south, being attended, through the courtesy of the *Correo* or Postmaster of Alamo, by a Mexican horseman as temporary guide. Half a league brought us to a high ridge where the Mexican left us, after pointing in a due southerly direction and exclaiming *"Sur, sur."* The man was quite picturesque and gave his directions in a dramatic manner. It had seemed to me that southwest was more nearly the proper course for us, but the positive "Sur, sur" was convincing and southward we turned, following the trail down a steep slope and through a succession of small valleys where the heavy growth of grass, the delightful red berries, the fine live-oaks, the dense chemise, the scurrying flocks of quail and the frequent deer tracks took my thoughts back to similar scenes in those northern mountains made familiar to all by Stevenson's "Silverado Squatters."

On the ensuing day, to our regret, we left a fairly good trail bearing southwesterly, doubtless to the olive-shaded ruins of the old Dominican Mission of Santo Tomás de Aquina, and followed a fainter trail which led in the southerly direction indicated by the Mexican. Our course, after taking us into lofty mountains from which we could see the distant ocean to the westward, led down abruptly to a deep canyon where there was an old shack, thatched with tule grass, and other evidences of by-gone Indian occupation. A goodly stream of water headed near the shack, and following along the stream for a league we made camp in an old brush corral, shaded by a noble group of live-oaks and sycamores. The grass was thick and the spot ideal for camping. In addition to his ministerial experiences, "Ben" had cooked at one time in a restaurant from which he had been invited to sever his connections because of the amount of fuel which he persisted in burning. Though such extravagant habits would have been as reprehensible on the desert as in the restaurant, they were not objectionable in the corral, where for many seasons the dead limbs had been falling in undisturbed heaps. His cooking operations, in consequence, succeeded admirably. One great bonfire threw its reflections upon the sides of the deep canyon, while over a smaller fire most appetizing dishes simmered and broiled to the delight of our anxious appetites. Even when sleep claimed us, a willow tripod arrangement of "Ben's" manufacture held suspended above the coals a slow boiling pot of beans. Quite undisturbed by the fact that we knew not just where we were, we slept soundly and entirely without forebodings for the morrow.

On the 24th we continued down the arroyo, passing another deserted corral and arriving shortly at a junction of two canyons below which the walls of the main canyon became extremely precipitous, while the stream pursued its course over a rocky bed which dropped in places in such a manner as to render the course impassable for our animals. To our delight we found horse tracks leading high up to the left. These we followed. Whoever guided that horse must have partaken of the loco weed or have carried under his belt a large amount of mescal, for the tracks led us through the densest chemise and deep down the most appalling declivities.

For a day and a half, each time that I had looked from the height of Pedro Ximenez, back upon my brave train of pack burros, with Coronado's bell tinkling so cheerfully and with Ben trudging along in the wake of the procession, my heart had throbbed with all the pride of a railway magnate watching his express trains whizzing along their double track road-beds. Now I passed through the anxieties of a railway president in flood season or in time of rebate investigation. Again and again the *alforcas* caught in the brush and the burros were "hung up," to the detriment of Ben's anti-swearing resolutions, for that worthy, having, on the first day, observed my swearing proclivities were not keen, had announced his determination to return to the pious language employed in the days of his pastorate in southwestern Texas. Eventually, Coronado slipped and fell, not through any fault of his, but because he was urged over a precipice and there overbalanced by his load. Gathering his small feet close to his body, down he rolled, to the bottom of the gorge, a hundred feet below, striking with a dull thud that sent shivers through me at the thought of broken bones and ruined *impedimenta*. Yet, after I had extricated him from his tangled pack, he arose, with a grunt, and calmly commenced cropping the sedge grass—but, for all his calmness, I think he was rather vexed at us.

Ben and I stood on either side of the burro and looked up at the precipices about us. We were in a box canyon where we seemed buried and so discouraged did we feel that we fell to and ate a good lunch, an excellent way of restoring a man's grit and increasing his resourcefulness. In this case we found our dismay perceptibly lessened and, by the aid of ropes, shortly hauled Coronado up the further side of the gorge.

On we went for three intense hours, breaking and hacking a course for our animals through the dense brush, avoiding chollas and Spanish bayonets, our eyes on the burros or searching in the dead leaves for tracks of that horse. Riding was out of the question; I was on foot cutting and smashing a way for the animals and Ben was busied in widening the passage for the packs. The scenery probably was grand —the plain at Alamo is reputed to be 4,900 feet above the sea level, and we had climbed to a much greater altitude, but I had no time for scenery. Cortez took his turn at rolling, then, in company with Coronado he was "hung up" in the brush. A jagged limb ripped into my forearm, breaking off by the side of an artery, where I dared not extricate it for the moment; I jammed my knee against the thorny extremity of a maguay leaf, which left a persistent throbbing pain in the knee-cap as a consequence. Neither of us had anything to say, but we both felt desperate, and it would have gone hard with the Mexican who gave us directions had he fallen in our way.

Meantime, the tracks led higher up into the sierras, the

brush giving way to great white granite boulders. At last, as the sun was setting and our spirits deeply depressed, we came upon the fairest scenery: a plain well-used *trail!* Down this we joyfully turned, descending toward the southwest. Hundreds of years and thousands of feet must have passed over that trail, for it was worn deep into the granite body of the mountain; in one place where I experimented with a tape, the trail was thirty-eight inches deep in the rock. Exhilarated in spite of our thorough exhaustion, we hurried on, noting tracks of a lion mingled with those of barefooted Indians. Finally we again came upon our water-course, now grown wider, and following it for a couple of miles, made camp on the sand with heavy darkness round about. We were both badly used up. My arms and knee ached acutely, and Ben also was subject for my medicine case, with its liniments and rolls of bandages. In addition, beyond the fact that we were among the spurs of San Pedro Mártir Sierra, we did not know where we were. We had every reason to believe, however, that we were in the neighborhood of some Indian *rancheria,* though of the possible attitude of its inhabitants toward us in such an unchartered end of the world we were rather dubious.

On the morning of the 25th we were so stiff that only our hearty constitutions enabled us to move forward. During the night a lion had come down to inspect us, marking up the sand with his great claws within twenty paces of camp, for, owing to the probable proximity of Indians, we had kept no camp fire burning. Continuing down the stream, we shortly crossed a small irrigating ditch, and beyond, upon a sandy bench of perhaps four acres, we came abruptly upon an Indian village.

As there are no complete maps or reports of the interior of Lower California, and as the reputations of the unvisited places are in nerve-racking accord with the mystery hanging over the entire peninsula, an exciting element of Lower California exploration exists in the fact that the explorer never knows what he may find at any turn of an arroyo—and it is a land of arroyos! In this instance, I found myself suddenly face to face with an Indian rancheria of half a dozen shacks and some fifty people, and what treatment to expect was beyond me, for I had never so much as heard of the existence of an Indian village in this particular region.

The bucks, garbed in a doubtful assortment of tatters, were lounging about at their ease, conversing with an Indian traveler, who was outward bound with two pack burros, laden with wild honey. The women were squatting on the ground before *metate* stones, a few crushing corn, but the majority reducing to powder a small black seed, the like of which is usually to be found in the crops of wild doves. Children were playing about in absolute nakedness, the boys practicing with stout bows and reed arrows. The babies of the village were in the care of the young girls, who carried them at their sides, the youngsters clinging, with mussy hands and straddling legs, to their comely foster mothers. They were a healthy, husky looking race of people, not unlike the Catarina Yumas in countenance but of heavier physique. Their shacks, also, were larger and more substantially put together than those of my *ladrone* acquaintances. As to what their treatment of us would be I was uncertain. Ben muttered, "Look out." We proceeded to do so.

The traveler, speaking in mongrel Spanish, informed us that they were Pais Indians (doubtless the same as the Pi-pis of the Salada and Colentura region at the southwest) and that we were the first white men who had ever come to the village. Though friendly in his address, he voiced the evident wonder of the village by inquiring how we had ever arrived from Alamo, coming from the direction which we had, and whether we were prospectors. Our arrival certainly created the confusion supposedly incident to the coming of first whites: the naked children were whisked away, the girls fled, the squaws became silent and the bucks looked at us with undisguised curiosity. A broad shouldered, strapping fellow, dressed in old overalls, tattered shirt, high peaked Spanish straw sombrero, and wearing a genial expression and waving Dundrearies, seemed to be the head man. Of him I asked permission to photograph the village, the traveler acting as interpreter. At first the big fellow seemed to think that evil lay in cameras, but when I showed him an Indian picture in a magazine he grunted a smiling assent, and entering one of the shacks conferred over the matter with a wizened ancient, who, judged by his parchment wrinkles, might have been a confrère of Cortez. The ancient proved to be the head chief and offered no objection to picture taking.

Meantime, the girls had reappeared with fresh coats of paint on their faces and bandanas coyly arranged upon their heads. If picture-taking was in order, they were prepared. To the general surprise, the ordeal consumed but an instant; then, in appreciation, I presented the big fellow with a cup of Scotch whiskey. This he passed over to the wrinkled one, who after downing all but the dregs, smacked his thin lips and returned the cup to his brawny understudy. The other bucks stood by and smiled half-heartedly as they watched the Scotch disappearing. They didn't get a taste! Talk about regard for the aged, we civilized beings are not in the same class with the Pi-pis.

Suddenly the head chief beckoned me to him. Already I had ostentatiously swung my heavy six-shooter into a prominent position and I approached him without hesitation. It seemed that my green riding bags, long the despair of my friends and the delight of my heart, had aroused his covetousness. Briefly he gave me to understand that the weather was cold and he was thin; that the trousers would do him much good, while at my age they were unnecessary —pointing, for verification, at the scantily clad young bucks of the village with their happy smiles, knife belts and *guarachas*. At this, the big fellow with the Dundrearies nodded smiling assent: it seemed time for America to retreat, and with hasty adieux, I left the Pais to their own resources, grateful to escape with honors of war—and my trousers, or with my trousers and without the honors of war. As I put spurs to the greatly surprised Pedro Ximenez, I turned in the saddle for a last look at the rancheria. All that I observed was a wizened ancient, following along the trail. He stooped pitiably, his face was parchment wrinkles, his claw-like hands were clasping his withered thighs and in quivering tones he called after me, "so cold, so very cold."

These Indians gather wild honey and raise beans, corn, grapes and melons from their fertile soil. Adjoining their village, and further down the canyon, there were signs which indicated that in some earlier day there had been a large population and many irrigated fields along the river-bottom. The Dominican Friars who established the missions about the northern portions of Lower California left few records of what they there found or did, but in one of their fragments they set forth that the Indians of San Vicente Mission were "unquiet, proud and fickle"; that those of Santo Tomás and Santa Catarina were "quick-tempered, treacherous, warlike and very difficult to govern"; that the Indians of Santa Catarina and Santo Tomás belonged "to the Yuma family," and that, "in 1781 the Mission of San Vicente was attacked by two thousand Yumas from the mountains who did great injury." As these Pais are within striking distance of each of these three mis-

▲   Mission Santo Domingo de la Frontera

Rancho Hamilton (Santo Domingo)   ▼

▲ El Socorro

Mission El Rosario Viñadaco ▼

sions, perhaps in those old days they were possessed of the entire combination of bad qualities named. At the time of my visit, however, they called their rancheria Dolores and were preparing—men, women and children—to take a long trip through the mountains to attend Mass at Santa Catarina Mission.

One primitive Indian whom we met below the village—he wore a coat and a belt and carried his *guarachas* in his hand—explained that, according to the customs of the Pais, a buck could have as many squaws as he desired, but that one squaw could do the requisite work and raise nine children, which was a sufficient family in these days. Talk about race suicide! This chap carried an ancient repeating rifle, which, as he told us, had suffered eleven distinct breaks in falling over a cliff and beneath a pack animal. It could only be discharged after wiring tightly in place all its parts. In consequence, this red man was hunting with a single cartridge in the barrel, and the lever and magazine wired fast to the barrel and stock. Probably, however, that single cartridge sufficed for the killing of a deer—or of some wandering beef, for I was later informed that the Pais were sad *ladrones* with a penchant for other people's cattle.

Learning from the hunter of the whereabouts of an *agua caliente* or hot spring, we hastened on, passing wonderful patches of wild clover and dense masses of pussy willow. By nightfall we reached the spring. According to our informant, who with other Indians of the *rancheria* was a stout Christian—and had in his shack some china marked "I. H. S."—this *agua caliente* though now little used, had been a favorite spot of the old Fraíles. Certainly, somebody in olden times had protected the spring with a well-built stone coping, fifty feet by ten, but sedges and tule grass had overgrown all save a nice clear pool, ten feet by six, and wild clover ran down to the edge. Such a camping spot!

While Ben exercised his culinary arts before a large fire in the shadows of the cottonwoods, I tumbled into the welcome spring and came forth leaving behind me pains and stiffness, dust and cholla thorns. Reclining on the yielding clover, before the companionable fire, a savory supper awaiting my keen appetite, close at hand a reliable Indian trail for the morrow, a contentment stole over me unknown in the narrow life against which I had become an insurgent. What cared I even though directions had been misleading and Indians numerous!

CHAPTER IV

THERE is a pathos in the ruins of past splendor which casts a shadow over the spirit of the traveler, bringing a sobering sense of the transitory works of man. Unconsciously, I gave myself completely to this feeling as I sat in the shade of the *casa* of the Señor of the Rancho of San Vicente late one January afternoon a few short days after my visit at the Rancheria of Dolores. I had just come in from a stroll among the ruins of the ancient Mission of San Vicente and was content to dream in the mellow light of the dying day.

There was food for dreams. On the summit of the green hill before me a Spanish fort had once frowned and thousands of Indians had vainly assaulted its walls. Now a squirrel crouched low in play on the ruined bastions, soldiers and flag were gone and the few miserable Indians in the hovel at the foot of the hill had welcomed the *centavos* which a passing traveler gave them. To the left of the fort there was once a high walled cemetery where Castilian officers and cowled Dominican Padres were placed at rest with the pomp of other days. Now the walls were broken, the graves fallen in, and garishly modern crosses, memorials to the recent dead, crowded from sight the neglected tombs of early dignitaries. Below the fort and to the right of the cemetery where, amid silent ruins, the dove now mourned and the raven cried discordantly, church and monastery and Governor's mansion had stood—structures,

43

some of them, full one hundred paces in length. Below
these ruins, in the great moat-like ditch now dry, ob-
structed, unused, shrouded by tall thickets of tuna and sugar-
cane, there had flowed in those earlier days a stream, precious alike for irrigation and defense.

Here was once the capital of *La Frontera,* the frontier
district. Here were swollen storehouses, broad fields, great
herds of cattle, sheep and horses, riches that now are gone,
like the spirits of those who controlled them, for naught remains save a few burros, horses and cattle, a small plot of
cultivated land, watered by a feeble stream, an atmosphere
of the past—and sombre, crumbling ruins returning, unhindered, to the jealous bosom of mother earth from whence
they came. Down at the base of the hill, where the clover
grows, stands a sentinel group of gnarled and blackened
olive trees, ancients guarding the ruins above—yet, when
travellers thronged *El Camino Real,* these were sturdy
trees, thick of foliage and generous of their shade.

While my thoughts were wandering, and I yielded to the
magic languor of the land, there came to mind the chronicles of the scribes and the traditions of my surroundings—
and close on their heels and before my heavy eyelids,
imagination unfolded the scenes which had been enacted at
San Vicente in the romantic days removed so far from
modern life. At the touch of the wand of Fancy, the ruins
disappeared and there on the hill stood a smoke-enshrouded
fort and just below it rose the Cross, high and clear, sur-
mounting a noble mission. Down there, amid spreading
tunas and young olives, I saw a cloud of red devils, bedaubed with war paint, decked with feathers and carrying
bows and arrows and spears. To the right, by the river's
curve, are more of the same ilk, for this is the year 1781
and the Indians from the Arroyo Grande and L'Encentada,
from San Miguel and Santo Tomás, their feuds forgotten,

have gathered to sack the sturdy young Mission of San Vicente Ferrer.

Even as the fiendish war-whoop rings out, the scene changes: the flag with the eagle and the snake now floats over the fortress, the mission granaries have grown and the fields are more extensive, for nigh half a century has passed. There, at a stout table in the refectory, sits a strange figure, a bronzed young man, long and lean of frame, with high cheek-bones and aquiline nose, with thin lips and square jaw; he is dressed in frayed buckskins and his worn leggins and moccasins have lost many of their beads. Seated facing him are two Friars, dark robed and rotund. The elder of the Friars is speaking: "Be of good cheer, Señor Pattie," he says, with a fatherly smile, "this detention is but a formality of the Commandante; he is a strange man with his regulations: he even desires us to take the oath of allegiance to his new Government." The young man half rises, exclaiming, "But this formality that he imposes upon us passes strangeness. Ah, had not the Colorado with its devilish tidal current wet our powder—aye, or that treacherous dog at Santa Catarina not deceived us—there'd be many in Purgatory waiting your prayers ere we'd been prisoners." The younger Friar waves a soothing hand. "Prisoners and perhaps heretics, also, you are, but our friends, my señor," says he, bringing forth a dusty wine skin, "and now over this bottle which is of the best port which our good brothers at Santa Rosalia de Mulege prepare, we will drink to Kentucky and you will tell us of those *amigos* of yours, Señors Bowie and David Crockett."

The face of the frontiersman relaxes from its harassed look and he cries, "Aye, that I will, for as yet you are my friends, but first I will offer a bumper: May the Mexicans at San Vicente pay with their blood for the indignity which they have put upon us men of Kentucky."

As the half-protesting Friars clink their glasses, the scene shifts: the Mission is unroofed, the fields are choked with weeds. Now the air is cleft by a wild, thrilling cheer that ends in a barking yell and a double line of tall warriors rushes up towards the fort, with bayonets fixed; from the port-holes there comes a murderous blaze of fire and many of the tall warriors crumple up like stalks of barley before a reaper: the line hesitates, and instantly the leader, a small, wiry man, bared rapier in hand, turns savagely upon them. "Oh, d—n you, d—n you, d—n, you all," he shrieks in thin high-pitched tones, "do you mind being killed! Dare you stop, dare you survive and return to Marysville, to Sacramento, to San Francisco—and admit that Greasers licked you? Do you want it said that mothers in Tennessee and Kentucky whelp white livers, mud-sills, Yanks?" He rasps out the last word with a bitter scream. "Yanks," that is what stiffens up the line. Again that wild barking yell, and the little man and his tall followers sweep up the hill and over the walls, carrying their two-starred flag into the fortress where a quarter of a century earlier Pattie of Kentucky was imprisoned, for this is February, 1854, and William Walker and his filibusters are planning the slave state of Lower Caliornia and Sonora.

From these realms of other days, I rouse myself with a start, for the Señor of San Vicente is standing before me and I feel that I have been dreaming. "Ten thousand Indians gathered from the mountains once to assault the mission over yonder"; he has seen me staring at the ruins and he waves his hand toward them, "and now on the whole Peninsula there is not a quarter that number." I now assent, and he continues: "Once your people fought my people here, but your country did not approve." I assented and he adds, "And once Mexicans fought Mexicans near the fort, but I do not know what it was about." I nod a third time:

how truly his closing statement would apply to most wars? and then, for conversation's sake, remark, "I'm going to ride my mule the length of the peninsula even to San José del Cabo."

"*Si!*" he exclaims in surprise, "*Baja California por tierra.*"

My Latin comes to the aid of my faulty Spanish and I mutter to myself, "Lower California Overland," aloud I say, "*Si, señor, Baja California por tierra,*" and shaking his head he murmurs, "Very far, señor, very far." Then he amazes me, by adding, "I have lived at beautiful San José del Cabo. There, too, you will find a site called San Vicente and there, as here, your people fought my people, only there your people were nearly overcome. But that battle was in a regular war."

"Yes?" I answered, my curiosity all agog, for then I knew not how Uncle Sam twice lost the Peninsula of Lower California.

Historians have an unfortunate faculty of omitting many interesting passages from their chronicles. Thus, in their accounts of the war between Mexico and the United States, they make no record of the Spartan-like defense of Chapultepec by the cadets of the Mexican Military Academy— they gave their blood, every boy of them, in heroic sacrifice to their country. Neither do the chroniclers mention the fierce engagements in Lower California between the United States Marines and the New York Volunteers on the one side and the native Californians and their Yaqui allies on the other, and yet the unfortunate conflict furnished no finer evidence of bravery. At Chapultepec there is a monument to the cadets, and grim war records attest the frightful losses suffered by the American regiments which finally swept over the bodies of the young heroes; but tradition and half-forgotten archives alone bear testimony to the stirring events in Lower California—for the chapter ends with Uncle Sam's surrender of Lower California!

The messages and private journal of President Polk throw a white light on the Mexican War; personal memoirs of the volunteers supplement these writings. The truth about the episode is that the occupation of the Peninsula by the United States forces, dating from the beginning of the struggle, was premeditated and in pursuance of a carefully arranged plan for its permanent retention. A treaty making slip set awry the arrangements. So Uncle Sam, our close-fisted Uncle, lost a province. Later, he lost the same land again, but the second time he was in the wrong even before it was won and offered to him. Before relating the incidents of the second fiasco, however, I must digress so far as to submit my first sources of information concerning the personality of that romantic but misguided character, William Walker, the "Gray Eyed Man of Destiny," one-time conqueror of Lower California.

As a child, I lived in the early California mining town of Marysville, whither my father, in company with many another young fortune-seeker, had journeyed in the exciting days immediately following the discovery of gold. In the evenings of my childhood, he was ever generous in satisfying my craving for adventure with his reminiscences of the golden days along the Yuba River. These reminiscences have never grown dim in my memory: there was the story of how Alcalde Field rose to be a Justice of the United States Supreme Court, of the heroism of the women of the Donner Party, of Lord "Charlie" Fairfax who preferred being a Speaker of the California Legislature to holding his English title; there were stern tales of the way the Unionists ended dueling in California by grimly naming double-barreled shotguns with buckshot loads at six paces as terms of combat with any southern challenger; and last but not lightly to be related, was the history of "Filibuster Walker," that man greater than a pirate or an Indian, who had even asked my father to go a-filibustering with him, first in Mexico and then in Nicaragua. And in those childish days I could not comprehend why such an invitation had been declined, for being a filibuster seemed greater than becoming president, or even being a pirate. In later years, while a law student, I saw much of one Barney Wolfe, an early Marysville friend of my father. "Handsome Barney" he had been called in the '50's when he was by Walker's side in Nicaragua.

Thus possessed of the American side of Walker's history, I found a peculiar interest in entering Lower California and listening to the old Indians and Mexicans who had seen and known him there, and it seems appropriate here to record the Mexican course of the "Last of the Filibusters." In 1850, at the age of twenty-six, Walker had made his appearance in San Francisco as a journalist. Prior to that date, he had trained himself for medicine, law and journalism, having studied successively at his native city of Nashville, and in Philadelphia, Paris, Göttingen, Heidelberg and New Orleans. In 1851, he came before the California public in consequence of an article in his paper, the San Francisco *Herald*, reflecting upon a certain Judge Parsons; because of this article he was fined five hundred dollars and, in default of payment thereof, sent to jail. A popular demonstration in Walker's behalf ensued and he was released on a writ of habeas corpus. Later, he went before the California Legislature and endeavored to secure the impeachment of Judge Parsons—judicial impeachments being a California epidemic at that time. In 1852, Walker appeared in Marysville as an attorney and as leader of the pro-slavery faction. In the same year he visited Guaymas for the purpose of discovering what the French filibusters,

Pindray and Count Raousset de Boulbon, were doing in
Sonora.   Impressed with the possibility of forming a pro-
slavery state out of Sonora, the young firebrand hastened
back to California where he found a hearty support awaiting him at the hands of the southern leaders, the "Chiv"
element, who, imbued not only with devotion to the slave
cause but also with a firm belief in the doctrine of "mani-
fest destiny," were watching the French filibusters with
hostile eyes.   Heartily encouraged, therefore, and accompanied by his friend, Henry P. Watkins, Walker revisited
Guaymas in June, 1853, only to be ordered away by the
alarmed authorities.   But before his departure many of
the affrighted inhabitants besought him to return with fighting men and protect them from the warlike Yaquis who
even to this day terrorize portions of Sonora.

Once again in the United States Walker opened a re-
cruiting office at San Francisco and issued to ready pur-
chasers bonds of the prospective "Republic of Sonora and
Lower California."   California was filled with venturesome spirits and many of them at once gathered about Walker's standard.   For the major part these recruits were
young Kentuckians and Tennesseans, imbued with southern
ideas and "spoiling for a scrap."   On October the 15th,
1853, Walker, with forty-six men and abundant supplies,
slipped out of the Golden Gate, bound on a filibustering expedition against a friendly nation.   No attempt was made
to stop his warlike brig, the "Caroline," for the very defi-
nite reason that, for preventing Walker's departure two
weeks earlier in the "Arrow," General Hitchcock had been
removed from his command of the government forces at
San Francisco!   In the '50's Jefferson Davis and his southern clique of Senators were anxious to make the way easy
for an adventurer who might bring a new Texas into the

Union and add new slave votes to their column in the United States Senate.

In due time the "Caroline" arrived at Las Paz, where Walker landed his men, took the city, issued a proclamation promising general protection, religious toleration and establishing the Louisiana Code, a simple method of introducing slavery. A flag, with two stars representing Lower California and Sonora and with two red stripes enclosing a white one, was immediately hoisted and a republic was proclaimed with Walker as President, Frederic Emory as Secretary of State, John M. Jernagin as Secretary of War, Howard H. Snow as Secretary of the Navy, Charles H. Gilman as Captain of Battalion, and Wm. P. Mann as Admiral of the Navy. These proceedings the natives viewed with complacency. Such opposition as they offered was speedily overcome by the invaders, who shortly departed taking with them the public documents—or such of them as they had not already shot away as cartridge covers—and Señor Robelledo, the Political Chief of the district. After touching successively at San José del Cabo and Magdalena Bay, the filibusters disembarked, a hundred miles south of San Diego, at Todos Santos Bay, where Walker established himself in headquarters, which he termed Fort McKibben, from whence he easily repulsed the attacking Mexicans.

Meantime, rumor and the press announced throughout the United States the accurate news that Walker was in control of Lower California, and throughout the South and West many were anxious to join his standard. One evening, early in December, 1853, the great double doors of an improvised barrack were thrown open in San Francisco and out upon the streets poured a body of well-armed recruits for "President Walker." Undisturbed, except by the clamor of many who desired to join them, they marched down to the water front and, two hundred and thirty strong, sailed at midnight in the "Anita" for Todos Santos Bay. These men were mainly Kentuckians and Tennesseans, with a sprinkling of Irish and Germans whom Walker considered the bravest of all foreigners and the only equals of his irresistible American warriors. In physique these filibusters rivalled the giant guardsmen of the Emperor Frederick; among them a man under six feet in height was a rarity.

Reinforced by these adventurers, Walker seized Santo Tomás and fought the battles of La Grulla and San Vicente, both victories for his flag. In referring to these contests the old Mexicans and Indians, to a man, characterize Walker in the same words: he was small, boyish appearing and very brave (*muy valiente*). Moreover, he seemed possessed of Berserker rage in battle. In describing this attribute an old Indian at San Vicente related to me how Walker rushed always ahead of his men when fighting and at such times seemed a devil. The general impression retained of the filibusters is that Walker feared nothing and was a wonderful Captain; that he was youthful looking and wished the people to be free from ill usage; that his men were sharpshooting giants seeking to ravage the land, but "all soldiers and officials did that in those days" according to one of my informants. At Ensenada, an old Indian woman gave me her recollections of the filibusters: she had been a mere girl, living at San Isidro where there were many young women, when *"Guillermo"* Walker and his *Americanos* marched by: he was a small, preoccupied *Capitan,* but his men were very tall and they waved handkerchiefs at her and her friends. I inquired what response was made: "Oh, we waved our hands to them, beckoning," she replied, with a crackling grin.

Walker was always restlessly busy. Besides fighting these small battles, he issued five more proclamations, organized a government and drilled his followers—and so incessantly that a body of them endeavored to desert, an unfortunate step on their part, however, for not only were they unsuccessful in their effort but two of their number were shot and many of the others flogged. Immediately after these proceedings, the filibuster leader gathered his men about him and offered them all their choice of continuing on or of returning to the United States. Only fifty turned northward. With the balance Walker went into quarters at San Vicente.

At this point Uncle Sam again might have acquired Lower California. He had allowed Walker to recruit and outfit in his territory and to sail, unhindered, through the Golden Gate; six months had passed and now the Peninsula lay in the filibuster's palm, ready for annexation. But Uncle made no move. The opportunity was lost.

There is no lack of interest in the further adventures of the filibusters even though they have had no chronicler. On the 20th of March, 1854, Walker sent a portion of his forces to San Quintin Bay and Rosario under instructions to hold the country. With the balance he marched into the mountains to the east of San Vicente and history has had no record of his doings thereafter until he appeared a month later, on the west bank of the Colorado River, intent on reaching Sonora and subjecting it to his rule. His every step, however, is recalled by the old Indians. According to their accounts he entered the Pais country, along the Colentura Arroyo, directed by a small band of Indian allies, and there some of his men met their death—just how or by whom the Indians do not relate. From this arroyo he swung around the northwest shoulder of the mighty sierra of San Pedro Mártir and entered the Valle Trinidad, the scattered inhabitants fleeing before him. Here he added to his stock of beef cattle and preempted an unbroken "calico" or pinto stallion which the departing Mexicans, with malice aforethought, had left behind.   It was a beautiful animal, and possessed of so wild and vicious a spirit that no *vaquero* had been able to stay astride its back.   When the boyish *Capitan,* therefore, in the presence of his men and of numerous Indians, not only mounted the stallion but subdued it, the Indians, delighted by such horsemanship—and the evident abundance of provisions—immediately allied themselves to the cause of the filibusters and showed them their ancient trail into the secret depths of the Arroyo Grande and thence across the desert, around the Sierra del Pintos, and down the Hardy River to the Colorado.   By this time, Pais, Kaliwa, Catarina Yuma and Cocupa Indians were following the *Americanos* and joyously sharing their diminishing provisions.

Crossing the Colorado River proved a disastrous feat. Cattle and supplies were swept away, lives lost and the rank and file discouraged.   Famine and a general break-up ensued, some of the filibusters traveling northward and surrendering to the American forces at Yuma, while Walker himself with the balance, recrossed the river and began his return march.   Provisions gone, the *Americanos* quickly lost their Indian allies and soon found them, as pitiless enemies, co-operating with a company of Mexican troops under Melendrez, a most resourceful officer.   Eventually, the remnant of the filibusters, their reputation for fearless bravery in no way tarnished, reached the American Line just south of San Diego, and surrendered, on the American side, to Captain Burton, of the United States Army.

Just before Walker and his men crossed the Line, the leader of the pursuing Mexican forces advised Captain Burton that he wished to capture the filibusters.   "Good," responded Burton, "that will relieve us of trouble.   You are five to one, go ahead."   Thereupon the Mexican troops advanced cautiously upon their crippled foe, but Walker, in place of escaping across the Line, faced his young warriors about and led them, wildly cheering, against the foe. The latter fled, incontinently, whereupon Walker marched his men into United States territory and surrendered. The filibusters whom Walker had sent southward from San Vicente overran the country while their ammunition lasted, then they died by the garrote and the dagger. For his action against a friendly country, Walker was tried in the United States Court at San Francisco—and acquitted!

When one recalls that in 1847-8 Uncle Sam fought for Lower California, obtained possession of the land, conciliated the people—and then gave up the country; that in 1853-4 he permitted Walker to outfit and recruit in San Francisco and acquitted him of the crime of so doing— and yet did not accept Lower California when the filibuster had it in hand early in 1854; when one reads that in 1859, our same Uncle, through President Buchanan and his Minister to Mexico, McClane, endeavored to take advantage of Benito Juarez's extremity and purchase Lower California; and twenty-two years later, if rumor runs truly, only the death of President Garfield interfered with an official sounding of Mexico as to her willingness to sell the California Peninsula: When one considers this succession of inconsistent actions, but a single explanation presents itself: assuredly, they all chanced at times when our Uncle Sam was off fishing and Miss Columbia was running the government and enjoying, to the limit, her feminine prerogative of being whimsical.

Persistently, however, the question arises, Will the United States acquire Lower California? And it is no unsafe prediction to reply that the Peninsula will not come under the Stars and Stripes by any filibustering doorway. The ill-advised persons, who buried stands of arms in the sands near San Quintin not a quarter of a century since, might well have known that, in endeavoring to emulate Walker, they were pursuing a plan not in accord with an age of Hague Peace Tribunals.

▲ Mission San Fernando Velicatá

Llano de San Agustín ▼

▲   Agua Dulce

Pictographs (Cataviñá)   ▼

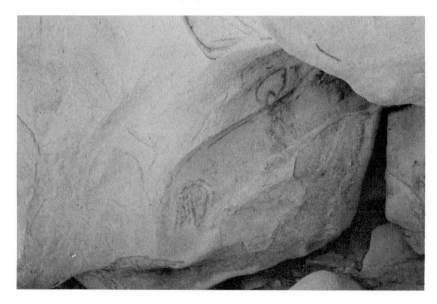

CHAPTER V

DECEMBER and January had passed and February was opening with a burst of rain that made the possession of a slicker a distinct blessing. San Vicente, with its romantic associations, was many leagues behind me, but my course still trended southward along *El Camino Real.*

On the fifth of February I rode into San Quintin, a small village of perhaps a hundred two-legged inhabitants and a hundred million fleas. It is situated on the edge of the Pacific, just above the thirtieth parallel of north latitude, and hard by five strange hills which, in the halcyon days of its buccaneering and smuggling trade, gave the port its early name of the *Bay of Five Hills.* Briefly, San Quintin has a harbor which needs dredging, wonderful salt beds from which, for some unknown reason, no salt is extracted, a flour mill which is enjoying a long vacation, and a lobster factory which does nothing to interfere with the numerous lobsters thriving along the coast. Also, there is a twenty-mile railroad—relic of colonization efforts—over which a locomotive once traveled carrying as its freight a bale of hay; being put to work, later, at running the flour mill! Finally, gulls and other sea fowl march and counter march in squadrons along the shore line, while the duck and goose shooting to he had at San Quintin is not to be excelled on the American continent.

In consequence of a "scene" with my erstwise Texas parson, I arrived at San Quintin in a most irritable mood. The trouble had arisen from the man's devotional methods. Of course an earnest desire for prayer at eventide—though assuredly most unusual along the Border—merits respect, but Ben's proceedings along this line early aroused my suspicions concerning his sincerity; for not only did he shout his supplications in good old southern Methodist fashion, but he shortly developed a vexatious habit of confessing his sins dolefully in my immediate presence at such times as I was tired and especially in need of sleep. The second night of these revival experiences had brought forth the fact that the fellow was in Mexico because of an anxious Grand Jury in Texas: admitting his crime and expressing his penitence, he called loudly upon his Creator for forgiveness, announcing his desire to return and receive the full punishment awaiting him at the hands of the law. My sympathy aroused—though my slumbers were disturbed—I advised him the following morning that upon the completion of our trip I would present his case, in its most favorable aspect, to the prosecuting attorney of his home county and arrange for a light sentence, the arrangement between us being conditioned upon his return to Texas and submission to the authorities. Texas prisons, however, are, it seems, places in which one has no leisure for continuous prayer, but much time for heavy manual labor; therefore my suggestion was not well received. Finally, the morning before our arrival at San Quintin, the wayward Ben petulantly disclosed his cowardice, declaring himself averse to facing the prospective dangers of the middle portion of the Peninsula and advising me to give up the idea of proceeding into such an arid region. To this I made bitter reply, stating that I intended to proceed, even though I had to travel alone, and as for him, if he planned to desert, he had best do so at the first town, for if he endeavored to leave me in the wilderness farther south, I would shoot him down like a dog.

Under such a happy condition of affairs, enhanced by the dampness of a driving rain storm, I made my entry into San Quintin. Almost immediately, however, matters became more cheerful, for a courteous and well informed Mexican, Sr. Gabriel Victoria, greeted me kindly and made me acquainted with the Englishman, Señor Dick. The balance of his name is immaterial. The "remittance man" of my Alamo burro show had first mentioned him to me. Some time a first mate in the English merchant marine and since the early '80's engaged continuously in Peninsular mining enterprises, no more romantic figure is to be found in Lower California than this sturdy, blonde, good-looking Englishman, Señor Dick. The more material part of his qualifications is, that you cannot find a better traveling companion for *El Camino Real* than he, or one more widely informed.

On the evening of my arrival at San Quintin, "Charlie," an extremely wise and enthusiastic Chinaman whose acquaintance I had just made, came to my tent with word that I was wanted in the hotel dining-room. On entering the room, five minutes later, I found that it was deserted save for two lone men who were seated at either end of a long table. One was Señor Dick, the other I recognized as the native mail carrier of the district. As the substantial distance between the two men was bridged by an alarming array of bottles, I accepted Señor Dick's invitation to be seated, with a mental thanksgiving for an extensive capacity that comes through a strain of Dutch blood. No sooner was I in my allotted place than the prompt opening of bottles assured me of the accuracy of what I already surmised: I was in for a serious and not-to-be-slighted ordeal, a frontier drinking-bout. And here let me parenthesize that San Quentin is pronounced San Cantéen, a pronunciation which no visitor is apt to forget, for assuredly the canteen is patron saint of this flea-bitten pueblo. As assistance in securing a new muleteer might depend on the manner in which I passed the drinking test, I committed myself to it with due deliberation. Fortunately, by taking port in place of the more fiery mescal chosen by my companions and by devoting considerable time to the consumption of crackers and apples, I was enabled to hold my own, acquitting myself to the evident satisfaction of my examiners.

Early in the game Charlie dropped in, inquiring whether I was acquainted with two of my compatriots who had passed through some months before. "Him catchee klyote," he exclaimed, disdainfully, "no good *carne*. Him catchee lats and mice, belly good, *muy bueno*," he added, musingly, at the same time indicating, with thumb and forefinger, the way in which he transferred similar choice morsels into his mouth. Subsequently I ascertained that the Americans had been engaged in securing specimens for the National Museum at Washington. The festive Oriental, however, had come to his own conclusions. Presently, inspired by the clinking glasses and the mellow light of dim lamp and flickering candle, Señor Dick and the Mexican grew reminiscent, recounting, in turn, a succession of weirdly fascinating tales of mines and lost prospectors, of buried treasure and haunted ruins, of game and poisonous serpents, of the camino and of thirst. Finally, when the bottles were nearly empty, the jovial *Chino* showed that he had sportive as well as epicurean tastes, for he gravely produced from within the liberal folds of his blouse a ragged pack of cards and innocently suggested a "little gama poka." This risk—the mail carrier averred that Charlie always had "full houses" —I avoided by coolly suggesting, as a substitute, that each man turn a card, "low" man to win, our watches the stakes and only to be produced after the "show down." But to this game Charlie objected as naïvely as he had urged "poka." The reason for his reluctance and my indifference was explained later when, being curious concerning the hour, we drew out our timepieces: his was a valuable gold repeater; mine had cost a dollar and was already out of order.

Astounded by the oblique position of the hour hand, we hunted our blankets, upturned glasses, drained bottles, empty lamp and guttered candle silently attesting the end of the "conference." And yet such were its auspicious results that before morning was far advanced Señor Dick and I were in the saddle, with pack animals swinging along before us. A capable well-mannered Mexican boy, duly indentured to me for three months, had taken my parson's place as muleteer, San Quintin was miles behind us, and my worries were forgotten. I had paid off Ben before leaving the village; so thenceforth there was prospect of my slumbers being undisturbed. The little I know concerning the unfortunate fellow's subsequent movements was related to me months later. Retracing his steps northward he had stopped by the wayside, evidently to enjoy the hospitality of a party of miners, when one of the latter suddenly demanded my whereabouts. Being somewhat slow in his response, the dazed Ben found himself unexpectedly face to face with that inflexible, though unwritten, law of the frontier, which declares that where two men enter the wilderness together and one returns, alone, that one must account satisfactorily for the absence of his fellow or suffer the consequences. That evening the unfortunate fellow slipped out of camp; he appeared later in Ensenada, but I never saw him again.

And now what a different and interesting companion I had! For three days our course trended southward, and except at Rosario, not a man crossed our trail. The sierras blocked the eastern horizon, the booming Pacific was down at our right and all about us were cacti, cacti and more cacti.

"Señor Dick, where are the Indians?" I inquired as we rode along. "In the States, Lower California and Indians are practically synonymous."

The Señor shifted his stubby pipe and answered shortly, "In the States and in the Old Country, people don't know anything about Lower California." Presently, however, he considered the Indian proposition. "They are dead, stone dead, the whole blooming outfit—except a few strays. Down along the Colorado and the Hardy there's said to be a fair handful of Cocupas. I take it that you've made the acquaintance of the Catarina Yumas and Pi-pis, and, by and bye, over there on San Pedro Mártir, you'll find the Kaliwas. But the southern tribes, the thousands of Pericues, Guiacuras and Cochimis—you'll have a hard time finding even a trace of them." I urged my mule forward. It is strangely difficult to catch the words of a man riding ahead of one.

"Weren't they hardy?" I asked.

"Rather." Then his blue eyes twinkled and he continued, "Did you ever hear of the Indian who ran from Santa Rosalia to San Francisco?"

"No, tell me," I urged.

"It is a true yarn," began my companion, and with this introduction narrated the following tale: A few years ago there lived on the Peninsula an ancient hunter, an Indian by the name of Juan. He was a great wanderer, spending part of his time at Loreto, part at Santa Rosalia and the balance in the "waist" of the Peninsula. On one of his periodic visits to Santa Rosalia, he found a snorting, clanging iron affair, running on metallic rails reaching from the Providencia Copper Mines to the milling plant at Santa Rosalia. The Rothschilds and other big French capitalists, having purchased the mines, had built a short railroad to connect them with Santa Rosalia, half a league distant, but this explanation was not vouchsafed to Juan nor would it have conveyed aught to him. However, for years he had watched with silent interest the steamers plying up and down the Gulf of California, or the *Mar de Cortez* as he called it, and upon being informed that the new creature was related to the *"Vapors"* he quietly slipped into the frame station at Providencia and asked for a ride. This request curtly refused, Juan forthwith fell into a bitter passion of anger from which he was aroused to action by the sneering whistle of the departing engine. Casting one disdainful glance over station, employees, engine and track, the lithe Indian swung away at full speed down the Camino and shortly loped into Santa Rosalia, somewhat in advance of the screaming engine.

Emboldened by this success, a month later Juan entered the steamship office at Santa Rosalia and begged for passage to San Francisco. A second time he met with a refusal. Again angered, the old hunter sought out his English and American friends and they, in a spirit of mischief, promptly backed him to vanquish the steamer *Curacao* in its forthcoming run to San Francisco, a six hundred league trip for the steamer, four hundred leagues for the pedestrian. With a final shriek of escaping steam, the *Curacao* nosed out of the harbor. With a twist of his breech-cloth Juan took to the cactus. Two weeks later the steamer entered the slip at San Francisco and there sat old Juan on a barnacled pile, calmly smoking a cigarette. He wore a trifle more clothes than on leaving Santa Rosalia and was a shade thinner, but otherwise the same old Indian. *"Vds. muy tarde,"* he solemnly remarked to the Captain, between cigarette whiffs, the which, freely translated, means "You fellows are mighty slow."

"Whether or not Juan's backers wired their friends in San Diego to help the Indian's legs with a passage on the Northern Express from that city to San Francisco," added Señor Dick, with a broad grin, "is no part of the story. I merely offer it as seasoning. The point is, that Juan made good and his backers gathered in their wagers."

"It's a mighty fine story," said I, rather emphasizing the last word, "but how did Juan carry his commissary while on the camino?"

The Señor disregarded this query, apparently, his eyes the meantime resting abstractedly on our mozos, now well in the lead with the pack animals. Presently, however, he broke the silence. "What is your Mexican boy doing there, off the camino?" he asked. I looked up and observed that the boy seemed to be enjoying himself greatly. "Why, he is extracting something edible from the flower of the aloe or maguay."

"Exactly! And that something is a dew as sweet as honey—and nourishing. Do you know what that green club is, which my mozo has so carefully bound back of his saddle?"

I shook my head.

"Well, to-night you will see him roast that in the coals and enjoy it as much as you would a sweet potato. It is the young stalk of the flowering maguay. And within that viznaga there, you may find a juice sufficient to lessen thirst."

Thus, as we traveled on I learned from the kindly Englishman the natural lore of the country, knowledge which in time was to save my life. About the fifth day out we approached the old Mission of San Fernando. Here our ways were to part, and here he advised me to look out for a high cliff marked with prehistoric hieroglyphs.

CHAPTER VI

IN the opening pages of his scholarly work on California, Padre Francisco Javier Clavijero, the eighteenth century Jesuit chronicler, dealt extensively with the native races of the southern portion of the Peninsula, and in his paragraphs concerning prehistoric peoples offered material calculated to excite the curiosity of any traveler in Lower California. Indeed, according to Clavijero these first settlers were of heroic size and given to hieroglyphic writing,

In line with his statements is the following, which is said to have been written in 1790:

" 'Throughout civilized California, from south to north, and especially in the caves and smooth rocks, there remain various rude paintings, . . . The colors are of four kinds —yellow, green, black and a reddish color. The greater part of them are painted *in high places,* and from this it is inferred by some that the old tradition is true, that there were giants among the ancient Californians. . . . One inscription resembles Gothic letters interspersed with Hebrew and Chaldean characters. . . . It is evident that the paintings and drawings of the Californians are significant symbols and landmarks by which they intended to leave to posterity the memory of their establishment in this country. . . . These pictures are not like those of Mexico but might have the same purpose.' "

Bancroft, in his "Native Races," discusses the paragraph last cited, locating the writings on a cliff near the old Jesuit

* Republished, in part, from *The American Anthropologist,* for April-June, 1908.

Misson of Santiago, some leagues below La Paz, and concludes with this statement, "The only accounts of antiquities (on the Peninsula) relate to cave and cliff paintings and inscriptions which have never been copied and concerning which, consequently, not much can be said."

These various passages concerning the prehistoric Californians had whetted my curiosity even before I entered Mexico and quite naturally, therefore, throughout my explorations, and especially in the cliff regions, I kept a sharp lookout for any evidence of the handiwork of these forgotten people. To my great delight I was fortunate to discover three new groups of cliff writings which I will here present in succinct order.

1.   The Arroyo Grande Petroglyphs.

In January, while hunting big-horn, I made camp in the Arroyo Grande. This Grand Canyon is an awe-inspiring chasm through which a dry river-bed takes its course, heading in the sierras southeast of Alamo and finally debouching into the desert immediately southwest of the mouth of the Colorado River. The product of volcanic action, the entire region is dry and barren. Dull red cliffs, honey-combed with caves, rise sheer above the white sand of the arroyo bed to dizzy heights where condor and big-horn make their homes. There are no known springs of water in the vicinity, but in one of the many deep and rocky gorges which intersect the Arroyo Grande from the northwest there are eight or nine *tinajas,* or natural cisterns, where rain water— when there is rain—collects. The petroglyphs are pecked shallowly into the face of a dark granite boulder set above the largest of the *tinajas.* In the lower right hand corner of the cliff there appears a figure which may have been intended to represent a human being. Aside from this it would seem as though the writer intended to make an in-

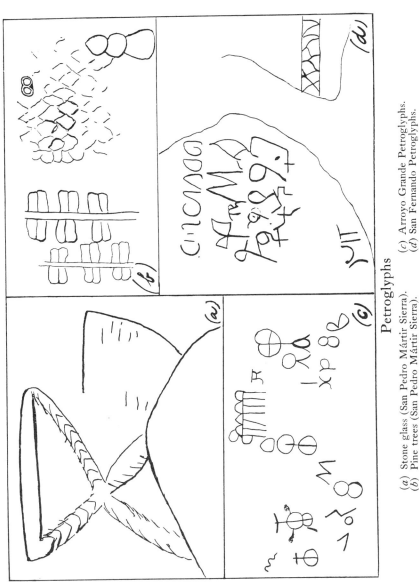

Petroglyphs

(a) Stone glass (San Pedro Mártir Sierra).
(b) Pine trees (San Pedro Mártir Sierra).
(c) Arroyo Grande Petroglyphs.
(d) San Fernando Petroglyphs.

scription rather than to delineate any figures. The design that at once catches the eye, however, is the rain sign of the Mokis, the cloud from which drops are falling. Two other characters of interest are the M and the Φ which stand out from the center of the group. Here, moreover, as in the San Fernando group which I will presently describe, are designs so far resembling the Phœnecian characters representative of Bh and N as to explain the eighteenth century chronicler's classification of the California petroglyphs as writings of the Chaldeans and other ancient peoples.

These Arroyo Grande petroglyphs, though barely exceeding in any instance a height of eighteen inches, stand out plain and distinct.

For untold generations the Arroyo Grande was an Indian highway to the desert and the Colorado River, and from its mouth, traversing the lava formation of the eastern portion of the desert, scar-like trails are still visible, although cacti, which require, the Indians say, two centuries for maturing, long ago overgrew these forgotten caminos and stretched their dead bodies athwart them. Until late in the last century the Arroyo Grande was a hiding-place for outlaws, the *tinajas* being unknown to the Mexican authorities. Even now they are visited but infrequently.

2. The San Pedro Mártir Petroglyphs.

As the crow flies, the distance from these Arroyo Grande *tinajas* to the base of San Pedro Mártir Sierra, is not over twelve leagues, but to the being not blessed with wings, the rugged sierras about the Arroyo Grande and the sweltering sands of the San Felipe Desert make the distance seem interminable. This desert has a gruesome reputation, for though but few people have entered upon its stretches, of those few, several have not returned. Mexicans and Indians, alike, speak of it with a shudder and there is no record of any man having explored all of its recesses and bounds. Out upon this dreary waste open the forbidding mouths of San Mattias, Esperancia, Copal and Diablo, grim arroyos slashed deep into the vitals of San Pedro Mártir Sierra. Before these openings worn boulders and scarred logs, borne down from the heights above by wild storm torrents, lie half buried in the sand, most inviting eminences for lion and coyote when hunger and the restlessness of night call them from their lairs. Even the Kaliwas, the Indians of the great Sierra, know little of these retreats: there is sufficient heat upon the desert, where some air stirs, they say, with a shrug of dark shoulders; why approach the mountainside, where there is no breeze from the Gulf, and enter a heat infernal, challenging death itself?

These arroyos open out from the northern side of the sierra. In one of them, a short distance from its mouth and to the west, there are three successive sets of petroglyphs, all of them facing the east. The Indians are unaware of their existence. I saw them, however, in August, 1906.

The first set is on a boulder not over fifty paces from the bed of the arroyo. The design of this petroglyph is that of a conventional human heart enclosing characters. The other sets are near one another and about one hundred paces up-stream from the first. They appear on bold granite cliffs, high above the bed of the arroyo. One of these last named sets represents several persons approaching two pine trees. As the only pines in the neighborhood are on the crest of the sierra in the direction taken by the figures, this petroglyph may be taken as a guide post of the ancient people.

Clavijero, in recounting the San Joaquin discovery, mentions that in one of the caves paintings were found representing "men and women with garments similar to those of the Mexicans, but they were entirely barefoot. The men had their arms open and somewhat elevated, and one of the women had her hair hanging loose down her back and a tuft of feathers on her head." Oddly enough, the figures of this group are not those of nude Indians of the Peninsula, but of people "with garments."

On a cliff, just above the pine-tree cliff, there are two figures either of persons with broad head-coverings or of a quadruped with human head and shoulders. Beyond this set there is a panel of figures on a broad and wide cliff and, at the farther side thereof, a sharp design much like an hour-glass. All of these last three sets of petroglyphs are over four feet in height, cut in outline on the granite rock and the peckings smeared over with an unfading yellowish paint. Distance plays strange pranks with them, for at first glance they seem plain and accessible, but after one has worked his way upward to a certain proximity their inaccessibility becomes disappointingly apparent. Indeed, the people who marked these cliffs either had an abundance of rope ladders at their disposal or else lower buttresses of the crag have crumbled away.

3. The San Fernando Petroglyphs.

It was in February, that as related in the preceding chapter, Señor Dick and I arrived at the ruins of the Franciscan Mission of San Fernando, founded by Junipero Serra in May, 1769, immediately prior to his departure for Upper California and his notable career in that favored region. San Fernando lies on the thirtieth parallel of north latitude. A short half-mile northwest of the mission ruins there are several high cliffs facing the east and on these I found the petroglyphs of which the señor had advised me. According to the native legend these *jeroglyficos* were made by a race of great stature who inhabited the country long before the coming of the Indians. The design or character, which appears by itself at the right hand of the group and resembles a Roman numeral, is identical with one of the characters in the Santiago group, which was located in the eighteenth century. At the very top of the cliff I deciphered certain letters, perhaps intended either for the Spanish Cruz, or the Latin Crux, a cross: anyway, it is said that these were added by the padres to destroy the spell of evil inherent in the *jeroglyficos* below!

4. *Other Evidence of the Petroglyph Makers.*

In addition to these various cliff writings, there are other signs in Lower California which bear testimony of the sojourn of this prehistoric race. Thus, a hundred miles and more south of San Fernando, there rises a barren range of lofty sierras, and while exploring certain of its higher ridges a prospector recently found remnants of an ancient road cut in the rock. Before he had followed the road any great distance the prospector's canteen failed him, so that he was compelled to retreat without having ascertained the objective of the camino. It would be interesting to explore this range—and with relays of Indians to pack water, exploration would be possible—for its course might disclose further traces of the Petroglyph Makers.

A hundred miles southwest of these sierras lies the little mining pueblo of Calmalli. But a few leagues to the west of the pueblo may be heard the booming breakers of the Pacific. On the cliffs of an arroyo down near the ocean appears the work of some bygone Petroglyph Maker who certainly possessed marvelous skill, for the human figures and designs which he here drew were extremely well executed and enduringly decorated with coloring matter. Southeast of Calmalli and just off the twenty-seventh parallel of north latitude lies San Joaquin, a rancho where,

▲   Cataviñá

Calamajué   ▼

▲   La Asamblea

Yubay   ▼

according to Clavijero, one Padre Robea, a Jesuit priest, found gigantic remains and a cave with "painted figures of men and women, decently clad." Near San Joaquin is the old mission town of San Ignacio, the junction of numerous *caminos* dating back to the days of the padres. Some of these highways are said to antedate the Spanish conquest and to be relics of the skill of the Petroglyph Makers. Certainly, a combination of many laborers with a remarkable knowledge of the art of road-building must have been essential for their construction.

To sum up: Of a character differing in many respects from those in the United States and on the mainland of Mexico, the cliff writings in Lower California form a chain extending down the Peninsula; furthermore, there is evidence in the sierras which indicates the existence of roads antedating the earliest Spanish settlements in the country.

In connection with the Petroglyph Makers, it is quite worth while gathering together such data as there is concerning the people who immediately succeeded them, the Indians of the southern portion of the California Peninsula. A crisp, modern description of these natives might, with slight exaggeration, be phrased in a brief sentence, viz.: There aren't any. However, their passing is of such recent date that an accurate knowledge of them has been preserved by book and by tradition even though they made no petroglyphs and left no monuments. When the first Europeans landed on the Peninsula in 1533, they found, near the present site of La Paz, a wideawake party of Indians who not only impolitely objected to being robbed by the punctilious Spaniards, but even ruthlessly proceeded to kill Ximenes, a pilot from one of the ships of Cortez. In this, the natives showed a fine though unconscious sense of justice, for Ximenes had, a short time before, mutinied and killed Becerra, his captain. During the period of slightly more than a century and half succeeding this episode, various Conquistadores and buccaneers visited the southern portion of the Peninsula and reported it as thickly peopled with Indians, brave in combat, skillful in diving, unaccustomed to the wearing of clothing, habitually possessing an abnormal hunger and always delighted by the receipt of any sweetmeat.

Then the seventeenth century came to a close and the Society of Jesus, through its missionaries, undertook the development of California and the Christianization of the "Gentiles" or Indians.   These Padres found two principal native tribes inhabiting the southern portion of the Peninsula: the Pericues, reaching from Cape San Lucas to the Mission of Santiago and some leagues beyond, and the Guiacuras, disputing the northern territory of the Pericues and extending northward to Loreto, the early Mission capital of the Californias.   The Cochimis, occupying the region from Loreto to the high mountains at the northern end of Lower California, occasionally reached over into the southern grounds.   In the aggregate these three tribes numbered twenty thousand members   Each of the three main tribal divisions was broken into many lesser tribes, with individual dialects and varied idioms.   Although they were a healthy people at the time of the coming of the Padres, the Indians did not remain so long, for measles, smallpox and the loathsome diseases of tainted civilization, introduced among them by the garrisons, spread with frightful virulence.   In seventy years the southern Indians were reduced to a scant five thousand.   By 1794 it is recorded that there were no Indians surviving about some of the southern missions, and thirty years later report says that not a single pure Indian was to be found below Loreto. Those who escaped disease, however, lived to extreme old age.   So indeed, do the Mexicans upon the Peninsula to-day, and one may meet

The aged Cochimi of Santa Gertrudis

even yet centenarians at Loreto and learn from them concerning the closing days of the Spanish sway when the soldiers branded with a red-hot iron each new herd of Indians brought into the Presidio!

The Pericues and Guiacuras are now practically extinct. It is not surprising. Of the thousands of Cochimis, perhaps a hundred still survive about the missions of San Xavier, Santa Gertrudis and San Borja. Those at San Xavier, however, I am inclined to believe should be classed as Guiacuras. The Cochimis are a good-natured, easygoing people, far more formally religious and far more fond of hunting than the neighboring Mexicans; they are more reliable workers than their neighbors, but they dress just as raggedly. A few years more and they will have disappeared entirely. A family of this tribe watch over San Borja Mission, down in the "waist" of the Peninsula. Rita, the head of the family, faithfully rang the mission bells the Sunday I spent at San Borja.

When I was at Santa Gertrudis, I slept by the mission and was awakened early in the morning by an ancient Cochimi who was croning over her beads before the mission altar. Later, as she sat on the steps, enjoying a cigarette and sunning her frail body, she told me that she was over a hundred years old. Had she said one hundred and fifty I should not have been skeptical, for she seemed well along in the mummy class. Crouched on the worn stone steps, she seemed the very epitome of the mission system, a poor, faithful old dame, the sole worshiper in the wilderness, dreaming of the last Padres, for whose return a half century of prayers had been vain, and peopling, doubtless, the deserted plaza with the figures of those now resting in the neglected graves hard by.

CHAPTER VII

FOR three days Señor Dick and I rested at San Fernando, waiting for a cessation of the downpour which met us there. San Fernando is conducive to waiting. Moreover, from both a geographical and an historical standpoint, it is a spot for consideration. But to appreciate San Fernando or any portion of the California Peninsula, for that matter, an insight, at least, into the mission history of the land is essential. Lacking such knowledge every step of Peninsula travel is deprived of the wealth of color with which it is illumined in the rich traditional and recorded history of the land. In the State of California the old missions are of romantic interest as landmarks of an earlier day. Yet so vast is the area over which they are scattered and so marvelous has been the growth of the country since their construction that a traveler might pass the length of the State without seeing so much as a single mission. In the Mexican Peninsula of Baja California, on the other hand, so completely were the garden spots searched out and preempted by the zealous mission builders that the chain of missions eventually included the vital watering places of the country. Reaching north, south and west from Loreto, the Mother Mission, and weaving in and out among the various missions, were three great highways, the *Gulfo,* the *Sierra,* and the *Pacifico,*

Caminos Reales.   So closely did these caminos follow the most feasible lines of travel and so slight has been the material development of the territory since the days of the padres that even now, in the twentieth century, the ancient mission chain is not an incident but the most prominent and essential feature of Peninsula travel.

It was in the closing years of the seventeenth century, over a hundred and sixty years subsequent to the time that Cortez first set foot in the land, that the Jesuits began their monumental series of mission construction in California. Later, after the Society of Jesus had dominated for seventy years, came the San Fernandines, adding, during their brief stay, one mission to the twenty-five erected by their predecessors.   The Dominicans quickly superseded the San Fernandines and, with nine missions to their credit, concluded the chain begun by the Society of Jesus.   Thus, although the missions seen in the State of California were constructed by the San Fernandines, alone, the more numerous missions in Baja California represent the labor of three Brotherhoods.   Furthermore, mission building in Baja California was practically completed ere it began in what is now the State of California.

A glimpse into early chronicles shows the Mission of San Fernando in the light of an historic link between the two Californias.   In the spring of the year 1769, the worthy Padre Junipero Serra, head of the Franciscan Friars, then new arrivals in California, accompanied by Captain Gaspar de Portolá, Governor of the Peninsula, and guarded by a strong body of soldiers and Indians, made camp at a spot twenty leagues northwest of Santa Maria, the last mission of the Jesuits.   Here, in a fertile, well-watered valley, surrounded by mountains rich in copper and iron ore, many Indians lived and an advance guard of the new Brotherhood had already erected a few

adobes. To good Padre Serra and the gallant captain the
site seemed favorable for a mission and therefore they
halted, laying, one morning in May, 1769, the foundations
of the Mission of San Fernando de Velicata. But the name
of Junipero Serra was to become historic in another California. After a few days in this pleasant spot the Padre,
with Portolá, and a portion of the escort, hurried forward
and in July, ninety-six days out from Loreto, he founded a
mission at San Diego and thereby began his illustrious
career in Alta California, for the San Diego foundation
was the first of the many missions erected in Upper California.

San Fernando de Velicata, in latitude 30 degrees north,
longitude 115 degrees 5 minutes west, and lying thirty
leagues southwesterly from the Mexican port of San Quintin on the Pacific coast, was the only mission of the Franciscan Brotherhood in Lower California. For in the year
1773, pursuant to a compact entered into with the Dominican Brotherhood, the San Fernandines left the Peninsula
and moved northward into Upper California. At the close
of the eighteenth century the mission produced abundant
crops, including a small amount of cotton, and the flocks of
sheep and cattle increased largely. In 1770 there were
five hundred and thirty converts registered at San Fernando;
sixty years later there were but nineteen souls all told; in
1849, "the only inhabitants" were "three old Indians," and
by 1867 the mission was "in ruins and deserted."

So much for the recorded history of the Last Mission of
the Franciscan Brotherhood in Lower California. To-
day, approaching from the southwest, the traveler comes
to a great, thick stone wall and passing through a break he
notices to his left an ancient stone-lined irrigating ditch.
Almost immediately thereafter, the arroyo, down which
the trail leads, opens into a wide valley containing several

hundred acres of land running east and west.   At the farther, or eastern end, rise the ruins of the old mission, guarded, seemingly, by a dozen adobe residences.   The trail
leads toward the mission across the old fields of the padres,
now overgrown with willows, save, only, for a few acres
planted with corn.   The line of the irrigating ditch is plain,
as one rides on, and finally terminates in a deep, square cistern where the padres utilized the native stone and cement.
The tradition is, that Padre Serra, before he rode northward, gave instructions concerning the "blasting" of rock
by heating it with fire and then cracking the heated substance
with a dash of cold water and that thus aqueduct and cistern were made possible.

The mission is now entirely in ruins, a mere fraction of
the walls remaining upright.   The *iglesia* was approximately thirty paces by ten, surface measurement, with a
small ell to the east in which there are several old graves.
To the west there were other adobe structures and a patio
approximately seventy-five paces by thirty, surface area.
The *iglesia* faced the southwest.   At this time it is extremely difficult to trace even the outlines.   To obtain a level
space for the buildings an excavation was evidently made
into the hill.   The structures of San Fernando were of
adobe and, in default of vestiges of broken tiling, I should
say that the roofing was of thatch.

About eight families, all, Mexican and Indian alike, seemingly in poor circumstances, live about the ruins in adobe
dwellings.   One small Mexican family merits notice for
uniformity of fine features.   The young husband is handsome, the baby pretty, the seventeen-year-old Señora an unconscious beauty.   In her delicately chiseled features the
student of heredity would trace ancestry of high degree.
Ignorant of the great outer world, however, this queenly

child cares for her home, content with an improvident husband, her dimpling baby and a tiny flower garden.

With the breaking of the rainstorm, I bade Señor Dick *"adios"* and at the head of my caravan and with Timoteo and Jesús (pronounced Hey-soús), my native mozos, dutifully bringing up the rear, I rode slowly out from the precincts of San Fernando. It was late in the afternoon of the 13th of February, 1906, though to dates I gave small heed. Had I not been spendthrift of time and eager for adventure I should have turned to the southwest with Señor Dick and ridden along the road bearing around via Catarina (not to be confounded with the mission of that name). As it was, I headed eastward having determined to trace out the old *Sierra Camino Real* and enjoy that freedom which only exists where there are no settlements and where a man must rely entirely upon himself in whatever adventures may befall him, a freedom which abounds in that narrow, rugged and almost unknown section of Baja California—the "waist" of the California Peninsula. Let him who would plunge into that delightfully mysterious region be slow in leaving San Fernando, however, unless he be well supplied with provisions, ammunition and fire-arms, with generous-sized canteens and with mules—or, still better, with stalwart, long-hoofed burros. And let him never take the plunge, if he be unfortunately lacking a bump of locality and an appreciation of the wildest haunts of Dame Nature.

On St. Valentine's Day, we crossed the Plains of Buenos Ayres, south of the mountain peaks of Matomi and San Juan de Dios, which were first visited by Padre Link, in the year 1760. They are almost as near the end of the world now as they were then. Some adventurous British hunter, having exhausted the fields of India and Africa and being desirous of new wilds, occasionally turns to these sierras for lion and mountain sheep; otherwise, they are rarely disturbed by foreigners. On the Plains of Buenos Ayres, we came to the *pozo* (well) of San Augustine, near which we found a deserted cabin and several splendid slabs of most beautiful onyx, which had evidently been brought from the onyx quarries a few leagues distant, quarries not worked at present.

At San Augustine we left the *camino* leading to the quarry and turned southward, traveling for some distance with no trail at all. Then we found traces of the old *Sierra Camino Real*. It was a strange country through which we passed, no vegetation save cacti, a wilderness of stones and on all sides sierras and buttes, resting against the sky with flat, leveled surfaces, mere truncated cones, their peaks snapped off by volcanic explosions of some by-gone age. Eventually we arrived at an arroyo in which a few tall, slender palms raised high their tufted heads. We made camp here, being no more than a furlong from a large pool of fresh water known as *Agua Dulce* (Sweet Water), and noted by the old chroniclers as a welcome spring beside which Fr. Junipero Serro and Gaspar de Portolá with their little retinue made camp in May, 1769, while en route to Upper California. Night was already upon us and while Timoteo and Jesús drove the stock down the arroyo for better food, I began building a fire.

Suddenly, a voice from the darkness called out: *"Buenas tardes, Señor"* (Good afternoon, sir). Turning about, startled, my hand on my revolver, I saw looming out of the obscurity, a young Mexican, with red serapa, white sombrero, tattered trousers and worn *guaraches*. He was decidedly handsome, but thin and distressingly bright-eyed. He asked if he might buy some flour. At this stage of the conversation, my men appeared on the scene and it shortly developed that the young Mexican, in company with his girl-wife and his father and mother had made camp at

The author and his party leaving the ruins of Junipero Serra's Mission of San Fernando de Velicata

Agua Dulce, where they had just arrived after four days' wandering in the sierras with nothing to eat except the pulp of the viznaga cactus. He soon disappeared with provisions, prayerfully exclaiming that we had saved four lives. Later on his parents appeared. Both of them were in a pitiable condition and both seemed to be above the peon class. With pathetically listless voices, the old couple told their story. They had lived on the mainland, it seemed, where, for years, the father had been a school teacher. Their only son having eloped with a girl, the old people accompanied the runaway couple across the Mar de Cortez and thence up the Peninsula. In the course of their wanderings, the mother had been taken ill, in fact she looked so hollow-eyed that I doubt whether the poor creature survived many more trials. Finally, while lost in the bewildering sierras, they had been overtaken by a fierce rainstorm and their provisions had given out. After one look at the snub-nosed girl in the case, the cause of their disasters, I pitied the old couple, anew, and thought the young fellow a fool. The following day as we passed Agua Dulce, I saw the wanderers camping in company with a party of Indians who had dropped upon the scene from I know not where. They were so picturesque a group that I longed to train my camera upon them, but I had not the heart to offend such half-starved people by attempting to record their forlorn condition.

From Agua Dulce we continued onward through a wild country. At times there would be no trail at all. Frequently the boulders would be piled high on the mesa in strange designs. Although I occasionally saw heads and skeletons of mountain sheep along the way, we fell in with no human beings and observed no signs of their recent presence. We had our difficulties. First I suffered from dizziness and nausea; shortly thereafter, Coronado, my bell burro, lurched against a cholla and had to be thrown and "hog-tied" before the thorns could be extracted; then Jesús, in riding up a steep incline, struck his jaw against a sharp cliff, laying open his lips and drenching his face with blood. Timoteo, however, came scathless through all.   Finally, we saw the waters of the Gulf, the famed *Mar de Cortez,* glistening down below us, and swinging away to the right, we came upon the brink of an immense rocky gorge.

Into this gorge we descended the following morning. Years ago the trail had been washed open and torn away and, according to Timoteo, even before that happening, this portion of the Sierra Camino Real had been neglected and out of use, travelers taking a less rocky course over near the Pacific coast.   Down went the burros, however, jumping from rock to rock like so many goats, for it is in accordance with his deserts that throughout the "waist" of the Peninsula the burro is termed the King of the Camino. Sliding, swaying, poising for a spring, jumping to the accompaniment of rolling stones and vivid Mexican exclamations, down they went, pack and saddle animals, bringing up with a sudden lurch at a spot where the gorge makes a bend and where nature has gently waved her wand of beauty.

In nearly parallel lines the mountain sides rise upward, seemingly a scarce fifty feet apart, their white boulders reflecting in the large clear pools of a meandering stream. Tall sedge grass covered the floor of the gorge and encroached upon the course of the stream, while the profusion of lofty fan-palms was such that we found ourselves, unexpectedly, in an enchanting tropical forest. High above were the fluttering green boughs of the palms, high and higher yet the boundless granite sides of the gorge.   A half mile of this grassy course brought us into a broader arroyo, dotted with palms.   After following this arroyo for a mile, the ancient Camino turned sharply to the right and, passing

▲   Yubay

Bahía de Los Angeles   ▼

▲   Punta Prieta

Mission San Francisco Borja   ▼

between white boulders, we arrived unexpectedly before two roofless adobes, the ruins of the ancient Jesuit Mission of Santa Maria. The great palm ridge-pole of one of the buildings was still in place, the palms growing beyond showing between the earthen walls and the pole. Roofs, doors and windows were missing. Otherwise the *iglesia,* or church, and parochial house have fared well at the hand of Time and man. A yard from the level of the ground and exactly in line with and beneath the ridge-pole of the parochial house, I noted a slight excavation.

There are not more than two acres of level ground about the mission, even including that upon which the buildings stand, and they require scant space. The patio, so usual in Baja California, seems here to have been omitted, though the two buildings were so erected as to obtain the wonted ell. The main building faces east and its ground measurement is thirty paces by ten. A pace distant from its northwest corner stands the other adobe, occupying a space fourteen paces by seven. The walls of the two buildings are composed of adobe with much straw and many shells and stones intermingled. Though the rains have beaten against these ruined walls and heaped much fine sand at their base, they still measure nigh a yard in thickness and seem to have been between seven and eight feet in height at the eaves. From ground to ridge-pole the main building, certainly an *iglesia* from the ruins of an altar at the western end, must have been over twenty feet in height. Three doorways pierced the walls, one at the east, one at the north and one by the altar, and in the south wall there were three windows, the apertures for which now measure thirty-six by thirty-three inches. In front of this building, the ground is level with the earthen floor within, the natural slope having been overcome by an artificial stone foundation. This bench merely extends a few paces out from the doorway. On looking through the windows in the ruined walls the visitor sees near by a wealth of date and fan palms, a spring and a ruined aqueduct.

The lesser building was evidently used as quarters for the padre. It contains two small rooms, narrow quarters for men of such rank in life as the brilliant Jesuits who came to California. In the bottom of the excavation made at the west end of this adobe, there are two hollows which, judging from their form, may long have been the resting place of two bowls or rounded jars.

Unquestionably this excavation was opened within recent years, and concerning it I had already heard this story: In 1893, an American, from San Francisco, visited Santa Maria. Upon his arrival he went directly to the west end of the parochial house, noting, with undisguised satisfaction, that it stood intact. Then he examined a writing while his Mexican guide, in obedience to instructions, ascended to the ridge-pole and dropped a plummet to the ground after which the American made a mark under the line of the plummet cord against the west wall, a measured yard from the level of the ground. The ensuing morning, without prospecting or even looking for game, the American announced his intention of returning immediately to Alta California. In the midst of preparations incidental to breaking camp the Mexican managed to examine, secretly, the adobe wall. Where the mark had been made there gaped the excavation which any traveller may now see—only then rust was in the hollows.

What had been stored therein? Consider the history and traditions of Santa Maria, then hazard a guess. The tradition is—and even the mines on the California Peninsula have been found through tradition—that a charitable woman of high degree lay on her death bed in her splendid mansion in crowded Europe. Family and servants, padre and chirurgeon stood anxiously by, awaiting the end. Suddenly the good woman rallied temporarily. When Death called, an hour later, her testament was written, signed, sealed and solemnly attested, and by the terms thereof a fortune was given to the founding of missions in the three most inaccessible retreats in the world. Tradition continues: the mission sites that filled the requirements of this strange testament were found all to be in California, and the Missions of San Borja, Calamyget and Santa Maria owed their existence to the beneficence of this testatrix.

History here steps in: "Again, in 1747, Dona Maria de Borja, Duchess of Gandia, left the Missions some 62,000 *pesos*," and, "there was money from the Duchess of Gandia's bequest for a new mission in the north and . . . site was found at the spot called Calagnujuet," and, finally, "New buildings were erected some fifty miles above Calagnujuet, and under the name of Santa Maria."

Should the actions of Dona Maria's trustees come before a court and the few foreigners who have visited the bleak sites of the Missions of San Borja, Calamyget and, most particularly Santa Maria, be allowed to testify, there would be abundant and unconflicting evidence in the record that the trustees made their selections in exact accord with the traditional behest of the grand dame, for assuredly no three more "inaccessible retreats" could have been found in the wide world.

In the fall of the year 1767, Padre Victoriano Arnes, who had suffered in his mission efforts at Calamyget where, between bad water and treacherous Indians, he had lost his crop, his improvements and almost his life, went northward into the mountains where a little stream with the big name of Carbujakaamang ran its brief course. Here there lived over three hundred Indians, and with their aid the Padre erected an adobe church and an adobe residence—and then,

one spring morning in 1768, a Spanish messenger of King
Charles III. arrived, bearing royal directions that every
member of the Society of Jesus must leave his mission without an hour's delay, and depart forthwith from Spanish
territory.   Furthermore, no Padre should take with him
any treasure or any possessions, save his habit, breviary and
two books, one on theology, the other on science.   At this
time Padre Arnes was thirty years of age and a man of high
attainments.   In substance this short paragraph embodies
all—except that the succeeding Brotherhoods did not occupy Santa Maria—that history has to record of the last
Jesuit Mission in California, yes, doubtless of the last foundation of the Society in New Spain.

Before his departure did Padre Arnes store his small
treasure in buried jars?   Did he vainly wait for a revoca-
tion of the decree, expelling his Society, and on his death-
bed confide the secret location to some fellow-padre?   Was
the secret handed down for nigh a century and a half until
it came into the possession of the San Franciscan?   These
are questions that appeal with pathetic and romantic interest as one thinks of the brilliant young priest who long ago
fought so hard endeavoring to establish missions in two of
the most inaccessible spots in the world.   Where did he
turn his steps, after being driven from his rugged California
sierras?   Where were his later years spent?   History
gives no answer.   Tradition says that his Indians missed
him; that after his departure death fell upon them and into
the gorge of the Carbujakaamang came a strange lion, a
lion which neither spear nor arrow could destroy, and that
the Indians fled before it.

And now for a century no Indians, no people have lived
about the Mission of Santa Maria.   When the Franciscan
Brotherhood succeeded the Society of Jesus, the newcomers
cast a single glance at the Last Mission of the Jesuits and

The ancient Sierra Camino Real, leading to the one-time Jesuit Mission of Santa Maria

then cautiously hastened onward. To-day no Mexican willingly stays any time in the mission precincts. When the shadows of night creep around the looming adobe walls and echoing down from the rocky cliffs comes the weird scream of a lion and the ghostly palms shiver and moan in the lonely night, then *Señor Mejicano* crosses himself and nervously curses the luck that brought him to the spot, piles wood on his fire and lies down to broken slumber, naked *machete* close at hand and *apprejos* in stockade about him.

CHAPTER VIII

FOR six days we camped near the old mission, resting our animals and ourselves. To distract my mozos, who were in continual dread of lions, I had them build a shady *remada* (arbor), cutting ocotilla shoots for the corner supports and ridge-poles and thatching the whole with broad palm boughs. To their delight, manifested by many a *"Viva la Mejico,"* I tied a small Mexican flag to one of the supports, then flung out the Stars and Stripes above my tent. At a near-by spring, Jesús discovered a flight of bees and, with Timoteo's assistance, gathered in an abundance of clear, sweet, wild honey which made a most acceptable combination with an excellent kind of bread which Timoteo provided by baking the loaf in the ashes and which he termed *"pan Italiano."* To make complete the enjoyment of comfort and shade, good eating and fine air, one should be a trifle weary. It is possible to become delightfully weary on the steep ascents above the Mission of Santa Maria, so every morning I clambered to a new height, ever enjoying the wild grandeur of each newly unfolded view. Moreover, on one of these lofty rambles, I bagged a noble supply of big game.

The shooting came about in this fashion: Accompanied by Timoteo, I had reached a rocky bench at an elevation of nigh five thousand feet. Full two thousand feet sheer above us rose a high, black truncated cone, swathed close in forbidding cliffs; for a league it stretched away with a width half that distance.   Doubtfully, we looked upward.

"Señor, there must be a great mesa above; but no man has ever climbed thither."

I could not help smiling at the gravity with which my man thus expressed himself in the vernacular, for, perhaps in consequence of the rarity of venturesome native hunters, virgin hunting grounds are not at all uncommon on the Peninsula.   I answered him gravely, however.   "Then we are going to be the first to ascend, Timoteo, for in these re-gions the old padres saw wild goats, and if wild goats are above, thither we must go."   As the worthy fellow looked impressed, I proceeded to explain that in the eighteenth century Padre Hernando Consag wrote of seeing wild goats near the thirtieth parallel of north latitude, which, as I re-membered, was but a few leagues distant.   Timoteo now smiled, showing his white even teeth.   Mexican mozos seldom wash their hands and have no idea of the properties of a tooth-brush, and yet their teeth are pearls.   I had used the word *chivos;* and among Mexicans the goat is an animal without character and his name ever calls forth a smile. Later, in studying first editions of the old Spanish chroni-cles I found that the Jesuits mentioned seeing *gamuzas* dur-ing their California travels, and from their descriptions of these animals and their habits I am satisfied that the rendi-tion of gamuza into *chiva* or goat, has been incorrect—*ber-renda* or antelope would be more accurate.

"Others than the padres have seen goats, hereabouts, señor.   Within the year past Señor Villavacensio's boy saw a large wild goat running with a flock of mountain sheep."

"*Bueno,*" I responded, "we must climb to that mesa and find that goat."

With that I handed Timoteo my heavy six-shooter—for he was unarmed and, like most Mexicans, deathly afraid of the larger variety of native lions—and started him off to the right of the sierra while I followed a sheep trail to the left, each of us in search of some break in the cliffs where an ascent might be made. An old Kaliwa Indian once explained to me the reason for the puzzling numbers of broad, well worn sheep trails in Lower California by saying that in his father's day the mountain sheep roamed in great droves over the sierras until of a sudden a terrible pestilence came among them, nearly exterminating the rams and killing the ewes by the thousands.

A quarter of an hour brought me to a point where the trail had been completely blocked by a landslide from a shallow arroyo above. I clambered over the boulders and loose shale and sauntered along. Within reach of my right hand rose the high cliffs, to my left yawned a vast mountain abyss, a full league across, and beyond rose great volcanic cones and mesas. There was grandeur enough in the view to turn one's head, so I promptly sat down to consider my surroundings; my glance at the same time chanced to wander upward just at the right moment to see a fine ram walk out upon a projecting crag, beyond and far above me, and proceed to scan the abyss. He was too far away for a shot and my efforts to locate him in the finder of my camera were vain. It was good just to watch him, however. He was careless of his dizzy position and, though plainly aware of my existence, he seemed unable either to place me or to decide what kind of a creature I was. Eventually he concluded that there was nothing to worry over, and turning about face, most deliberately walked out of sight. As he disappeared the morning sunlight brought out his glistening white sides and across my mind flashed the thought:—far above on that untrodden mesa, there is a WILD GOAT! and then:—that wild goat you *must* shoot.

Beyond me there was no prospect of ascent. I turned back to the pile of shale and looked up. The outlook was bad. There was no help for it, however, and I began swarming up among the broken cliffs following the course of the landslide. A friend of mine, a Scotch big game hunter, once said that no man placing too high a valuation on his neck should never hunt big-horn in Mexico, and that only bachelors, or men with wives well adapted to widow's weeds should follow such venturesome creatures at all. There's sense in his statement. It was a bad climb; looking down was out of the question. From childhood I've roamed the mountains—thank God for the free exhilaration of their heights—but this climb was about the worst I have ever undertaken. After having rebelliously concluded that my neck was forfeit and the goat lost, I gratefully surprised myself by attaining the crest of the cliffs, where I recovered my breath, pressed a cartridge into the chamber of my carbine—it's foolish to tackle bad climbs with a cartridge in the chamber—and looked around. Before me stretched a long narrow mesa, covered with volcanic rock through which sheep trails criss-crossed to the right and left. Stray blades of grass and two or three scrubby bushes were in sight. A small dry arroyo marked the bottom of a single swale in the mesa. No goat or sheep was in evidence. Seemingly I was on the roof of the world—and it was a deserted world.

I went slowly forward, drawing in great breaths of the air and looking carefully for game. Sheep love to sun themselves beside a boulder or to meditate in some shallow cave. Soon I reached the place where the goat or sheep had been. It was as dizzy a spot as the overhanging rock off Glacier Point above the Yosemite Valley. A foot or two outward advance satisfied my curiosity and then, as I peered over, a rolling stone—the bane of many a poor buck and sheep—caught my attention and I looked up to see, not a goat, but a lordly ram three hundred yards distant making for the swale. I was crouching on the crag. Up came my left knee, down upon it dropped my left elbow, the palm of my left hand closed upon the carbine barrel and the sport began.

As the first shot rang out two more sheep suddenly appeared and rushed away in the wake of the leader. If you are fond of Nature, kindly reader, imagine yourself on a projecting crag with a mighty abyss below and range on range of wild, barren sierras beyond; a golden sun tinting the world and warming your blood and Dame Nature in her grandest, most majestic mood pausing beside you. If your life is dear to you imagine yourself filled with vigor, drawing in deep breaths of mountain air, your muscles swelling out like great steel bands and that life which ten minutes earlier seemed about to be forfeited, thrilling you with wild abandon. If you enjoy shooting imagine yourself on the edge of a mesa with nigh a league of fair view before you and three mountain sheep, the noblest of all creatures of the wilderness, bounding away from you, their great horns held proudly aloft, while your sharp-voiced rifle calls to them to halt. The three conditions were mine; the suggested possibilities were facts; moreover, fifty miles distant there was a mining camp where men and women and children were half starving for meat.

Such moments are worth living. I remember regretting that there was no one to share the excitement with me and feeling certain that I should bag all three sheep, even though they had not faltered an instant in their flight. The second in the procession, a cream colored ewe, got in the line of my sight about the fifth shot and I let drive at her. The seventh shot was directed at the third sheep, a yearling ram. At the sixth report the leader, already near the edge of the swale, sank in his tracks; thereupon the other two, apparently imagining that the attack came from the front, turned about face and trotted laboriously toward me. My right arm always trembles when I am "shelling" big game, and at this unexpected happening it wobbled disgracefully. Fortunately an empty magazine created a temporary diversion. As I pressed in fresh cartridges I noticed that the barrel was decidedly hot.

After another shot I put down the carbine and took a camera snap at the mesa and the sheep; then the carbine resumed its sharp play, snarling quickly like an enraged hound. The cream colored sheep dropped suddenly all in a heap and the young ram at once rushed diagonally across the mesa, his right side plainly exposed to me. As I again reloaded the magazine, the heat of the barrel blistered my thumb and first finger. At the same time I heard the sharp, discordant notes of two ravens. *"Sangre, sangre"* (blood, blood), as the Mexican hunters interpret the cry, and on hearing it in the sierras they will aver success with all the surety of a gillie hearing the same sound in the stalking season on the Scotch heather. Certainly the Mexican raven has a remarkable faculty of being on hand at the killing and when he deserts you, rest assured there are no sheep in the vicinity.

The young ram, after drawing eight bullets in his direction, disappeared from sight over the farther side of the mesa; thereupon I climbed off my crag and proceeded to examine my game. Perhaps two or three minutes had been occupied by my shooting; it had seemed an immeasurable time. The cream colored ewe I found stone dead, pierced by three bullets. Although doomed by two fatal wounds the blood of which besmirched the white blotches on his tawny sides, the big ram was endeavoring to rise when I approached him. His majestic head and massive curling horns held defiantly aloft and his greenish eyes scintillating with rage made me involuntarily feel for him the respect that bravery and noble mien ever command. While elation is naturally the first sensation of every sheep hunter upon killing his game, it must give way to pity and regret as the grand, independent creature sinks limp and lifeless before him. What hunter of the high sierras can help having a feeling of comradeship for the ram that shares with him the solitary fastnesses and puts up so brave a race for life! Silent, and even ashamed, I turned away and the mighty ram sank down, gasped shortly and was dead.

A trail of blood led across the mesa to the yearling; he had reached the farther edge with seven bullets through him! A .30-.30 is no weapon for an animal of such tremendous vitality as the big-horn.

Eventually Timoteo, wild-eyed over my rapid-fire bombardment, arrived, having found a fairly passable ascent from his side of the sierra. There are three ways of carrying a sheep: one is to sling him to your side and give up after a few rods; another, is to carry him on your shoulders, the left legs and the right legs being tied before your left and right shoulders, respectively; the third way is to have some one else do the carrying. I adopted the second method, but for comfort I would recommend the third. By the time we had carried and dragged the sheep down to our pack mule the afternoon was far advanced, our shoulders ached cruelly, and we were exhausted. And how the mule ever scrambled down in the darkness among rocks and boulders is beyond me.

Finally, after traveling for hours, lighting our way by firing dead maguay stalks and dried fan-palm boughs, we piled the meat upon a rock for the night, turned loose the mule and followed him to camp, carrying the sheep-heads suspended over our shoulders. It was a weird ending of an exciting day: at regular intervals, high up among the rugged cliffs, smouldered the maguay plants, winking eyes in the cloaking darkness; in the trough of the arroyo down which we picked our way tall ghostly palms raised high their shadowy heads, their flaming boughs lighting up the somber depths of the arroyo and bringing out in sharp outline our slowly moving figures.

And thus, with an abundance of supplies, with great pans of wild honey, with wild mutton hanging to cool in the old Mission, with my few selected books, with my mozos anticipating my every wish, with the atmosphere of romance and early history about me, I spent six delightful days, so veritable a king that I made note in my journal that there was nothing particularly farther that I desired, unless it be that I might continue forever in this retired spot in the rugged wilderness.

With a sigh and many a regret, I left my kingdom of Santa Maria on the morning of the 22nd of February. By the vilest pretense of a trail and through the rockiest country that I had ever experienced, we climbed out from the arroyo and passed over a sierra ridge to the southeast. It is small wonder that horses are never used with any advantage in this region. Coming down to a plain, we traveled for ten leagues over a most rocky and barren stretch where there was virtually no trail, unless the line of graves along the way be considered a camino. Graves of men who died gasping for water, graves, not merely of foreigners but of Mexicans as well, and even one of an Indian, for these were the dread *Llanos de Santa Maria* (Plains of St. Mary) which have exacted a frightful toll from those who have ventured out upon their arid stretches. San Franciscito, or "Little San Francisco," lying on the southern edge of these plains, proved, though located on the map, to be nothing but a few old arastras, a small mining shaft and a waterhole from which we were driven in disgust by the presence of a dead coyote. A few miles beyond San Franciscito, we found a deserted miner's shack and a well, and out from this

▲　Mission Santa Gertrudis

Mission Santa Gertrudis　▼

▲   Desierto de Sebastián Vizcaíno

Turtle fishing camp, Laguna Scammon   ▼

place there was a road leading toward the gulf coast.   Several ragged trails led off from this highway.

For a time we were at a loss concerning what course to pursue, fearing lest unwittingly we might pass the mining camp of Calamajuet,* which I was desirous of visiting. Finally, leaving my Mexicans with my outfit, I rode on a few miles, alone, and passing through a gap in the hills, came unexpectedly upon Calamajuet.   Yes, there was the house of the proprietor, my friend Señor Dick, with its thick stone walls and palm thatched roof; off to the right stood a mining engineer's tent and over near the arroyo a shack made of ocotilla stakes and thatch, and in this shack Mexican women and their Indian helpers were serving a hearty lunch to the men.   Señor Dick, it seemed, was absent at his other home near the *playa,* or roadstead, where he was awaiting the arrival of a cargo of provisions and machinery from Guaymas.   His head man, who greeted me, knew little English; my Spanish was not extensive, and as I had taken him from lunch, his temper was rather uncertain.   In consequence our interview was growing stormy when a tall blond chap, in corduroys, hobbled out from the shack which served as a dining room, and accosted me in English.

With his thick, gold-rimmed eye-glasses, carefully parted curly hair, his neatly cropped beard and eminently respectable moustache, with his well-tied necktie and general aspect of the proprieties, I knew in an instant that this new-comer was one of those wanderers who go forth from the British Isles to the "uttermost parts of the earth" in pursuit of big game.   His opportune appearance cleared the atmosphere and I soon had my outfit at Calamajuet.   In the two or three days which I spent at the camp, awaiting Señor Dick's arrival, I became acquainted with the young Britisher and learned that he was from the north of Scotland, had served in the Boer war, smashed a shoulder in

* Pronounced Calamawhay.—A. W. N.

polo, had had African fever, and, for the time being, was most decidedly under the weather, thanks to cactus thorns and a diet restricted, for several weeks past, to meat and hardtack. We soon made up a compact, agreeing to travel southward together, for he was anxious to see more of the Waist of the Peninsula. Moreover, his purse having mysteriously disappeared early in the month, he had a most natural desire to reach Guaymas and get in touch with his bank account. Later, finding that he wore well on the trail (than which I can think of no higher compliment), I expressed my appreciation by giving him a nick-name, sinking his very proper Scotch name beneath that of the "Laird."

The afternoon of the 26th, Señor Dick arrived on the scene and shortly thereafter two American miners, "Señor Santiago" and "Charley" Howard, put in an appearance. Santiago, an agreeable, widely-traveled man of thirty, was in high spirits, having just made a good "strike," which had instantly filled his mind with visons of gaieties in New York, Paris and Vienna. To the Simon Pure prospector, gold is made simply for "blowing in" purposes. Howard, for years a resident of the Peninsula, had come to Calamajuet to oversee the installation of the expected mining machinery. Santiago's spirits were infectious, and during the evening he and Señor Dick, the Laird, Howard, Sanchez (a young Mexican mining engineer), and I chatted, told stories and related hunting experiences until long past midnight.

Santiago began the yarning by telling me, in all seriousness and doubtless with a foundation of truth, how he awoke one morning in the sierras, half-starved and miles from everywhere, to find a welcome supply of rice in the folds of his blankets where it had been stored during the night by an industrious pair of pack-rats, and how, later, it developed that a Mexican, sleeping ten miles distant, that very night had mysteriously lost an equal amount of rice.

I countered at once by relating the story of the credulous Indian which I had obtained from an eighteenth century Peninsula chronicle. Here it is: A Padre, having obtained some particularly good bread, dispatched an Indian courier bearing a loaf and a note to the Padre of a neighboring mission. On the way the courier sat down to rest beside a water-hole; the bread and note he placed upon a large stone. Suddenly the pangs of hunger assailed the Indian and he devoured the bread to the last crumb. The note, however, was faithfully delivered. Upon its perusal the Padre naturally inquired for the bread. At this the Indian was dumbfounded, but, as he recovered his self-possession, he denied all knowledge of any bread. A week later the first Padre dispatched the same courier with another note and another loaf. Again the Indian stopped beside the water-hole, again hunger came upon him and once more the Padre at the neighboring mission received only a note. This time the worthy man was angered and accordingly berated the untrustworthy courier severely, whereupon the Indian, in bewilderment rather than shame, spoke out, "I confess, Padre," said he, "that the first letter told the truth for it did see me eat the bread, but this last one is a storyteller, affirming what it did not see. Padre, before eating this last loaf, I carefully hid the letter under a large stone, where it could not, by any means, have seen me eating of the bread."

Santiago laughed. "Give me a whole new hand," he said, "perhaps, then, I'll recover."

"Did you really find that in a book, an old book?" asked Señor Dick, in all seriousness.

"Certainly," I replied, "in a book dated about 1789."

"I expect it is a true story, then," said he, "for an old Indian at San Ignacio once repeated it to me as having come from his grandfather when he was a child."

"That is the way of it," remarked "Charley" Howard, "all the old Indians confess to Señor Dick. They think him equal to any Padre. You know the *paisanos* (natives) think that a *medico* is the whole show, so after I had cut a rattlesnake bitten hand from a man, using for the operation a meat saw and a razor, I quite plumed myself on my standing in a community where licensed physicians are unknown. Then I came here into the Waist of the Peninsula and found that my name had no weight beside Señor Dick's. 'He would have saved the arm,' said the *paisanos* on hearing of my famous exploit, and then they related some of his surgical operations. I'll give just one instance. A man was bitten by a *salamankaser,* a venomous kind of lizard. His friends howled mournfully their sorrow, carried the man some distance away and left him, supplied with food and water, to meet his horrible death. Along came Señor Dick. At once he noted the tainted air. 'What dead animal are you leaving about?' he inquired. They told him of the man and that he was not dead. 'Huh,' said Señor Dick, 'you are children.' Then he visited the cave. The bite had been on the arm and the discolored, decaying flesh was already falling away in chunks before the ravages of the poison. 'Get me water, earth mold, clay and boards,' roared the Señor, in quick anger. The *paisanos* obeyed and, after scraping, cutting and cleaning the arm, Señor Dick plastered it with wet clay and mold and then tied the boards about arm and plaster. The man is at work to-day with that arm—it's wizened, of course—and Señor Dick is the Grand Padre of the Waist of the Peninsula."

The good natured Englishman joined in the laugh that went around as Howard sprung this new name on him. "You are jollying me," he chuckled, "but I do love to carve."

CHAPTER IX

FILLED with eager anticipations of adventures in the wilderness, the Laird and I bade farewell to the mining camp of Calamajuet and turned southward, together. Two subsidized fellow travelers, Señor Rita Otero and his genial spouse, Cochimi Indians homeward bound, accompanied us. With my boy Jesús, four pack burros and a colt trailing along with us, our aggregate of man and beast formed a caravan of no mean length. By the presence of the Señora a new element, the softening feminine atmosphere, was added to our rugged life. I casually remarked on this to the Laird. He showed no enthusiasm, however. A fluttering bandana covered her head; an expansive smile wreathed her kindly face; a light red "mother Hubbard" draped her figure; *teguas,* or native shoes, completed the costume. She occupied the right side of her burro, a manner of riding entirely new to us. Her novel seat in the saddle she maintained by resting her right foot in the right stirrup and swinging her left knee over the pommel. Despite the shortcomings of her training and apparel—the Laird, in his extreme modesty, blushingly meditated upon presenting her with a pair of socks—the good Señora was kindly and eminently matronly.

We entered *El Camino Real* a short mile from the mining camp. Americans are wont to think of this Royal Camino as a broad roadway. It is not. It is historic, it is romantically interesting, it is deeply worn, it extends countless leagues, but it is a trail, a bridle path a scant yard in width.   In mission days sections of this Way assuredly were roads of generous breadth, and yet he who now would truly describe *El Camino Real* must picture a deeply worn, ancient way, historic and fascinating, but narrow—a long, long narrow trail.

Continuing steadily southward we passed to the right of the ruins of Calamyget Mission, some three leagues and a half from Señor Dick's camp, and made camp for the first night (February the 27th) at an old stone corral two leagues farther on.   In this latitude the old padres located on their maps a spot styled "San Francisco."   Doubtless we were in San Francisco—only we didn't know it!   A warm spring of arsenic water was near at hand.   This water the Oteros declined to drink, advising us that their people had always deemed it possessed of dangerous properties.   After ascertaining the presence of the arsenic, I laughed at their fears and astounded them by saying that American girls not infrequently enhanced the whiteness of their complexion by drinking from such springs   Later Jesús tasted the water, whereupon the Señora promptly accused him of endeavoring to change his color.

That our conversation might not be understood by our people who had heard enough English to misconstrue what we might be saying, the Laird and I lapsed into French— and such French!   His had been picked up in Cambridge days on sundry trips to the Latin Quarter in Paris, and mine was commensurate with the reading, a dozen years earlier, of "Le Roi de Montagne."   It served its purpose, however.   The Laird was pleasant company, a thoroughly alert explorer and a most delightful woman-hater.   To my intense amusement, he remarked most simply, while speaking of life in English country houses: "It's just eating, dancing, piano-playing, dressing, ladies, flirting, and all such damned nonsense."

Although the country through which we passed was barren and rugged, the mountains frequently rising to five and six thousand feet, the frequency of arroyos and the long stretches of mesa enabled us to make fair headway. The surface of the country was a *pedregal*, or mosaic of stones. Every form of plant or tree life bristled with thorns. The *visnaga*, or barrel-shaped cactus, green fluted, devoid of leaves and armed with orderly arranged ranks of fishhook-like thorns, dotted the mesas and stood sentinel along the arroyos. Giant *cardones*, or tree cacti, gracefully erect or misshaped and fantastic, cast the only shade found along the camino. The trunk of this cactus is from one to three meters in circumference and sends forth and upward from two or three to twelve or fifteen gigantic columnar branches. These branches are leafless and of a greenish-brown color; like the visnaga, they are fluted and thorny. Here and there prostrate *cardones* revealed, in death, their interior structure: white rods, gathered together like a bunch of faggots, and surrounded by and surrounding the dead pith. Overtowering the *cardones* were frequent groves of the slender *cirio* or *milapa*, an inviting and most strange cactus, indigenous to the Waist of the Peninsula. This peculiar and graceful tree grows to a height of sixty or seventy feet without a single branch. Its bark is not unlike that of the aspen; its inner pith frequently decays, making magnificent retreats for birds, snakes or hiving bees. Again and again we would bow low in our saddles or slash quickly with ready machetes as the thorny bough of some *ocotilla* swayed across the camino. This cactus sends upward from its tentacle roots a circle of greenish, thorny stalks that sway in the breeze like so many sinuous snakes. In the course of many years these stalks attain lengths of from five to ten

metres; in the spring time they blossom out with scarlet
tassels. Encroaching close upon the camino the black,
snake-like limbs of the tart *pithaya* or *tajua,* armed with
needle-like thorns, were a constant warning for us not to
stray from the trail, while its close ally, the *cholla,* most provoking of the whole cactus tribe, again and again dropped
its bristling sections in the way of the fetlocks of our animals. The branches of the *cholla* are composed of various
subdivisions, each two or three inches in length, an inch in
diameter and covered with innumerable thorns, both large
and small. As these sections not only break away and
cling to the man or beast that touches them but in seasons
drop of their own accord, littering the caminos, they are an
ever present menace to the traveler. To the birds, however, the *cholla* evidently is a blessing, for again and again
we observed their nests built beyond the reach of predatory
snakes in the midst of protecting *cholla* branches.

But even though frequent and unmistakable signs of
mountain sheep were to be seen along our way, water was
as scarce as cacti were abundant. In the thirty leagues
southward from the mining camp we passed but one good
watering place, the Agua de Youbai, a well several rods to
the left of the camino and with nothing to indicate its presence. On the high mountain summits above this water,
according to Otero, the padres had trees felled and used the
timber for doorways and casements of the Missions of San
Borja and Calamyget. During the day time our people,
fearful of thirst, were all activity, urging on the burros to
surprising speed for such animals. Their energies were
spasmodic, however.

The second evening, after unpacking, Otero sat restfully
on his heels and watched his wife, sitting restfully on her
heels and watching him. The Laird and I at once pitched
our tent and Jesús gathered wood, all of which seemed to

The Aqua de Youbia

A rocky section of El Camino Real

please our couple; to their further evident approval, we next made a fire. Then the Lairds' Scotch burst forth. But although he verbally trampled all over Otero for being so confoundedly slow and dull, the Indian merely smiled and failed to understand. The "Madam"—as we had named his spouse—for her part, smiled, also, and added several spoonfuls of lard to the *tortillas*—a favorite, detestable trick of hers. Things grew lively and the festive Otero flashed sharp glances at my companion. At this I ostentatiously opened up and dusted my ferocious six-shooter and, intoning, padre-fashion, recited liberally from the *"Beatus ille"* of Horace. Wide-eyed, and sure that I was some sort of a Padre—a heavily armed one, too—the devout Indians crossed themselves. The tension of the situation relaxed, the Laird retired to the tent.

After he had made himself comfortable within its narrow limits, I entered, closing the flaps securely. Scraping aside a few stones, I threw down four mountain sheep hides and over them spread out my blankets and *serapa*. Quickly undressing I snuggled into the simple bed, for the night was cold. Already my companion had tied a lighted candle to a maguay leaf and jammed the thorn end into the earth between our shoulders. Although I could see that he was admiring his candlestick, I purposely failed to notice it. He shortly sought to arouse me.

"Such an uncivilized American savage, traveling without a sleeping-bag," he announced.

"Such a pampered Scot, overladen with a forty-pound sleeping bag," I retorted. "Why doesn't he carry a feather bed? Will he use his half-pint share of water for his morning tub?"

He pondered deeply. "Have a smoke?" he ventured finally.

"No, but I'd like your Kipling."

"And I your Balzac."

For a moment there was much fumbling in the pockets of his sleeping bag and among the compartments of my saddlebags. Then the books, being produced, were read with every satisfaction until sounds of slumber without and sputtering candle within announced proper time for sleep.

"Good night," I muttered. "Your gun handy?"

We traveled early and we traveled late, for where there is no water one dares not linger. In the evenings Otero and I usually dismounted and stretched ourselves by leading the advance at a jog-trot. South of Youbai we crossed the tapering ends of two level valleys extending down towards the Gulf and containing several thousand acres with grass and brush. According to Otero a few antelope ranged in this section. The Laird considered these valleys similar to the veldts of South Africa. Like the *Llanos de Buenos Ayres* and the *Llanos de Santa Maria,* which are also inhabited by small bands of antelope—this region is barren of springs. After passing beyond these valleys we went through a succession of hills well covered with undergrowth and small trees. We saw several deer, or rather our guides (?) did, for having burros, the Oteros and Jesús usually managed to keep half a league in our lead, so that their guiding services were of the minimum variety. From these hills we gradually ascended into higher mountains, each of which Otero termed the "Cerro Colorado." During this entire forced march the nights were crisply cool.

The third evening out the Laird and I talked over the alluring details of a future hunt together.

"There's a jolly good bit of country down south of Mazatlan," he remarked across the camp-fire.

"Lake Chapala way?" I inquired, snipping a green and yellow spider off my knee.

"Somewhat. Just off the Guadalajara road."

"Ah! That's where there are so many charming wom-
en," I murmured, smiling indulgently, for even mention of
the name Guadalajara calls forth visions of winsome "nut
brown maids."

"Women! Don't for Heaven's sake trail them in." He
shoved a piece of maguay fiber into the coals and lighted a
cigarette in the blaze. "Plague take 'em, anyway, they're
always in the way. It's the lions we want." The approv-
ing nod with which I greeted this ungallant remark indicated
that I, too, was in a slaying mood. For a time the two of
us were silent, the Laird puffing forth contentful wreaths of
smoke while I studied the coals. Suddenly a twig snapped,
sharply, throwing out an unwonted blaze.

"Oh, confound that female, she's at it again!" I sputtered, as the light showed me the Madam diligently heaping lard into the batter for the morning *tortillas*. "Hi,
there! *No mas manteca!*" I uttered the words in an
aggressive tone, and either that, or the reproof, itself,
brought me a scowl from the worthy dame and a grunt from
her lord. She paused in her labors, however. Otero,
meantime, wrinkled his brow in deep thought.

"Señor, don't you care for lard?" he ventured, presently
—only he used the Spanish.

"No," I snapped out.

"Nor coffee?" he continued.

"No," I answered, more unconcernedly.

"Don't you care for mescal?" This he asked with some
hesitancy.

"No," I replied, laughingly. "No, I don't like mescal."

Such strange lack of appreciation of the good things of
life was altogether too much for the Madam. *"Mira!"*
(Lo, behold!) she exclaimed, rocking herself back and
forth in the dim fire light. *"No guste manteca, café, mescal. Mira, mira!"* For a moment the old Cochimi was

speechless, then he had a new idea. He gave it immediate expression. Had I a substitute for these luxuries; were there three other things that I did especially desire? I promptly answered in the affirmative. First, I wanted "a buck antelope." But Otero here interrupted, his eyes shining with approval. "Ah! excellent meat," and the Madam echoed, *"Muy bueno carne."* Also, I wanted "two big lions." This incomprehensible desire called forth an "Ugh! Lions are very fierce. Bad, bad!" from Otero, while with an amazed *"Mira!"* the Madam hunched forward nearer the protecting coals. I had expressed, however, only two separate wishes. They were anxious to hear my third.

"What shall I add?" I inquired of the Laird.

"Why, tell 'em," was the response, between puffs, "that you want some gentle little maid whose tendrils will cling to your rugged being, whose eyes—"

"Cut it, man, cut it," I interrupted, laughingly. Nevertheless, addressing the expectant Oteros in Spanish, I oracularly recited, "A buck antelope, two big lions—and a pretty girl." The climax was unexpected. Otero's mouth opened in surprise, then extended in a wide grin. The Madam, meantime, chuckled, approvingly, repeating my statement with many *"Miras."* "That's enough for the savage mind for one night," growled the Laird. "Let's turn in." And turn in we did.

Before sleep came, however, we heard the old fellow suggest to Madam that I might make a good life's partner for their younger *muchacha.* With an appreciative feminine eye, the Madam at once urged the claims of the Laird as a blond and more handsome man, but the calculating Otero silenced her by replying that *"El Americano"* could kill the most *carne,* which was of far greater importance than looks. The Laird felt hurt. During his convalescence in the States, after his polo injury, society girls whom he had not even met had showered him with flowers. Here, when he was too crippled to hunt mountain sheep, local society cast him coolly aside.

On the 2nd day of March, we reached the Mission of San Francisco de Borja, an unusual stone structure, which unexpectedly loomed before us as we came around a mountain spur. With its magnificent carved stone portals, its high battlements and extensive adobe outbuildings and corrals, certainly grim San Borja is a most unexpected as well as an impressive mission. On nearer approach we found that the *iglesia* was built entirely of hewn stones, many of them extremely large and all firmly keyed in place. Even the lofty vaulted roof was constructed of stone and cement, with massive keyed arches supporting it.

Otero, who seemed to be a self-appointed guardian on the mission, directed us to take our choice of any of the adobe outhouses. Accordingly, selecting one that seemed clean and was heavily carpeted with green grass, we pitched our tent within its walls, for San Borja is a place of much dew and the mission out-houses have long been unroofed. The Oteros resided in a shack, built against the wall of the *iglesia* and within its patio. After she had dismounted from her burro and entered into her mansion, the Madam seated herself and, to our amusement, began sharply to order about her numerous daughters and granddaughters, in a most magnificent and authoritative manner. Her own small children were hardly to be distinguished from her grandchildren, but the latest baby in the aggregation she frequently clasped in her arms. Otero also experienced a change, becoming an hospitable caretaker, quite far removed from the Indian of the camino to whom the loss of teaspoons and other incidentals of camp outfit might be ascribed.

Two or three families of Yaqui Indians and one family

of ancient Cochimis resided in old huts near the mission. Otero, however, was the one who climbed to the belfry on Sunday morning and sounded the bells for matins, though none but the elderly people seemed to gather for the simple prayer services.   Hanging against the interior walls of the *iglesia* there were a few fairly good oil paintings of saints, and in one of the dark, dungeon-like rooms off the altar two skulls grinned.   Perhaps, if these yellowed jaws could now voice words, vivid scenes would be recalled; for tradition and ancient chronicles alike give to the Mission of San Borja a most romantic history, dating from those eighteenth century days when the Duquesa Dona Maria de Borja (or Borgia), first decided to make an endowment for a mission at Adac, the ancient Cochimi name for the San Borja site. Its medicinal hot springs had made this spot famous among the Indians.   The establishment was founded in 1762, by the Jesuit explorer, Padre Winceslao Link, a brilliantly educated native of old Bohemia.   The first buildings were made of adobe and covered a large space of ground.   Subsequently these structures were in part superseded by the present stone *iglesia,* or church, on which, according to tradition, the Dominican Frailes labored up to the end of the eighteenth century.   In the opening years of the nineteenth century, the Superior of the Peninsula Missions sent a circular letter to his friars asking for suggestions and reports. The response of the *Fraile* of San Borja still exists.   In polished periods he describes his loneliness, cut off from all intercourse with the world and from all conversation, save in a mongrel tongue with treacherous savages, and pathetically inquires whether friars may not be assigned in couples at such remote missions as his own.   Poor Fraile!   According to their own tradition, the Cochimis ended his life by gently dropping a heavy boulder on his head.

The church is a substantial building, seven and a half by

▲ Calmallí

Mission San Ignacio Kadakaamán ▼

▲   Las Vírgenes

Santa Rosalía   ▼

thirty-nine paces within and probably a dozen paces in height; the walls are over a yard in thickness. The main doorway is guarded by massive hewn timber doors, and just beyond the threshold stands a font, cut out of a single block of stone; a southwestern doorway is walled high with boulders. At either side of the altar, doorways open into dark, forbidding, circular rooms, intended doubtless for confessionals. To the left and just within the main entrance, a spiral stairway, with thirty-five worn steps of cut stone, leads to battlements, overlooking the main arroyo; similar battlements guard the northwestern corner of the church. Immediately before arriving at this balcony, the stairway branches and one set of steps enters a belfry where two copper bells are swung. The bells are inscribed thus: "179 * s e n o r s a n i o c e p h" and "7194 * S a n V I S-G U O S a g a n o d e." Facing slightly east of south itself, the church is joined on the southeast by a flat-roofed stone building containing a series of rooms and forming an ell within which lies the patio. A high arched gateway, such as one sees in old castles on the continent, opens into this court. Indeed, the entire mission has the atmosphere of a grim, massive fortress.

On the evening of our arrival at San Borja, the sound of string music attracted me toward the ell, in one of the large rooms of which I found two Yaqui musicians seated beside an ancient square table, on which burned a dim rush candle. One of the Yaquis was extremely good looking, the other jovial and burly. They played, in excellent time, on guitar and violin, while Martin, Otero's obliging eighteen-year-old son, waltzed slowly up and down the room. Soon a small Yaqui boy, with large, serious eyes and wrapped close, like his fellows, in a red *serapa*, entered and immediately fell to waltzing in solitary state. Ultimately, the fiddle was too much for me and I, likewise, took to footing it on the old stone flags where once the Padres had knelt in prayer, and where, on welcome occasions, they had enjoyed good wine with passing officials and dignitaries. Speaking of wine, in the mission garden we observed, during our stay at San Borja several large stone vats, which, according to the old Indians had been used in early times by the Padres for the making of wine and the pickling of olives. In the same garden, there are trellised grape vines, olive trees, date palms, orange trees, pomegranate shrubs and alfalfa, while evidences are near by of a former extensive irrigating system. Once upon a time a cloudburst played wild havoc with the gardens of San Borja.

The second day after our arrival at the Mission I visited San Ignacito, a *rancho* situated about five miles to the west. The proprietor of this *rancho* proved to be one of Señor Dick's numerous mining partners, Señor Fidel Villavacensio. In consequence of an early education secured in the United States, Señor Fidel not only addressed me in excellent English, but, to my greater surprise placed at my disposal copies of *Harper's Weekly* and the *Black Cat*. He entertained me also with much history and many interesting anecdotes concerning the days of the missions, and particularly of the closing days immediately preceding the Secularization Act, for he had known many an Indian who, in early youth, had been a neophyte. Modeling a system of intense irrigation with well, cistern and ditches after the one employed on the same land by the Padres a century ago, the Señor has recently cleared the ground at San Ignacito and is putting to practical use his knowledge of the history and tradition in so far, at least, as pertains to the making of a delightful garden spot in the barren wilderness.

Among my host's books I was delighted to find a Spanish edition of the California writings of Padre Javier Clavijero, the eighteenth century Jesuit chronicler of whom I've already made mention.   An Italian version of this invaluable work I had seen years before in San Francisco.

As modern naturalists seem to consider the mountain sheep one of their nineteenth century discoveries, I will quote an illuminating passage from chapter sixteen of Clavijero: *"El taje de la California es el ibex de Plinio y el bouquetin de Bufon. 'Sunt ibices pernicitatis quamquam onerato capite vastis cornibus.' "* Plin. Hist. Nat. Lib. VIII, c. 53).   Which, roughly translated, means, "The *taje* of California is similar to the ibex of Pliny and the bouquetin of Buffon.   The ibex is extremely active, though his head is weighed down by great horns."   This passage is followed by a statement that what has been written concerning the ibex and bouquetin has been observed to be true of the California *taje*.

In this connection I will here add a quotation from Alexander Humboldt, written prior to 1803.   "The Sierra de la Giganta," wrote the great traveler in his notes on California, "is inhabited by an animal resembling the mouflon (*ovis ammon*) of Sardinia . . .   The Spaniards call them wild sheep (*carneres cimarones*).   They leap, like the ibex, with their heads downward; and their horns are curved on themselves in a spiral form.   This animal differs essentially from the wild goat . . . . these goats, which belong perhaps to the antelope race, go in the country by the name of berrendas."

And as Padre Jakob Baegert also wrote on California mountain sheep in the eighteenth century, before Shaw, Cuvier, Desmarest, Audubon and Doyle, the first accredited writers on the subject were born, a quotation from his "Nachrichten" is here proper: "Where the chain of mountains that runs lengthwise through the whole peninsula reaches a considerable height, there are found animals resembling our rams in all respects, except their horns, which are thicker, longer and much more curved." The old Padre was evidently the author of that ridiculous jumping yarn for he concluded his account thus, "When pursued, these animals will drop themselves from the highest precipices upon their horns without receiving any injury." But what may not be expected in the sheep line when it is considered that that champion story-teller, Marco Polo, with his *ovis poli,* or sheep of Central Asia, began the discovering of mountain sheep way back in the thirteenth century!

Two modern hunters have written happily and with particularly good sense concerning the big-horn. In 1881, the Earl of Dunraven, an Irish big game hunter, thus referred to the Rocky Mountain sheep: *"Ovis montana,* locally and variously called the mountain sheep, big-horn or taye, is very closely allied to, if he is not identical with, *Ovis Argali,* the wild sheep of Asia, and he is akin to the European mouflon. . . . To find the big-horn the hunter scales giddy precipices and climbs to soaring peaks and confronts nature face to face in her grandest, her most terrific moods." And in his "Hunting Trips of a Ranchman," Colonel Roosevelt says, "Hunting the big horn is at all times the hardest and most difficult kind of sport. . . . Its chase constitutes the noblest form of sport with the rifle. . . . No other form of hunting does as much to bring out the good qualities, both moral and physical, of the sportsman who follow it."

A few years ago the mountain sheep of the Grapevine Mountains between Nevada and California was named after that industrious naturalist, Mr. E. W. Nelson. If the Lower California sheep is to receive any distinctive name, I suggest that the honor fall to Francisco Clavijero.

But I have wandered far from San Ignacito. The purpose of my visit there had been to bargain for a burro, one of mine having become too foot-sore for further travel. Unfortunately for me, the Señor had no burros to sell; how-

ever, though we might not traffic in live stock, he kindly gave
me some dried beef, gladly accepting in return a small gift
of coffee, beans, flour and tobacco from us, the end of his
own supplies being in sight.   The worthy Mexican particularly appreciated the tobacco, while his wife stated that the
coffee would bring quiet to her head, which had been rebellious for six days.   She informed me that without coffee,
neither she nor her women could do efficient work, so de-
pendent had they become upon the beverage.

Though my visit failed of its purpose I enjoyed it greatly, for my kindly host was an interesting and observant
man; moreover, he was resourceful.   Toothache, scourge
of the wilderness, he cured in a novel way: With a thread
and sheet of writing paper he made a cornucopia, the open
end of which he placed flat upon a dish; he then set fire to
the upper end of the cornucopia whereupon the burning
paper generated a drop of yellow liquid.   This liquid—it
is extremely bitter—he applied, with a toothpick and cotton, to the cavity and the toothache perished amid the howls
of the possessor of the tooth.

Teguas, or native shoes, if made by Señor Fidel, are
highly prized in the Waist of the Peninsula.   To their
value I can testify, for he kindly prepared a pair for me
"while I waited."   His method was simplicity itself: Using
a draw knife, he first smoothed off a piece of heavy tanned
beef hide and from this he cut out two pieces of leather,
measured to my feet; then he cut out two more pieces of
similar design and, by the aid of small cobblers' tacks, soon
had double thickness soles prepared.   The uppers he made
of a single thickness and with lighter weight leather.   Each
upper consisted of two parts; the front piece, resembling, in
appearance, a plasterer's trowel, covered the toe and instep
and served, also, the purpose of a tongue; the other piece
lapped over the tongue with its ends and extended around

the heel of the foot: These uppers were attached to the soles with extremely small cobblers' tacks driven, from the outer side, through the lower edge of the uppers. Holes having been made through the upper portions of the extremities of each of the overlapping uppers, shoe strings, in the shape of buckskin thongs, were passed through these holes to bind the *teguas* to the feet. Heels he omitted. For comfort and noiseless travel *teguas* are unequalled. I used mine in hunting until they were worn out and then purchased another pair at Loreto. Although the Señor could not inform me concerning the invention of these native shoes, inasmuch as my Scotch friend wore similar footgear made by Kaffirs for use on the African veldt, I hazard a guess that the widely-traveled Jesuits originated the California *tegua*.

While he was working over the leather Señor Villavacensio asked me whether I was collecting botanical or zoological specimens. Upon my negative reply he related to me this yarn: A few years ago, when Señor Dick was yet in charge of the San Juan Mine above Los Flores, the quarterly supply boat brought to Los Angeles Playa a scientist from the United States. Señor Dick received the stranger hospitably and supplied him with a native mozo under whose guidance the scientist easily secured many new and unclassified specimens. As the time for his departure drew near, the scientist became uneasy. At last he stated his case to Señor Dick. He was possessed of a camera and he desired a picture taken which would show the dangers through which he had passed. "Good," said Señor Dick, "we'll arrange that." Accordingly, Señor Dick, Señor Fidel, the American and the mozo repaired to a convenient and not too dangerous precipice. Near the brink they arranged a mining crane and a heavy rope, the farther end of which was tied about the waist of the American. With the Señors and the mozo managing the crane, the ambitious scientist, a handful of his new specimens in his hands, was swung over. After paying out forty feet of rope, Señor Dick withdrew to a good vantage point and snapped the camera. "After the scientist's return to the States," concluded Señor Fidel, "the picture of the feat was developed and published in the papers with thrilling headlines which secured for him an honorable position. He had never written us his thanks, though."

On my return from San Ignacito, I found that my companion had been successful in engaging two burros and their master, one of the musical Yaquis, to journey any reasonable distance with us. Accordingly, as the Laird was still under the weather, we decided to swing down to the Gulf and visit Los Flores, where there was said to be a mining proprietor who had at one time practiced medicine. This matter agreed upon, I congratulated my friend upon his burro bargaining abilities and accepted his invitation to visit the further corner of the mission gardens and inspect some hot springs in which he planned to bathe his injured limbs.

The springs proved to be decidedly warm, well shaded by cottonwood trees and partially lined with flat stones. To the Laird's discomfiture, however, two of the Madam's daughters and one of her baby granddaughters were resting calmly by the larger spring, evidently preparing for the baby's bath. Even his ostentatious throwing aside of his coat and unlacing of his boots failed to induce them to depart.

He paused with blushes on his cheeks and soft swear words on his lips, and courteously made signs to the Indian maidens to take their departure. The latter giggled and made response to the effect that they were not in the way and that their people had used the *aguas calientes* since the beginning of the world. This was too much for my risibility, but though I rallied him unmercifully my companion, having had experience in India with natives, positively declined to take the needed bath while the Indians were in the neighborhood, saying that the question of *caste* must be respected. Accordingly, I herded the pair away to a lesser spring and then devoted myself to the diversion of a party of half a dozen small Indians who were en route for their hot bath. These little people soon became accustomed to me and played with all the glee of Anglo-Saxon children; laughing gaily, then creeping quietly towards me with small hands outstretched, only to turn and rush away in feigned alarm. Whenever I made pretense of seizing them their delight became ecstatic. Of my camera, however, they had so real a fear that I had not the heart to turn it upon them. Though they were all pretty, bright-eyed toddlers, their one-piece garments were ragged and wofully unwashed.

Refreshed by his bath, the Laird finally rejoined me. Returning to the mission, we climbed the battlements whence we could view the surrounding rugged country at our ease. Here he explained to me the proper military manner of defending the mission against Indians, while I threw stones at a large iguana which, hearing our voices, had thrust his beetling head inquisitively from an aperture among the stones of the arched roof. A century ago the Cochimis besieged San Borja and endeavored to scale its walls. Now Otero, a Cochimi, is its sole guardian. His intense faithfulness is measured by the fact that, when an earnest Padre attempted to remove one of the mission bells to an *iglesia* where services were more frequent, Otero trailed down the good man, laid a charge against him before a *juez* (justice) and secured the return of the bell.

After descending from our station, the Laird and I visited the Madam and presented her with a worn pair of riding-bags for the use of her growing male progeny; in token of her appreciation she gave us a large dish of wild honey. Meantime, Otero appeared on the scene bearing two fiber *soladeros*, or saddle sweat blankets, which I had agreed to buy and which he had made from the *palma del monte*, a species of palm growing extensively in the region of San Borja. These fiber *soladeros* keep an animal's back cool and save it from sores. The knack of their preparation is doubtless a survival of the art of weaving which the Jesuits introduced among the Peninsula Mission Indians in the eighteenth century. Good mattresses are made in the same way, but the mattress market is rather slack about San Borja.

While Otero was in the midst of a minute description of the process of making fiber *soladeros*, the Laird veered away toward camp where I joined him half an hour later. As I appeared choking with laughter he gravely inquired concerning the cause of my mirth.

"Great things, those *soladeros*," I began, "and, fortunately, the Kitten understands their preparation."

"I grant the usefulness," he replied, seriously, "but who's the 'Kitten,' and why 'fortunately'?"

"The 'Kitten' is the *muchacha* for whom our friends desire a life's partner. As I have just explained that the hot baths have restored you to shooting condition, the Señor has given his approval and the Madam is delighted over the near prospect of a blonde son-in-law."

"Get out! You're stringing me."

"Stay here twenty-four hours and see," I replied, challengingly.

"Lord, man, I've never seen the woman—don't desire to, either."

"That doesn't matter. She's heard about you. When I told her that you had a big *rancho* on a distant island with

lard, coffee, sugar, and candies by the barrel, she clapped
her hands in wild delight.   She's almost thirteen which, as
I gather, is a proper nuptial age among the Cochimis.
Laird, the greatest thing you ever did was to be born blonde
—and the second greatest was when you gave Madam some
of your tobacco."

"If you're trying to string me, keep on," he growled,
hotly.   I shrugged my shoulders and made ready to prepare
supper.   My silence disturbed him.   "Suppose we break
camp," he observed, presently.   "I've always made it a
point to keep my distance with savages."

"Good," I cried, applaudingly, while the Laird looked
fiercely toward the mission as though expecting a savage
wedding party to issue from the ancient arched doorway.
Presently I continued: "All I have to add is that if you
should decide to take this Cochimi princess, Pocahontas like,
to be your Lady, do not let it disturb our friendship.   I
won't be jealous.   Honest, I wont.   I've seen her!"

That night was intensely cold, so cold that I slept fitfully
and was awakened by the tinkling of Coronado's bell.
Looking over the wall of our adobe, I saw the last of our
animals vaulting the bars which kept them within a walled
field of alfalfa—which they were leaving with the plain intent of dieting on shrubs and cacti.   A comical sight they
made, stalking seriously along, single file, in the bright
moonlight.

Our departure the following morning was too exciting to
be interesting.   To begin with, rest and green feed had
made broncos of our burros so that even our powerful
Yaqui servitor, assisted by my active little mozo, was unable
to persuade the festive Cabrillo, my big white burro, to be
saddled until both forefeet were tied and a blind placed over
his eyes.   Meantime one of my other burros and a Yaqui
burro inopportunely took to the hills.   On top of this the

Indian muchachas kept pestering me for *"ropa."* We had already made the family many presents and our supply of rope was short. In the confusion, I lost my temper and told the girls most sharply that I had not an inch of rope to spare. Undiscouraged, however, they hung about the adobe clamoring for *"ropa, un peso ropa,"* to which they received no response, except a short reply from me to the effect that all our rope was required for our packs and that not five pesos would secure them a piece of it. Only too glad to escape from the pertinacious *muchachas* and their cries of *"ropa, Señor, ropa,"* I slipped into my saddle and rode over to the mission gateway where I was bidding the Madam a touching farewell, when I heard an exclamation from one of the younger members of her family. Looking backward, I saw the form of my friend stretched on the ground. I learned later that just as he was mounting his burro, one of the Yaqui's *broncos,* the animal had leaped forward and fallen with him, pinning his already injured knee beneath its shoulders and against a sharp fragment of broken stone. That the leg was not fractured is a marvel. After assisting the Laird to his feet, I found him grittily persistent in remounting his vicious beast. He was gravely anxious to quit San Borja.

CHAPTER X

FROM San Borja, the Laird and I journeyed north-westerly and then northeasterly, finding faint signs of an ancient and very broad highway, marked by lines of stones on either side, lines which must have been surveyed with every care. No well defined trail remained, however. We were now in the Waist, proper, of the Peninsula, the distance from Gulf to Ocean being but thirty-seven miles. Indeed, as we crossed the divide of the main cordillera, I was able to see the Pacific Ocean to the west; the Gulf of California being only a few miles to the east I felt willing to concur in the belief that, in an earlier age, the ocean swept across this section of the Peninsula, form-ing an island of the southern portion.

Passing through the divide we found a considerable pond lying in a sheltered valley, joyous with the gay chorus of quail and song birds and fragrant with the perfume of myriad wild flowers. At this stage of our journey, while engaged in my frequent occupation of delving in my Spanish dictionary, my eyes fell upon the word *"ropa,"* the English equivalent following gave me a feeling of deepest mortifi-cation and chagrin. I had assumed that *ropa* meant "rope": it means "clothes, clothing, laundry!" On my ar-rival at San Borja I had arranged with the Madame for the laundering of a bundle of our clothes. Her girls had done the work and in my absence at San Ignacito, left the bundle in our tent where it had lain unobserved and had finally been thrust with my blankets into a dunnage bag. Thus the Laird and I, representatives of two highly civilized nations, had coolly ridden away without paying the poor, anxious *muchachas* their well-earned *peso* laundry bill. As it was too late for us to return and correct our mistake, I pity the next foreigner who endeavors to have washing done by the Indian girls of San Borja!

The second day out, my companion's burro renewed his bronco tricks, developing a strange faculty for falling un-expectedly down. The Laird's vocabulary grew extraordi-narily, but it was unable to keep pace with that burro's new wrinkles of deviltry. Our people, also, were provoking. In one instance we had delayed, that I might extract several thorns which had jammed their way through my shoes. They kept blithely on; in fact, they were full two miles away when we eventually caught sight of them. Even to frequent discharges of our rifles they gave no heed until we had so far advanced that the Laird was able to drop a rifle ball from his long-barreled .30-.40 Winchester, in their imme-diate neighborhood. When one is in a country minus a trail and pays a man to act as guide, it is not gratifying to have that man hasten out of sight and leave one to his own tracking resources. Such experiences as this finally led me to trust to my own mountain sense and to enjoin my mozos to confine their attentions to the animals, cooking and pack-ing and leave to me the course of travel.

On the afternoon of the second day, I witnessed with keen relish and delight a gusty passage between my irate com-panion and our stupid, burly Yaqui "guide." The latter had been particularly doltish and the former, having exhausted all his sign language and native swear words without effect, stood before the wooden faced Indian, his little soft hat awry on the back of his curly blond head, his usually mild face flushed with anger, his lips white, his elbows close to his body, his clenched hands before him, beating the air. The words that I caught were these: "Oh, curse you! Oh, you cursed Yaqui! I have damned you in four tongues and your face is still impassive. Oh, if I only knew your language so that I could swear with a feeling that what I said was being appreciated! Oh, oh! Can't you even *see* that I am cursing you?" So earnest a denunciation, delivered in entire ignorance of my proximity, could not be spoiled, so I fell back before exploding with laughter.

That evening, with the glint of a smile in his eyes, my Scotchman suddenly remarked, "Do you know what the Yaq.'s name is?"

"Julio, I believe," I replied.

"A portion of it. His full name is Julius Cæsar. Your boy's name is Jesús, and it is beyond reason for any two men to expect smooth traveling when trying to follow, at the same time, both Great Cæsar and Je—"

"Here, let up," I interrupted, laughingly, "must I tell you that, to save my conscience from a feeling of sacrilege, for days—every time I've written it in my journal, in fact— I've followed that boy's name, religiously, with brackets, enclosing the decent Spanish pronunciation, and now you, you dissenting, Covenanting, Scotch Presbyterian, impious, irreverent—"

"Oh, man, man, I'm more than weary; let's sleep," and sleep we accordingly did.

The following day we descended along the course of a rattlesnake-infested arroyo that brought us out upon the Gulf of California. Half a league from shore there lay a rocky island, stretching as far as the eye could see to the north and making a beautiful, land-locked harbor with a beach unsurpassed at any of the American watering places. This was the Bay of Los Angeles of the Gulf, a broad sweep

of twenty-five miles, for many years the retreat of the cheerful buccaneers, in more recent times the haven of *contrabandistas* and beachcombers.   Here our eyes were gladdened
by the sight of a group of palms and a small clump of sugar-
cane, clustered on the rising ground just above several
shacks, old stone corrals and the shattered ribs of ships'
boats.   This oasis proved to be the *Aguaje San Juan*
(Spring of St. John), of which I had read in chronicles
written a century and a half ago.   Shadowing the palms, a
white granite mountain lifted its craggy shoulders a sheer
mile towards the clear sky, while from the Aguaje a sparkling stream bubbled forth and rushed into pools.   For the
convenience of stray crafts, a rusty iron pipe carried a steady
flow from one of the pools to the shore, a furlong distant.
In 1746 the Jesuit explorer, Padre Hernando Consag,
visited this coast and named the harbor the Bay of the
Angels, the island, Guardian Angel (*Angel de la Guardia*),
and the strait between shore and island, Whale Channel
(*Canal de Ballenas*).   This channel has always been noted
for its whales, called California Grays.   Upon the passing
of the buccaneers, the New Bedford whalers hurried hither
and waged war upon the "Grays."   The New Englanders
got the worst of it, however, and now these warrior whales
play and splash about and bring forth their young, undisturbed by harpoon or rifle.

Making camp in a corral, we found, in a cave near by, a
choice assortment of skulls and other "human various."
In early times the Indians from San Borja frequented the
Aguaje San Juan, catching turtles, fish and oysters in the
Bay, while the Yaqui and Seri Indians crossed the Gulf from
the Sonora coast for like purpose, not infrequently meeting
with sanguinary results.   We, however, found but one
visitor, a pock-marked ancient, seemingly a beachcomber,
though he may have been a retired pirate.

▲ French locomotive, Santa Rosalía

Arroyo Magdalena ▼

▲　Visita San José de Magdalena

Río Mulegé　▼

The night we passed near the Aguaje was perfect, a moon, nearly full, bringing out the massive, ghostly white sierras, the glistening sand on the wide beach and the glassy water of the crescent bay. Awakening at midnight, I arose and, leaning against the ancient wall of our silent camp, revelled in the brilliant beauty of my surroundings, thinking of the sixteenth century Spanish voyagers that first had ventured into this Adriatic of the West, this Sea of Cortez, and of the freebooters, *contrabandistas* and naval explorers of later days, until their shadows seemed to rise up against the clear outline of silent *Angel de la Guardia*. I slept again, most peacefully now, in the balmy air, but with the first soft light of early morning I slipped down to the sandy beach and, finding among the timbers of a broken ship's boat, two great turtle shells, I dragged them nearer the rippling water. Upon one I piled my clothes, resting the while in placid comfort upon the other. After a keenly invigorating plunge—though the water was a trifle cold and sharks had to be considered—I raced along the warm sands, converted to primitive life and quite ready to lapse into a primeval existence.

On leaving the Aguaje, we followed the line of the beach, passing the deserted reduction works of the Santa Marta Mine, and winding our way along a narrow path in the cliff high above the breaking waves. Here one of the burros became alarmed by a rolling stone and, turning half about in the trail, frightened the others, placing my whole outfit in imminent danger of falling over the cliff and into the surf far beneath. The stolid Julius, who was nearest to the tangle, was too lazy to retrace his steps and extricate the animals, nor did he come to time until subjected to the persuasiveness inherent in the staring muzzle of a carbine. Farther along we descended to the shore once more, and shortly passed a forlorn wayside grave with its grim pile of stones and pathetic little driftwood cross. Another mile brought us to a warehouse, a boat landing and a deserted frame house. In the latter a rusted telephone box catching my eye, I at once called for "Central." To my extreme surprise, a woman's soft voice answered, promptly, in English, and much abashed, I was soon announcing my name and my intention of paying my respects to the residents of *Los Flores* (The Flowers), the other end of the line.

Accordingly, we now turned from the coast. After journeying two leagues along a sandy road, leading in a southerly direction, we came upon a charming region of densely growing wild flowers where the presence of shadowy buildings, rampant burros and barking dogs advised us of a settlement. This according to Julius, was Los Flores. Night having fallen we went into camp without investigation. The following morning we made the acquaintance of the proprietor of the place, an American by the name of Dr. Plank. Not only was he a fellow countryman but also a Good Samaritan, for he made room for us at his hospitable table, introduced his wife and son and placed his home and his books at our disposal. Here we stayed for three days, during which we thoroughly enjoyed ourselves. A large mining plant is situated at Los Flores in connection with which there is a seven-mile railroad with a baby engine. When I boarded this engine, young Plank soberly informed me that one of my burros was weeping with surprise and jealousy at the sight.

Throughout the altogether pleasant hours spent at Los Flores, I sought eagerly for additional news in regard to the Seri Indians concerning whom I had read already in old chronicles and of whom Julio had frequently spoken with latent bitterness. These people inhabit *Tiburon,* or Shark Island, a barren, rocky stretch of land some ten leagues in length by four or five in breadth, lying off the Sonora coast, opposite the Aguaje San Juan.   Though its greatest heights attain an elevation of 5,000 feet, there are only three considerable water-holes on the entire island.   From the summer of 1540 when Hernando de Alarcon, one of Cortez's admirals, finding the surrounding sea swarming with voracious sharks, gave the land its name, Tiburon Island has been a place of ill repute amongst men.   A race of splendid physique and marvelous fleetness, its inhabitants, known as the Seri, were reported by Don Rodrigo Maldonado, an officer of Coronado, as being "so large and tall that the best man in the (Spanish) army reached only to their chests." Indeed, there is excellent reason for believing that out of the Spanish tales of the Seri were created, through an author's imaginative brain, the Brobdingnagians of Dean Swift.   At the same time it is no wild phantasy to surmise that Tiburon is really the island which Cortez had in view when he sent his admirals in search of California, "the land of Amazons"; certainly the Seri women exercise an unusual control of affairs on Tiburon, and all kinship is reckoned in the female line.

Prior to the middle of the seventeenth century the inhabitants of the island were reputed to be cannibals, a stigma which still attaches to them; by the opening of the eighteenth century their animosity toward strangers had become proverbial.   Neighboring Indian tribes, Spaniards, Mexicans, Americans, indeed, all visiting aliens have found the Seri inexplicably treacherous and hostile.   Non-agricultural barbarians, scantily garbed in pelican skins, partial to meat uncooked and to the unspeakably disgusting "second crop" of the cacti, these isolated aborigines are possessed of a pride of blood so fierce and intense that to intermingle their own with that of an alien is an indefensible crime.

The Seri are essentially warriors.   During the three centuries last past over fifty recorded attempts have been made

to subjugate them.   Cunning, possessed of unequalled endurance and a demoniac lust for blood, they have repulsed
or eluded all comers.   If as many as five hundred members
of the tribe yet survive, then a moderate estimate of their
cost merely to Mexican war parties, would be two hundred
dollars per head.   While they carry long bows, they seem
more partial to *hupfs,* or handy boulders, and to their teeth
and hands.   That they use poisoned arrows is a charge
that has been made against their warriors these two centuries past.   It is said that they obtain the deadly venom
by pressing their arrow points against partially hollowed
putrified livers within which a repulsive mass of centipedes,
tarantulas and rattlesnakes have been stored, warring until
death.

Lithe, deep-chested, of rather comely figures and well pro-
portioned bodies, the strength of the Seri is as extraordinary
as their lust for slaughter.   Separated from the Sonora
mainland by the treacherous waters of a narrow strait,
well termed *Boca Infierno* (Mouth of Hell) and *Infiernillo*
(Little Hell) they dextrously propel their frail cane *balsas*
across the swirling waves, carrying with them plunder from
the inland natives.   Indeed, at low tide it is said they breast
these waters without artificial support, carrying on their
stalwart shoulders great reeking quarters of stolen beef.
Working in concert, moreover, four Seri will run down a
deer or mountain sheep, beating out its brains with *hupfs.*
Many of the men exceed six feet in height.

Meager in its vocabulary, the language of these people
has been variously ascribed to Arabian, Welsh and Pata-
gonian original.   In their worship, the turtle and the pelican are chief tutelaries.

So many of the visitors to Tiburon Island, however, have
disappeared, leaving no sign, that most knowledge of its
people and their customs is traditional and veiled in uncer-

tainty. Of recent travelers who have never returned from the Seri, I will mention two San Francisco correspondents, murdered there in 1894, a party of prospectors who effected a landing in 1896, two traders who were made away with in 1898 and, finally, the Grindell party of last year. Well, indeed, did a scientist of the Smithsonian Institute characterize the natives of Tiburon as "the most primitive, the most bloodthirsty and treacherous of the Indians of North America." So much for the 'cross-the-Gulf neighbors of Los Flores. The knowledge that leagues of water intervened was rather comforting.

On the third day of our visit at Los Flores, our kindly American host professionally advised my Scotch friend against traveling farther overland in his debilitated condition and invited him to remain in his home, until such time in the near future as a steamer from Guaymas might appear. He even seriously remonstrated with me concerning my venturing southward by the lost *Gulfo Camino,* stating that it was reputed to lead through a dangerous and untraveled country. I parted regretfully with the Laird. Taking the miner's advice in so far as it concerned the carrying of Mexican currency in place of coin, and providing myself with a new Indian guide, Lario, by name, and two new rented burros, I left Los Flores late the afternoon of the 11th of March and rode southward into the wilds.

A rainstorm soon burst upon us and continued unceasingly, but we covered ten miles before darkness and the pelting storm compelled us to halt. Then, having been forewarned by Dr. Plank, I had my mozos tie the burros for the night so that they might not stray away into regions abounding in the poison weed, *la yerba,* and the poisonous little creature *el animal,* both of which are deadly to grazing beasts. Seemingly satisfied, the tethered burros munched away on boughs of *palo verde* cut for them by the mozos.

The following morning we continued on in a flood of rain, from which my companions sought to protect themselves by covering their shoulders with mountain sheep hides, which I permitted them to take from the packs, while I revelled in my slicker. In places we saw parallel lines of stones marking the ancient and now unknown *Gulfo Camino* of the Padres; the greater portion of the time, however, we had not even a sign of trail to follow. Finally, late in the afternoon, we reached a sinister appearing *rancho,* beyond which Lario suddenly declined to move, in person or by burro. In extenuation he stated that he was unacquainted with the country and feared its dangers, that I might better have taken the open Sierra Camino over *Paraiso* way.

As I was unwilling to turn back or aside, I at once paid off the fellow and then, after much bargaining, engaged two burros and their owner, the least murderous looking of the unprepossessing mestizos gathered at the *rancho,* to journey with me as far as the Mission of Santa Gertrudis. Rapidly transferring such of my belongings as were on Lario's burros to the newly engaged ones, I pressed on and managed to place a league between the *rancho* and myself before darkness and the rain compelled us to camp on the edge of the arroyo down which we were riding. In the middle of the night I looked from my tent and observed a curious phenomenon. Rain drops were falling though the sky was cloudless and the stars shining brightly!

After a dripping night, we hastened on into a region of lofty and rugged volcanic sierras, the favored retreat of several varieties of big game. Of watering places, however, we found but one, the "buried," or sand-covered *Tinaja de Santa Marita.* At this *tinaja* we replenished our canteens and then turned southwesterly into the sierras. As we were ascending a brushy slope, I experienced a sharp pain and a short period of uncertainty in consequence of a

An unprepossessing Mestizo

bite, just below my left knee made by a small, greenish-brown beetle. I captured the creature and at once endeavored to ascertain from the mestizo what degree of evil might result from the bite, for the pain was intense. Finally, I was advised that the beetle's bite, though as *mala* (evil) as the sting of an *alacran* (scorpion) was not as *mala* as a beweiner.* With this differentiation I was obliged to to be content and proceed.

Unexpectedly, a dip in the sierras gave us a view of the Gulf spread out below us with two successive islands in the middle distance and the outline of a third against the horizon. Surmising that these were the *Sal si Puedes* (Get Out if [thou] Canst), I pointed them out to the mestizo and he at once informed me that the two nearer islands were San Sebastian and San Lorenzo while the distant one was Tiburon. Then, extending his arm dramatically seaward, he cried out in the vernacular, "There, Señor, the home of the Seri! Señor, they are cannibals, fiendish cannibals." I gazed at the distant shore in horror and fascination, for much had I heard of ill-famed Tiburon. Then I shivered, thinking suddenly of the various explorers, even down to Grindell, not yet a twelve-month lost, who had disappeared forever on those shores glistening in the rays of the setting sun.

Swiftly, the clouds darkened the sky and hurled down upon us a deluge of rain. Then night fell and we made camp.

It was not a pleasant evening. Santa Gertrudis was full two days distant, we were in the uttermost corner of the American continent and I had grave doubts concerning my newly acquired and dangerous appearing mestizo. However, under the soothing influence of the patter of the drops

* General local term for rattlesnakes of all varieties.

on the canvas, I finally fell asleep under my small tent, supplies about me, carbine at hand, revolver tied to my wrist—and my mozos at my knees, partially sheltered by the tent flaps.

CHAPTER XI

SOME forty-eight hours later we emerged in safety from the lost *Gulfo Camino,* regaining the sierra trail near the Mission of Santa Gertrudis. Here, as a fitting, though altogether unpleasant, climax to the varied experiences which had marked our travels since leaving San Borja, I found myself face to face with serious trouble. Throughout the day the insolent eyes of the greedy mestizo had been fixed covetously on my outfit. Now, the very evening of our arrival at Santa Gertrudis, he discovered in the currency which I tendered him a pretext for the quarrel which he seemed only too anxious to bring about. His pay must be in silver, he cried. To this I made brief response, saying that I carried only currency and the smaller coins. For a moment he stared at me with lowering brows; then turned aside, muttering a surly rejoinder: silver he would have—and by morning.

There's unlimited picturesqueness about the old Spanish missions. Take Santa Gertrudis, for instance. Founded down near the twenty-eighth parallel, early in 1751, by Padre Consag, the noted Jesuit explorer, it has a cut stone *iglesia,* and a renaissance-style separate campanile. Sometimes, however, one is not interested in the picturesque. As I hunched my shoulders up against the massive stones of the southern wall of the *iglesia* of Santa Gertrudis, slipped my wrist through the buckskin cord about the butt-ring of my Colts .45, fixed a weather eye on the swathed form stretched out not three paces distant and realized that a long night was before me, I paid no heed to picturesque surroundings, my mind being occupied exclusively with the thought that an angry mestizo with a treacherous six-inch blade rested within the *serapa*. Indeed, crouching against the mission walls for the interminable hours of darkness proved a degree too romantic for any comfort.

Early the next morning an ancient crone, staff in hand, tottered past, entering the mission. While she told her beads within, I took the mestizo for a little walk beyond the native graveyard. As we strolled along I held forth— to a sullen auditor, I'll confess—on the equality of national bills and coin, plainly a most unappreciated dissertation. Presently, however, the fellow brightened visibly, his eyes fixed on just what I was in search of—a big, long-eared jackrabbit, sitting bolt upright near at hand. Some minutes later we returned to the mission—again past the cemetery. One chamber of my revolver was now empty and a thoughtful mestizo, carrying the remains of a badly mangled rabbit, had concluded that national bills were legal tender. Shortly, possessed of the right amount of these bills, he rode peaceably away, taking the back trail which led to his *rancho*.

This matter thus settled and breakfast disposed of, I dispatched my small mozo in search of a Mexican with a rentable burro and a willingness to tackle the alleged antelope country down on the eastern border of the *Llanos de Ojo Liebre*. I, for my part, undertook the luncheon proposition. The appetizing odors evidently reached the boy, for he quickly returned, reporting several mestizos and Indians near at hand, well provided with burros and anxious for meat and *pesos*, but mightily averse to entering upon a trip where the prospect for water was bad. Knowing what I do now, I would have been equally reluctant myself. As

The Mission of Santa Gertrudis

it was, I became provoked, according to my wont when the natives seemed timorous. In another moment, however, the jangle of merry bells diverted my attention toward the camino from the west.

I looked up in time to see a long cavalcade approaching with much show of high peaked sombreros and silver mounted saddles, of daggers and clanking spurs; altogether an unwonted and unusually fine outfit. The leader was a tall, slender Mexican, his black hair splashed with white. In single file, following close in his wake, came a pretty little girl, a thickly veiled young woman, dressed in somber black, two young fellows—one a handsome chap with an unexpected lettered red sweater—next numerous pack animals loaded with hampers—one even bore a large trunk—and finally three or four mozos. The entire party were mounted on long-legged mules, zebra-marked, sure-footed beasts. The cavalcade halted beside a stream some rods from the mission, whereupon the mozos began to unpack, under the supervision of the leader, while the veiled Señora, accompanied by the child and the two young men, approached the *iglesia*. Attracted by my mountain sheep hides, the little party swerved over my way and he of the red sweater, after introducing himself as "Frank Reavis, of San Francisco and Mexico," and acquiring my name, made me acquainted with his companions. Though alone in speaking English, Reavis was joined by the others in extending to me the hospitality of camp. In fact, every member of the party was most civil. The tall man proved to be no other than Don Emaliano Ybarra of Calmalli, leader of the *Pronunciamento* of 1875, and one of the last of the Mexican revolutionists. With his commanding manner, piercing black eyes and sharp acquiline features, the Don fitted the part to a theatrical nicety.

Siesta time over, the cavalcade turned into the mountains

to the southeast, bound for Santa Rosalia.   Don Emaliano,
however, took the opposite direction, first advising me that,
if I did not mind taking chances, he would find at Calmalli
an old Mexican willing to enter the antelope country with
me.   To Calmalli, therefore, I decided to turn my steps,
and at sunset that afternoon my small mozo and I got under
way and, with the stars to guide us, traveled northward for
nigh two leagues before unsaddling for the night.   The ensuing day, after eight leagues of travel, west and northwest,
we arrived at the small pueblo of Calmalli where we spent
St. Patrick's Day and a portion of the 18th, waiting for the
Don's old Mexican to bring in from the hills two burros.
This man's name was Castro, a designation as indefinite on
the California Peninsula as is Smith in Uncle Sam's California.

According to a lost Indian tradition, Calmalli signifies
"the lion at the spring"; it is said to have been visited by a
roving Spaniard in the year 1544.   I'll wager on the incor-
rectness of that date, however.   In 1883 gold placers were
discovered in the neighborhood and prospectors from the
four quarters of the globe forthwith flocked to the diggings.
One of these gold seekers was described to me by Don
Emaliano, his eyes the meantime sparkling brightly.   She
was a pretty young *Americana,* traveling alone, her outfit
packed on a gray mule, her garb the regulation miner's red
shirt, overalls, felt sombrero and heavy boots, her ready
six-shooter strapped to her belt.   Around her claim the
mercurial Mexicans flocked at once, intent on fond demon-
strations.   But the fair prospector had views of her own.

"I come from Tombstone," she asserted, in perfect Spanish, "Tombstone, Arizona, where three times a day the
Coroner makes his regular rounds, and I have always done
my modest share in furnishing him with employment.   You
must understand that I do not want any Greasers making

▲ Mission Santa Rosalía de Mulegé

Bahía Concepción ▼

▲   Mission Nuestra Señora de Loreto

Plaza, Loreto   ▼

love to me." And with this she nodded in a most cordial manner, swinging forward the holster of her formidable revolver. "I do hope, *caballeros*," she concluded, smilingly, "that there will be no misunderstanding of my views."

"She was a novel type for our gallants," chuckled Don Emaliano, reminiscently, and since the courtly Revolutionist, like most men who have braved danger, admitted a weakness for an attractive face, I should not be surprised if, in his presence, *La Americana* forgot her armament. No suggestion of this possibility, however, came from Don Emaliano.

Some years ago three million dollars of placer gold, together with the mining excitement, passed away from Calmalli, leaving piles of torn up earth and a small, slumbering pueblo where water is scarce and a vendible commodity, where provisions are limited and cartridges sell at eight to the dollar. Also, it costs one hundred and fifty dollars to be married, devoutly and legally, in Calmalli. Consequently, not more than three couples have been thus united there. Divorce being out of the question, the three may, the hundred lacking formal certificates assuredly will, stay in harness together, for, with a strange spirit of fidelity, Peninsula women cling most faithfully to their men so long as the latter provide, even in the meagerest measure, for them and their children.

My stay at Calmalli was made unexpectedly pleasant by the kindly attention of a Mr. Hall, an American mining man, near whose home I had made camp. As soon as we met, he invited me to his house on the strength of my— color, I was about to say, forgetting for the instant that three months' exposure to the Mexican sun had given my complexion the hue of an Indian. Before accepting his hospitality, however, I insisted that he examine my credentials, bringing forth, even as I spoke, a sheaf of gun-per-

mits, passports, etc., which I kept stored away in my saddle-
bags. As he waved these aside most good naturedly, the
gorgeous seal on one of the documents caught his eye. This
seal, intended primarily for Indians, had been my salvation
with at least one tribe. It had come into my possession
through the courtesy of Governor Pardee, of California,
who had kindly provided me with an open letter to the Mexican authorities. His Secretary of State had attached
thereto an immense red seal, stating that the latter would
serve to impress the natives.

This document held Mr. Hall's attention for a moment,
then, after scrutinizing the official signatures, he hurriedly
re-entered the house, leaving me bewildered by his actions.
Indeed, in my surprise I had begun to reperuse the letter,
seeking some clause that had perhaps escaped my notice,
when Mr. Hall returned, bearing a generous sized bottle
and two formidable looking glasses. "Had you only mentioned at the outset," he explained, proffering a glass, "that
you were Charley's friend," and he nodded toward the seal
and signature of the Secretary of State, "I should have understood your immediate needs." With that he filled high
my glass, regardless of protestations. "Charley's my
friend, too," he remarked, attending to the second glass.
"Here's how!"

Mrs. Hall, for a Mrs. Hall there was—also a visiting
friend from Los Angeles—joined with her husband in cordial hospitality. With the three I partook of a good American dinner where bread took the place of everlasting *tortillas*
and where fried chicken, salad and vegetables were generously served. The table cleared, we chatted together
with rapidly increasing intimacy after the fashion of exiles
come together in a strange, wild land. "Don't be too much
impressed," explained the hostess, laughingly, "for, where
visitors only happen in about once a year, why—even you

are an event." Ultimately the ladies made a planetary
wheel—they both seemed partial to the occult—cast my
horoscope and read my palm, gathering from these sources
that the future held in store for me a vital danger, a vast
fortune and several other interesting prospects. As I had
picked up a few ore specimens which Mr. Hall considered
of some value, we at once proceeded to discuss methods of
enjoyment of the coming fortune. Indeed, we presently
imagined ourselves dashing bravely down the Bois de Bou-
logne behind six pure white trotting mules, their tall ears
ornamented with the yellow flowers of the blossoming
maguay plant, and attended by eight outriders on galloping
burros—altogether a picture quite sufficient to send every
self-respecting Parisian motor-car into a panic.

On the forenoon of the 18th, after bidding these kindly
Americans good-bye, I went on to the main part of the
pueblo where Castro was to join me and where I expected
to have a bit of soldering done to one of my large canteens.
I had no difficulty in locating Castro and his two sonorous
burros. The soldering proposition, however, was another
matter, for the mining man with the necessary tools was
deep in *fiesta,* the occasion therefor being the Saint's Day
of young Josefa, the belle of Calmalli—her birthday, that is,
for in Lower California an infant is named after the saint
on whose day he is born. The mining office being deserted, I directed my steps, necessarily, toward the house
of the charming Señorita, where, as I had, on the previous
day, been formally introduced, a cordial reception awaited
me. Indeed, I was invited and urged and invited again to
dismount and enter the *casa.* Josefa and her sisters, in
gala attire, altogether attractively pretty and neat, were receiving. The postmaster, the revenue official and the judge
were there, also the mining surveyor of soldering abilities
and two or three other good looking young fellows. Two

of these *caballeros* were making music with guitar and mandolin, while one of the sisters served cognac, mescal and sherry.

"The American gentleman is in the nick of time," they said.

"Thank you all," replied the American gentleman, "I cannot delay, for the day advances and the next water is two days distant. If I may impose a moment on the Señor's time for soldering—"

"Soldering? It will be no imposition. First, however, you must join in Josefa's *fiesta*. Anyway, the middle of the day is the best time for starting on a journey."

To temporize was my only hope, so I took refreshments in turn with each of the Señoritas and then, revolver and cartridge belt, camera and spurs temporarily discarded, I waltzed with Josefa and later with her sisters. Though it was a poor, plain little shack, this *casa*, with earthen floor and but a single room, with rude chairs and beds pressed back against the walls to provide space for the dancers, no stately ballroom was ever more radiant with the spirit of hospitality and welcome. The Señoritas danced gracefully and were extremely decorous. Josefa, just fourteen, was decidedly charming; her oval face, lustrous eyes and warm coloring would attract attention in any company. At length Don Emaliano, with all his lithe grace, came upon the scene, glasses were filled again, Josefa's health was drunk, so also was mine, the Don and I made speeches, then the other Señors made speeches, the pretty girls dimpled and smiled irresistibly; more refreshments were passed, the guitar and mandolin twanged merrily and every one talked a gay streak. These grown men, the principal citizens of the pueblo, were having as happy a time as children on a holiday, for such is the temperament of the Mexican. Meantime, my departure seemed a forbidden subject.

When I again urged the necessity of going, therefore, the
Señors argued seriously that the middle of the day was a
bad time for the beginning of a journey, that the evening
was even better. Finally, at noon, I parted from the hospitable people but only by rushing away with my canteen
still unsoldered. As I spurred to the head of my caravan,
Don Emaliano exclaimed, sorrowfully, "Ah, how can you,
how can you! Is not the sweet hostess far more attractive
than any antelope?" while the Señoritas murmured softly,
"*Adios, Señor, Adios,*" and the mandolin and guitar
twanged a parting song. Surely, there is no hurrying in
Mexican California; there one is not supposed to hasten
even after antelope!

Anxious to make up lost time, we traveled south and
southwest from Calmalli, without pause, for five leagues,
passing through a hilly country and ultimately making
camp at dusk by the camino-side, where the presence of
much excellent bunch grass attracted the burros. Before the
camp-fire I amused myself by taking note of the proportions
of coffee and water employed by my Mexicans in making
their beloved beverage; something more than one of the
former to four of the latter! Next I turned to serious study
of Don Emaliano's table of distances between waters.
Here it is: Calmalli to Ojo Liebre, twenty leagues; Ojo
Liebre to San Angel, twenty-four leagues; San Angel to
San Ignacio, ten leagues. In other words, only two watering places intervened in a stretch of one hundred and sixty-
two miles—and even the Don, himself, was ignorant of the
country between Ojo Liebre and San Angel, a seventy-two
mile stretch of desert.

Early the ensuing morning we continued our journey
southward. As we were now in a fine grass country where
the tall *cholla* made excellent hiding places for antelope, I
walked in the van of my outfit with carbine in hand, first

causing the bell to be removed from Coronado, the plucky leader of my train. Nevertheless, though we advanced thenceforth in absolute silence over the sandy trail, no sight of game rewarded our efforts throughout the entire forenoon. After making a short halt for a mid-day siesta, we pressed on again, with an exceedingly hot sun overhead. Presently, leaving the rolling hills behind, we entered upon the *Llanos de Ojo Liebre,* or Plains of a Hare's Eye, sometimes also called Antelope Plains, an immense barren expanse, bordered by the San Pablo Sierras on the east, the Santa Clara Sierras on the south and a low horizon on the west. With its numerous curving swales and rounded sand hills, the vast field, covered with waving grasses, bobbing wild flowers and small, fretful leguminous plants, spread out before us like some billowy sea.

Soon I saw my first prong-horn or antelope. He was to our left, some three hundred yards distant, scurrying away for all the world like some big, awkward, white-rumped calf unexpectedly disturbed by an approaching train. However, despite his haste, he had an inviting, feminine trick of looking over his shoulder at a fellow, so I started in pursuit, on foot, with carbine and camera in hand. For several miles I followed that provoking beast, frequently waving my bandana in the most orthodox, story-book fashion, but, though he stopped twice, peering at me inquiringly from the high grass, I was unable to get a shot. Finally, settling down to business, he whisked out of sight with the speed of a greyhound.

After staring vainly at the heat-waves and sand hills that had swallowed up my tantalizing quarry, I concluded that it was time to return to my outfit; but look as I might, I could see nothing except the undulating plain with its sand and grass. Moreover, the sun was hot and the excitement of the chase gone. I realized that I was deadly thirsty and that my canteen was tied on my saddle. Alarmed over the situation, I circled about most wildly, signalling with my revolver, waving a bandana from hillock tops and carrying on generally like a lost child. Finally, collecting my wits, I back-tracked—no easy trick where the grass grew. Next, I found the camino, but my outfit was not in sight. By the time I caught up with my people darkness had fallen and my thirst was maddening. Invigorated by great gulps of water, I roundly abused Castro for deserting me. He, however, explained that Jesús had understood the first handkerchief waving to be a signal for them to move forward. After some growling, I simmered down; under the circumstances there was nothing else to do.

We rode on for a time in heavy silence and then, dismounting, proceeded on foot, thus resting the burros. The side-winders, however, were also using the camino and their presence robbed pedestrianism of all its pleasure. A "side-winder," let it be understood, is a short, extremely poisonous, rattlesnake that prefers the night time for his travels; he acquires his name from the peculiar manner in which he throws his coils when in motion. First Coronado, and then the other burros right on down the line, would jump aside with a wild snort of angry terror whereupon we would do a bit of side-stepping, ourselves, for the commotion signified that some vicious side-winder had the right of way. This jumping business got on my nerves so completely that at 8.30 P. M. I ordered a halt for the night, much to Castro's disapproval, since it was a dry camp, we had but a half pint of water on hand and Calmalli was fifty wilderness miles behind us.

Daylight, on the 20th, showed tracks of side-winders about our blankets and a small clump of young cottonwoods a half league dead ahead. Hastening forward with our thirsty burros, we shortly arrived at the clump. In the shade of tne trees were two pools of water, known as the *Pozo de Ojo Liebre,* or Well of a Hare's Eye, though why so named I am unable to explain. I will, therefore, merely submit Castro's dictum that "the tradition is lost, Señor." My first information concerning this water-hole had come from an old journal. Before entering Mexico I had provided myself with copies of such logs and journals of Lower California travel as were to be found—a strangely limited number. From the Ross Browne collection of 1867 I was aware that to cross the Llanos de Ojo Liebre was a venture that his party dared not essay; indeed, it had been reported to them that "from San Ignacio to San Angel, a salt, almost undrinkable water, is seven leagues; from San Angel the next water is Ojo Liebre, thirty leagues. Ojo Liebre is much resorted to by coyotes and wild animals, many of which are drowned in it and the water is said to be unendurably foul. From Ojo Liebre the next water is twenty leagues. The water is not to be depended on." However, this data had not deterred me, for, in my foolishness, I was rather hankering after adventures, and there is nothing venturesome in exploring known regions or keeping to open trails. Therefore, after drafting Castro into service on his reputation of having crossed, in boyhood, from Ojo Liebre to San Angel I had entered this sinister region heedless of consequences; Castro on his part, had come to me inquiring concerning my public offer of wages: a bonus of five *pesos,* extra, for a sight of a *berrendo* within two hundred yards, and a promise of much *carne,* after such sight, had won him completely.

We spent a day at Ojo Liebre. During the forenoon we boiled and strained water, a precaution which greatly amused my companions, who could see no objection to swallowing the myriads of small red insects inhabiting the well. In the afternoon Castro and I explored a vast salt bed a few miles distant, being amazed by the marvelous mirages flitting above the brilliant salt; next we swung away toward the Pacific Ocean. Between floundering in the salt bogs and slipping about the sand-hills, we had a sad time of it. Not far distant was grim Black Warrior Lagoon, the scene of the wrecking of many whaling vessels and the loss of many lives from the time of the ill-fated *Tower Castle,* whose crew, in 1838, escaped the waves only to die of thirst. The last survivor of this ship closed his journal with these hopeless words: "I have observed the symptoms of my companions; it is but reasonable to expect that my time will soon come, for I now experience those same symptoms." As this historical data, gleaned from a coast report which I carried in my saddle-bags, rather gave me the shivers, I swerved away from the treacherous coast and hunted until evening for antelope, getting better acquainted, the meantime, with Castro. Well past the threescore mark, he was quick-witted, full of dry humor, something of a philosopher and a born tracker. In appearance he was slight and wizened. After supper I set him to work—while I boiled more water for the journey—soldering the leaky canteen, which he did with metal taken from an empty meat can.

During our absence Jesús, urged on by a boy's appetite and keenly alive to the prospective dry camps and consequent limited cookery before us, had prudently fried some twenty *tortillas.* In the preparation of these cakes—a staple article of native diet on the Peninsula—a liberal supply of water is required, for though a mozo may at other times neglect his ablutions he never fails to rinse his hands before mixing *tortillas.* This preliminary rite concluded, the Mexican proceeds to mix flour, salt—and lard, if he possess it—with sufficient water to produce a thick dough, which he then breaks up into balls the size of a hen's egg. He next takes these spheres, one by one, between his palms and by a rotary motion of the hands, varied by occasional kneading between the fingers, flattens each one into a circular cake some twelve inches in diameter by an eighth of an inch in thickness. *Tortillas* are cooked, one at a time, on any sort of an unswabbed iron griddle that may be available. Not infrequently they receive a delectable further browning by being unceremoniously cast upon the embers. If made with little or no lard and well kneaded, these cakes are excellent to eat and easily digested. The evening well advanced, the *tortillas* cooked and the water boiled, we sought our blankets, ready to enter the desert on the morrow.

CHAPTER XII

THIRST!

EARLY in the morning of Wednesday, the twenty-first, we broke camp, bound for San Angel, the next water, distant, according to Castro, just three days. To meet the prospective thirst we had my saddle canteen, containing half a gallon, the mended canteen with two gallons, and a third holding two and a half gallons. Before taking our departure, we drank abundantly and, for the sake of future wayfarers, I planted several palm seeds about the *pozo,* while my Mexicans, less altruistically inclined, drove the burros to the water's edge. The animals, however, having slacked their thirst the previous day, stubbornly refused to drink. We headed for the southeast, following a faint trail which, Castro averred, had been made by the gold seekers bound for the Sacramento Placers in 1849-50, many of whom came from Panama to La Paz and thence overland, hundreds of leagues northward. For half a century the trail had not been used. It was dead. Fragments of glass from broken bottles, a line of grass slightly darker than that at its sides and as erect as the trimmed mane of a mule—these were all that marked the course of the old pioneers.

Finally we came to a number of stones laid upon an alkali surface of barren ground. They were in the form of a cross and their points indicated the four quarters of the compass. We agreed that this was the work of the ancient Padres. I even thought it possibly a relic of Padre Sigismundo Taravel, who crossed these plains and explored Cedros Island in 1730. Beyond this cross there was no sign of a trail. Once, indeed, the track of a burro crossed our course but, on examination, Castro and Jesús pronounced it to be that of a wild burro, though how they reached their conclusion concerning this *bronco* when all Peninsula burros are left unshod is more than I can say. However, accepting the track as a possible token of our being in the neighborhood of the old camino, we immediately spread out like a fan and traveled in that order for several fruitless hours. Then the ground became decidedly rolling, with thickets of *cholla* and *palma del monte* growing on the swells and making it difficult for us to pick our way forward even in single file. In one of these thickets Jesús got lost at dusk while pursuing a rabbit, so Castro and I, after vainly calling, made camp and built a large fire. After climbing a *palma del monte* the boy perceived the brilliant reflection and reached camp rejoicing.

That night a heavy fog moistened the grass, to the great relief of the thirsty burros. In the morning the mist was so dense that Castro had a wearisome chase and lost time in locating his burros, which had strayed away during the night, doubtless searching for water; and next my compass came into play. I led off on the course we had been following when the trail pinched out the preceding day, that is 17 degrees south of east. The fog lifted about ten—I could only estimate the hour, for my watch had been broken for over a month—and soon after, while crossing a *cardon* and *cholla* covered hill, I came upon a cinnamon colored wild cat enjoying a sun bath on the limb of a giant cactus. Two quick rifle shots disturbed pussy's slumbers and he disappeared from sight, sliding into a hole in the limb. Hearing the racket and thinking of extra *pesos* and much *carne*, my Mexicans rushed up, crying out, "An antelope, an antelope?"

They were crestfallen when I replied, *"No, un gato de campo."* (No, a wild cat). Unfortunately, the beast had not fallen to the ground; in fact, the blood-stained edge of the hollow in the limb evidenced the necessity of someone's ascending the tree and making investigations. When I suggested that one of them climb after the *gato,* both Castro and Jesús looked troubled, and accordingly, to preserve that surest safeguard vouchsafed to the exploring American, his reputed national disregard of all dangers, I pulled myself into the *cardon,* revolver ready. Facing the retreat of an angry cat not being especially attractive, I was decidedly relieved to find the creature lifeless.

Meantime, the burros had wandered away and, upon rounding them up, my Mexican called to me in sudden alarm. Hurrying forward, to my dismay I found that the burro carrying the recently mended canteen had run into a *cardon* with the result that the solder had come loose, letting the water, save perhaps a cup full, leak out. This was more serious, for we had been drawing heavily on the other large canteen, and in my saddle canteen there was barely a pint remaining. Nor was this all: In the blankness of the situation Castro confessed that he did not know where we were, that he had never before crossed this section of the great plains. In other words, expecting to find the old camino distinct, he had been tempted to undertake the trip for the sake of the promised *pesos.* However, he said he knew the *Agua* of San Angel and that it could not be over a day distant.

It was now nearly noon. We pressed on and very shortly the face of the country changed, becoming more open and very sandy. In many places, moreover, the earth was honeycombed with underground runways of gophers or similar burrowing creatures so that the burros broke through at every step. Their consequent jolting gait was overlooked by us in the more serious consequence of the resulting slow advance. The heat, also, now became intense and at lunch time Castro, realizing our condition, advised against the eating of any kind of meat lest our thirst be thereby increased. A few lettuce leaves, the remnant of a present given by the Halls, were so fresh and cooling to the palate that we relished them greatly.

Early in the afternoon we came upon three antelope, though I, personally, saw only one, a fine prong-horn buck. I was off my riding burro instantly, and signalling my men to keep the train in motion, dropped on one knee and began pumping lead at the buck, a fair mark, facing me at two hundred yards. Certainly that antelope had never before seen a man, for he stood calmly for two shots before turning tail. Running forward I saw no blood, but immediately caught sight of my game racing down a wide swale. After three shots, he fell, kicking violently. I rushed in pursuit, dropped my carbine and was drawing my camera from its case when the poor creature stumbled to its feet and made off across the swale. I supposed the buck would fall again, immediately, but he kept on until three more shots grounded him. Then I hurried forward to observe this, my first antelope. Five bullets had struck true, two of them coming out near together, just below the spine, and making a rent as large as a man's hand. He was a true Mexican prong-horn—a delicate, beautiful creature; white and tan and black, with graceful, black prong horns set just above large eyes, and with the long, well-turned head of a blooded greyhound. The flashing eyes of a cornered stag or the green orbs of a fighting big-horn have never appealed to me as did this dying antelope. His great, frightened, gazelle eyes looked up to me with so pathetic and reproachful an expression that I would gladly have given him back his life had such power been mine. Even now I feel regret rather than pride as I recall those great limpid eyes.

That night we made camp in a small clump of *palmas del monte,* our stock standing disconsolately about, too thirsty to seek their food. Dried biscuits and lettuce leaves sufficed for our supper. I sat up quite late preparing the antelope's head, intending to have it mounted for an approaching birthday of my sister-in-law. Before turning in, Castro and I put out several tin plates for the sake of a possible fall of dew. We did not sleep much. I awoke about midnight with my throat craving water. I drained nearly a cup, more, in fact, than my share for the time.

Friday morning there were a few drops of dew in the plate, we licked them up thirstily; then, careless of the antelope steaks, ate dried biscuit and baked potatoes. After this slight repast, we drew in our belts and pursued our easterly course, the fog saving us from the heat for a couple of hours. Our stock of water now consisted of two cupfuls, and all that relieved the seriousness of the position was Castro's assurance that by noon we would strike either the Calmalli-San Ignacio camino or the *Agua* of San Angel.

For two leagues we traveled over firm ground, radiant with wild flowers growing to the shoulders of the burros. Then the soil once more became loose and yielding, *cholla* and *cardones* superseded the wild flowers and, to the increasing torment of our thirst, was added the constant menace of cactus thorns. Gradually, we ascended the rising slope of the sierras, the ground changing to a rock heap, densely grown with the pernicious *cholla, palmas del monte* and *cardones.* With our advance came the greater heat of the day, bringing intense thirst and grave anxiety. Ultimately, noon grew near, and with sinking spirits we were forced to admit that there were no signs of any camino approaching our line of march from the northwest—Calmalli way. By midday we had arrived at a small arroyo on a high mesa; here we paused briefly, to extract thorns, rest and relish a half spoonful, each, of water.   White-limbed, fresh-looking *palos blancos* were growing about us, but in the absence of water their very freshness was derisively cruel.   Castro now urged that we bear away into the sierras to the north. Mindful of the advice given me in February by my friend, Señor Dick, however, I refused to consider this suggestion and later in the day, with threatening revolver, enforced my determination of pursuing, without the slightest variation, the course which we had adopted Wednesday afternoon.   Could we but hold out, this would bring us to some one of the caminos running into San Ignacio from the north or south, while straying would merely serve to eat up our endurance.   For twenty-four hours, dead ahead against the eastern horizon we had seen, except during darkness and fog, a mighty cleft peak, our adopted landmark, indicating to us the direction we had chosen—17 degrees south of east.   From this course there should be no turning.

After our brief rest, we pressed on over flat rocky ridges and across sandy arroyos, the whole country being nearly impassable because of the dense thickets of cacti and undergrowths.   In the forenoon, we had crossed several small water courses, parched, salt-stained by the evaporation of alkali water; now each successive arroyo wore a fresh, verdant carpet that deceitfully invited us to hasten forward but, on near approach, always proved to be flowering creepers, entangling gourd-vines, stubborn cacti—Dead Sea fruit for our terrible thirst.   Meantime, Castro and I were compelled, again and again, to dismount and hack a passage through the deterring growths.   Finally, we continued on foot, grim, silent figures, moving forward, forward, ready machetes in hand.   Early in the afternoon the Mexicans had split open a young *viznaga,* or barrel or fish-hook cactus,

▲ Sierra de la Giganta

Mission San Francisco Xavier Viggé ▼

▲   Arroyo Comondú

Mission San José de Comondú   ▼

and carved out great chunks of the firm, interior flesh; following their example, I was soon chewing some of this to a pulp. It looked like an apple and yielded considerable juice, but our bodies had become so dry and our throats so parched that we craved great gulps of water rather than this impalatable moisture. Perhaps an hour later Castro bent down suddenly, with a low gasp of delight, and wrenched loose from a crevice among the rocks a small plant made up of a number of pale delicate shoots. Explaining that this was the *siempre vivens* and *muy bueno*, the old fellow equably divided up the shoots. We chewed them greedily. The *siempre vivens* in its appearance greatly resembles the lily of the valley—always a favorite flower with me, now doubly so, for the leaves and flower stems of this, its desert cousin, proved to be juicy and an astringent, by no means unpleasant, to the throat and tongue.

Over seventy hours had elapsed since our poor burros had had water! Now, however, I shortly noticed a wise old burro of Castro's, and Cabrillo, my large, half bronco burro, tearing at a small, cylindrical cactus. The Mexicans at once nodded approvingly, and sighting another similar cactus, tore it loose for the burros. This cactus—not over an inch in diameter by four in height—they termed the *chiquita pithaya*. It contained much moisture. Almost immediately we were still further encouraged by the sight of two doves which, according to the Mexicans, betokened the proximity of water. As the hours dragged by, however, without materialization of these hopes, our spirits fell lower than ever.

Darkness found us on a rocky mesa where we unpacked. After pushing aside the large loose stones and opening our blankets on the half cleared spots, we sank down apathetically, heedless of the numerous stones remaining. For supper we ate baked potatoes, lump sugar and prunes. Each of us also gulped down a spoonful dole of water: this left us less than a cupful in stock.

Neither of the Mexicans had as yet uttered a word of complaint, nor did they now. Jesús, poor boy, lay forlornly on his blanket, careless of the stones beneath. His eyes looked preternaturally large and pathetic. Feeling that death was probably near at hand, my main regret was for him. Castro was reaping the chances of his speculation. I had challenged fate by attempting to explore the country, but poor Jesús was a mere pawn indentured to me by his father. Eventually, I made a few entries in my journal, smiling grimly as I noted that they filled out the last page in the volume. By this time Jesús had sunk into broken slumber; Castro, swathed in his serapa, crouched by the small fire; with tired muscles relaxed, I was stretched out at length on my blankets, disheartened and hopeless. Fortunately for me, sleep came, bringing temporary relief.

With a feverish start I awoke, possessed by a maddening thirst. The air was cruelly dry. No dampening mist had rolled in to cool us. The night was silent and starry. At other times in my life I had been on long stretches without water and had suffered from thirst—but never like this.

With a ghastly alertness ideas and thoughts came marching down the pathways of my brain and instantly I thus summed up the situation: We have little water and no supply is near—San Angel has evidently been passed to our right—and yet our parched condition is such that our systems imperatively demand refreshment. However, we have but a few drops of water and the nature of the country is such that even with fresh animals or greater individual energy there could be no hastening forward more rapidly toward San Ignacio. Unquestionably even more terrific thirst will come and with it—Death.

And yet death always seems the other fellow's portion, and while one is possessed of vigor its immediate personal proximity is hard to realize. Then it came over me that the many other poor devils who had met death by thirst on the Lower California deserts had doubtless found a similar difficulty in realizing the nearness of the end. On the heels of this thought there flashed across my mind the closing entry made by the last of the crew of the "Tower Castle," and I repeated to myself, *"It is but reasonable to expect that my time will soon come."* Yes, reason pointed that way for, face to face with the domination, the angry gripping of such maddening thirst, our minds certainly would shortly lose their balance, their grasp, and from an experience with tragedies of the desert I knew that such mental unbalancing —insanity—was the prelude, the first step, incident to death by thirst.

At this I grew rebellious. I would not give in. I was not fated to die in such manner—not yet, at least. Moreover, I belonged to the superior nation and I must keep up my end before my Mexicans. With this there flitted across my mind the gay pictures of fortune predicted by the kindly ladies at Calmalli and I found sardonic amusement in blaming them as false prophetesses. My thoughts hurried on and I began to consider a plan. Meantime I ate a few biscuit crumbs and lumps of sugar, moistened with a teaspoonful of whiskey. Next I seized upon my journal and made a brief closing note across the margin of the last page; then, scrawling on its cover my brother's address and a simple direction in Spanish that it be sent to him, I tied the book with a strong cord and slipped it into my saddle-bags.

Looking up from this, I saw Castro's eyes upon me. He evidently had understood the intent of my actions, for he nodded approvingly. Passing from him my glance wandered across the mesa, with its *cholla* and kindred shadows;

it noted the mist that had stayed on the plains below; for an instant it viewed the clear sky giving sinister promise of an early day of heat, then again fell upon the old Mexican in his serapa. On the spur of the moment I addressed him in English: "How now, old boy?" I said, forcing a grin. Though the words were meaningless to him, the spirit he appreciated and a smile, brave but frightfully ghastly, crept over his wizened features and seemed to run like some stray electric current out into his crisp gray curls. Presently in hollow tones that I even yet recall, he made his answer. *"Señor,"* he said, *"mañana, mañana no agua, mañana tardes —nosotros muertus."* (Sir, to-morrow morning no water, to-morrow afternoon—we die.) His words voiced the conclusions that I had not dared express. I shivered, and then, *"Si, señor,"* I replied, quietly.

For a long time after this we sat by the coals, brooding silently. Then he made inquiry whether I had wife and children. I shook my head. *"Bueno,"* he muttered, and without further words I knew the trend of his thoughts. Later I secured an hour of broken sleep, but long ere dawn Castro roused both Jesús and me that we might lose no possible chance of travel before the heat of the day. Suffering though I was, I could but note the quiet, even way in which both Mexicans went after the burros—poor creatures, they had stayed near by, their heads hanging disconsolately—and put on the packs, performing their wonted duties as faithfully as though the brightest prospects were before them. In response to a query as to how he felt, Jesús answered simply, *"Muy mala, Señor."*

To lighten the loads of our weary burros, I had regretfully directed Castro to throw aside the forequarters of the antelope. At the same time I divested myself of my camera, spurs, cartridges, even of my revolver, placing them all in my *cantinas;* thus lightly accoutered, and armed only with a short *machete,* I was prepared for the finish of the chapter. I now submitted the plan on which I had determined: if we found no water or camino by midday, the burros should be unpacked, unsaddled and turned loose, the Mexicans should put up my small tent and lie quietly in its shade while I, as the hardiest in the party, should push on ahead, find San Ignacio—if possible—and then hasten rapidly back on a fresh animal, bringing with me a supply of water. Castro approved of this scheme, Jesús nodded and we began the day's march.

This was Saturday, the 24th of March. For three days we had been traveling in a dry, smothering atmosphere, where extreme perspiration is the rule. On Wednesday we had had a reasonable amount of water, some five cups each. Thursday we had had probably three cups each, Friday not over three spoonfuls—and on this day Castro and I had been on foot most of the day and the brush had been dense. We began Saturday with a spoonful each: three spoonfuls remained. A personal experience of this nature is not pleasant to recall, and I shall hurry over our further sufferings.

A deep chasm soon confronted us, but after much difficulty we found a place where we could descend and down which we persuaded the burros to venture; poor creatures, they seemed to realize that it was no time to be stubborn over steep places for, with Coronado leading bravely, they jumped after me from boulder to boulder. In one place we found a number of the *siempre vivens* growing and these we seized upon with avidity. On we went, down one mountain side and up another. None of us had anything to say. Once or twice the Mexicans were disposed to stray from our course, but I grimly persuaded them into line. About eleven in the forenoon, while searching in a side arroyo for a possible *tinaja,* I came across a group of graves. This dispiriting discovery I kept from Jesús, though I made it known to Castro. The old man shook his head, briefly remarking that doubtless some considerable party had died of thirst and that we would soon be in the like fix—only we might have to wait a time for stones to be piled over us! This set me to thinking of an ancestor hunt I had once made in an overgrown cemetery at Newtown, Long Island, and I began to chuckle over the recollection that even the most magnificent tombstones in that cemetery were entirely neglected. The note of insanity which rang in my laughter checked these thoughts, sharply; but in another moment ghoulish memory was picturing the appearances of the various dead men whom I had chanced upon at different times and particularly one found near Lake Tahoe; above this man's body I had helped place a rude board, inscribed from the Psalms, "The mountains shall bring peace."

The recollection of this inscription still sharp in my brain, a dull effort to find a proper translation in Spanish engrossing my attention, laughter on my lips—to such a state had I come, when I saw near at hand the familiar parallel lines of stones which mark a roadway of the time of the padres. My wild cry, *"Un camino, un camino!"* brought my companions hurrying forward with strained, doubting expressions that were pathetic.

After following this trail—it came from the southwest, San Angel way, we learned later—for a few rods, we halted and wet our lips with the few drops remaining in the canteen and which we had been keeping, tacitly, for the first who should give out. Assuaging the further poignancy of our sufferings by chewing viznaga pulp, we kept on for about ten miles. Then, unexpectedly, the blank rocky mesa, over which we were traveling opened before us. At the bottom of the chasm, five or six hundred feet below, lay a long, narrow valley, of perhaps two thousand acres, with water—pools of fine, rippling water flowing through green masses of sedge—and palms—thousands of tall, graceful palms, shading numerous thatched houses—and over to the further side a beautiful stone church with spires and belfry rising aloft. Up the trail came a homelike cow, closely followed by three little barefoot girls, clad in pink and red.

Off came my sombrero. "Hurrah, hurrah!" I cried hoarsely.

"San Ignacio, San Ignacio," mumbled old Castro, while Jesús, hysterically laughing, cried out, *"Agua, agua!"*

PART II

THE WIDENING OF THE TRAIL

CHAPTER XIII

SAN IGNACIO, THE FAVORED

DOWN the camino we plunged, following hard in the wake of our thirst-crazed burros. Some slow dragging moments brought us into the midst of a group of natives lounging in dreamy apathy before the open doorway of a small shack built against the base of the cliff. *"Agua, agua!"* we demanded, gaspingly, with naught by way of preliminary greeting. Our hoarse, broken voices, our dry, mumbling lips, our frenzied manner, our burros wading belly-deep in the stream beyond: no need to amplify such signs to children of an arid land, to a people reared amid tragedies of the desert. On the instant, seizing cups and gourds they dipped up cooling water from an earthen *olla,* splashing our dry faces, our dry necks, our dry arms with large gourds of blessed water, then they gave us each a brimming cup, a great, cooling, life-renewing cup of water, cautioning us the meantime lest we drink overmuch.

And thus I came to San Ignacio, the favored. That we were in an out-of-the-world place was now brought home to me, for my accent disclosing my nationality, one of the natives exclaimed, "Ah, Señor, you are an *Americano!* Ten months past there were here two of your compatriots, bird collectors from your great city of Washington. But they came hither safely, having taken the upper, the well-beaten camino. Ah, three strange *Americanos* within the year!"

Soon we made camp in the shade of two great olive trees

where my tent opened out upon the stream and where palms and orange trees were near by. Thoroughly exhausted, we stretched out in the shade, now and again drinking more water or eating luscious fruit, for we were well supplied with oranges, lemons, dates and sugar-cane, gifts of kindly people who had come quietly to our camp with their offering as soon as the news of our fearful experience had reached them. In the late afternoon, with sharp clatter of hoofs there dashed by a party of gentlemen mounted on spirited Durangian horses, with silver mounted bridles and saddles and carrying long swords thrust under the left knees. Later, a gay party of these *Caballeros,* with Sigñoras and Señoritas in their midst, swept by, bowing gravely as they passed, and calling forth in courteous tones, *"Buenas tardes, Señor; buenas tardes."* Though seated in strangely designed side-saddles, the ladies rode with extreme grace. The peculiar features of these saddles consisted in the hanging of the stir-rup at the *right* side of the horse and in the presence of a high back or support which arose above the cantel and extended to the left.

Noting, in a dazed manner, these passers by, I rested quietly in camp, accepting the readily given information of not infrequent visitors. Meantime I drank water; by nightfall I had absorbed over two gallons and yet I craved more; indeed, there seemed no abatement to my thirst, my parched system absorbing the moisture as the desert sands drink in the drops of a rare August thunder shower. The following day found me feverishly nervous. Fortunately, however, a delightful young *caballero,* Señor Villavacensio, soon appeared and, seemingly appreciative of my mood, took me for a stroll along the winding, palm-shaded streets of the pueblo and through the quaint precincts of the ancient mission. Before my interest in these scenes had even begun to abate he turned toward a substantial residence where

I was formally presented to a dignified Señora and her two daughters, who inquired kindly concerning my home and my welfare. From this pleasant home we passed on to another and another, finding in each the same genial hospitality. With their bright eyes, soft voices, fluttering fans and easy grace the Señoritas were altogether adorable; winsome, nut-brown maids, every one of them, their pretty faces set off by the fascinating *rebozo,* or Mexican headdress.

Our calls concluded, we dropped in at a *cantina* and then another and another, finding in each drinking, smoking and billiard playing, but no drunkenness. We drank mediocre imported beer at four *reales* the small glass and a fine quality of native wine at half a *real* the generous sized glass. With evening came the sound of guitars and violin and I was ushered into an adobe where a *baile* or ball was in progress. The principal citizens of the pueblo were in attendance, dancing gravely with the Señoritas while the Señoras looked on with seeming content. I was courteously introduced to several of the young ladies and I found them excellent waltzers even though our dancing floor was earthen. Between the dances *mescal* was passed for the men and wine and beer for the women, but none indulged too freely. The scarcity of bachelors was noticeable. This was explained to me by the statement that the majority of the young men were employed in the copper mines at Santa Rosalia, too far distant to permit of their attendance at the *baile.*

Surely of San Ignacio I can write only in the kindliest vein and such, I am sure must also be the attitude even of those who have neither been rescued by its streams nor taken captive by the charm of its history and traditions for, with its oasis-like aspect and the impulsive hospitality of the inhabitants, the little pueblo is a delightful place, marvelously inviting to the traveler. By whatever camino he may ap-

proach, it comes as a surprise, the rocky mesa opening
unexpectedly before him and disclosing the verdant arroyo
below, with its tens of thousands of waving palms, its glistening orange trees, its green sedges gemmed with pools of
limpid water, its thatched roofed *jacales*—shacks made of
thatch—its substantial, flat roofed adobes and magnificent
stone mission church.   There are a thousand inhabitants in
the narrow valley.   They cultivate about two thousand
acres of rich, well-watered, ashy loam, volcanic in its origin
and of surpassing fertility, which rewards them with prosperity.   In the arroyo of San Ignacio oranges, lemons,
sugar-cane, olives, figs and grapes mature, unchallenged by
frost, while palms—sixty thousand, it is said, grow in profusion; the fan palm, useful for thatching, and the red,
green, yellow and black date palm all are there.   Enough
grain is raised and enough leather prepared for home consumption, while long trains of burros and mules carry away
for export cargoes of fresh and dried fruits, wine and a
native sugar called *panoche.*

The history of this favored valley is that of its mission.
Nigh two centuries ago a Jesuit explorer, one Sistiago, came
exultantly to Loreto, reporting the discovery of a deep
arroyo with much water and sedge grass and many Indians.
Happy coincidence: even then a caravel was entering the
offing bringing to California Padre Juan Bautista Luyando,
a brilliant and socially accomplished missionary, eager to
establish, personally, a mission dedicated to San Ignacio, the
founder of the Society of Jesus.   To Kadakaman, or the
Valley of Sedges, therefore, the two padres, pioneer and
aristocrat, hastened, founding there the Mission of San
Ignacio de Kadakaman.

This was in the year 1728.   Some three decades before
Padre Juan Maria Salvatierra, a priest of the Society of
Jesus, a native of Milan, of noble parentage and ancient

Spanish descent, had landed, with an escort of six soldiers, on the east coast of the Peninsula. In the seventy years succeeding this event and ending with their expulsion in 1768, the Jesuits established such a network of missions throughout the Peninsula that, although the eighteenth century was pre-eminently a fervid period of mission construction in their Spanish Majesties' realms, in no portion thereof was more ardor shown than in California. Not the California of these days, but the *Isla de California* as it was termed by the early chroniclers, the mysterious "Island" of pearls, mermaidens, Amazons and treasure, now classed as the Mexican territory of Baja California and, aside from its name, relatively as much a *terra incognita* as in the days when voyagers charted it as an island and peopled its valleys with roving and alluring Amazons.

Of the substantial work accomplished by the energetic Jesuits during the threescore and ten years of their California service, San Ignacio was the pivotal point, second only to sacred Loreto. From the year of its dedication the mission was the starting point for their venturesome explorers and an enticing field for their scholarly priests. At the time of the expulsion of these padres the church and subsidiary buildings at San Ignacio were still in course of construction; completed, a few years later, by the Dominicans, they were thereafter considered among the finest in the country.

The Mission of San Ignacio has its traditions as well as its history: A queen of Spain, it is said, gave a million and a half of pesos for its construction and over fifty years of labor were required for its completion; in the distant Santa Clara Sierra, within sight of the lofty spires of the church, lies hid away the mysterious Lost Mission of Santa Clara; finally, saintly padres have been interred before the altar of San Ignacio and beneath it there is secreted a

mighty chest of treasure.   Short has been the shrift allotted
to the wickedly avaricious who have sought this treasure;
for should it once be disturbed then the slumbering volcanic
fires in the mighty Tres Virgenes will awaken and over-
whelm San Ignacio with lava.   It is a pity that the volcano
did not give a few threatening rumbles a short time since,
for by so doing it might have saved the altar from being
pillaged, under the cloak of legal authority, of many of its
precious gold and silver ornaments.   The long knives of
the natives, however, will doubtless protect the traditional
treasure.

It is part history and part tradition that in early times
the Padres gathered at San Ignacio a library of rare books
and precious charts.   Even less than sixty years ago these
treasures were seen.   After diligent search I found, in the
hands of an old San Ignacio family, the remains of this
library: two poor, lone volumes.   Both were printed in
illuminated type, done at Rome *"Superiorum Permissu,"*
one under date of 1723, the other, 1783.   The ancient
leather and wood bindings, the broken iron clasps and the
quaint print of these relics would cause any normal anti-
quary to thrill with covetousness.   Church ceremonials, Holy
Days and other religious matters were the subjects considered in these books.   Near Santa Gertrudis I had found
others not unlike them, but with this greater interest: the
illustrations had been designed to appeal to the natives, the
Roman Centurions, for instance, being mounted on mules
accoutered with the shoulder and crupper straps in use on
the steep caminos of the Peninsula.

The Mission of San Ignacio is remarkably well preserved.   In outward appearance it is so like the Franciscan
Mission of San Luis Rey in the State of California that I
rather expect the latter must have been designed from it.
The church, the usual ell and the wall surrounding the patio

▲ Bells, San José de Comondú

Arroyo Comondú ▼

▲   Arroyo Comondú

La Purísima   ▼

stand practically untouched by time. At all hours of the day veiled Señoras and smiling girls enter the wide portals of the church to kneel in prayer before its ancient altar. The Post Office and the village school—with soft voiced urchins repeating aloud their lessons—are located in the commodious ell, while an elderly, rotund and jovial maker of leather, father of a sloe-eyed Señorita, inhabits still another portion of the priest-forsaken quarters. All the buildings are of cut stone. Approaching the church, which opens upon the usual plaza, one climbs two flights of steps before entering the lofty arched doorway with its massive hard-wood double doors. The walls are four feet in thickness. The interior, though but seven paces in width, floor measurement, is even of greater length than the church at San Borja, while the extreme height, under a superb dome, must be over twenty metres. Above the altar there are a number of magnificent oil paintings done by Italian brushes in the eighteenth century, while below and to the right and left are extensive alcoves, each with its individual shrine. Finally, the floor of the church is composed of hewn stone cubes, set closely together.

As the junction of numerous caminos which lead away to the north, south and east, San Ignacio even now is an important pueblo. Three of these trails connect with the Gulf port of Santa Rosalia, twenty leagues to the northeast. This was my next objective. Accordingly, selecting the most favored of the three trails, I set forth early the third morning after my arrival at San Ignacio. Anxiety for home news and the recollection of a promise given the proprietor of the mines at Los Flores, relative to the delivery of a certain letter to his factor at Santa Rosalia, urged me forward; otherwise, I would have rested longer, for my caravan still suffered from the effects of our experience on the Plains of Ojo Liebre.

In fact, my old mozo Castro was so feeble and unfit for travel that I left him in the care of his friends at San Ignacio. His parting message was a prayerful request that if death came, "would the *patrón* take the compass and fix the direction for my soul to reach Paradise?" Once on the road my poor Coronado, unable to continue his former vigorous gait, was compelled to see his place and leader's bell given to the younger and more recuperative Cabrillo. It was affecting to observe the evident humiliation with which the plucky burro accepted the change. Such were some of the effects of our struggle against thirst, an ever impending danger for those who wander in the fastnesses of Lower California. Now, however, we were to see the more settled portions of the Peninsula.

CHAPTER XIV

ALTHOUGH in Washington and San Francisco I had frequently heard mention of La Paz as the largest settlement on the California Peninsula, concerning Santa Rosalia I had found no data in the United States beyond the bare statement of some financial and shipping men that it was a small port on the Gulf of California where a wealthy French syndicate was quietly engaged in extensive copper mining. As I proceeded down the Peninsula, I began, to my surprise, however, to hear Santa Rosalia referred to as a French city and the largest municipality in Lower California. I left San Ignacio, therefore, filled with expectations.

For two days we traveled northeasterly, passing through lofty volcanic sierras and wearing around to the right of three massive peaks, the Three Virgins, two of which shyly hid themselves behind their sister. These peaks approach seven thousand feet in height and even in modern times have rumbled with volcanic life. During a portion of this journey we rode along a broad and ancient highway, bordered with stones and dating into prehistoric times. Late in the afternoon of the second day we entered a long valley in which we found habitations and small plots of garden land. Finally we came upon quite a settlement called Sant' Agueda and first developed in the days of the Padres. Here and there were palms and orange trees, a watercourse and a number of frame houses, at the farthest of which we stopped for the night. Our host and hostess were a French couple, Monsieur and Madame Rosand. From them I gathered that the residents of Sant' Agueda were engaged in raising "garden truck," which they marketed at Santa Rosalia, two leagues distant. Madame Rosand was an industrious little woman of twenty-eight, possessed of such a wealth of maternal love that she generously cared for a small orphan in addition to her own sturdy brood of six. Remembering her good deeds I bow to Madame Rosand, a brave little woman, and such a culinary artist! So pleased was I with this kindly couple that I arranged to leave Jesús with them while I pushed on to the Gulf.

I was in the saddle early the morning after my arrival at Sant' Agueda. The trail immediately broadened out into an excellent road, marked by a line of telephone poles. Soon I passed a succession of gaping mining shafts and then arrived at a small railroad station protected by a series of frame residence barracks. This was El Providencia, one of the three great copper mines of the Santa Rosalia group. Between San Ignacio and Sant' Agueda I had seen thickets which, though they were composed of small varieties of trees such as the palo blanco, were more extensive and numerous than any I had observed since leaving the region of thick mesquit near the 29th parallel, north latitude. Now, however, I had arrived in an absolutely barren country, devoid of any trees or shrubs.

The station rests in a narrow arroyo which gradually widened out as I rode forward. Twenty minutes burro travel brought me past a long shed—a public laundry, evidently, judging from the washtubs and hydrants under its shelter—into a town with side-walks, well-kept streets, frame houses and *"Rurales"* or mounted police. This was Santa Rosalia, the most modern and largest town in Lower California. At the foot of the street before me I could see

Santa Rosalia

a harbor and many ships; on the bluffs to the right and left of the town there were residences, while high above those at the left rose the mighty smoke-stacks of the smelter. After the rare interest of quaint San Ignacio my first impression of this new, mathematically laid out town was far from agreeable. The salt air from the harbor, however, was welcome. Eyeing my surroundings with curiosity and surprise I rode slowly down the main street, guided by the first urchin I observed, and crossing a plaza dismounted before the Correo, which I found just beyond.

Here I submitted identifying credentials to the Postmaster and asked for mail. The official carefully examined my documents, then smiling in a friendly manner delivered to me a packet of letters. These contained my first home news in over three months! With nervous fingers I opened the letter with the oldest postmark, then the one with the most recent. They contained no bad news. The official seemed to read the evident relief in my face for he smiled again and offered to conduct me to the neighboring office of the principal Mexican shipping merchant, Señor Rudolfo Garyzar, for whom I had made inquiry, as he was the factor of my mining friend at Los Flores.

Señor Garyzar proved to be a middle-aged Spanish-Mexican gentleman. Though he spoke little English he had full command of the pure Castilian. After accepting the letter which I delivered to him and thanking me courteously, he introduced me to the Mayor of Santa Rosalia, one Señor Bouchet. After greeting me in English, this gentleman proceeded to read, with every care, the credentials which I presented to him. Meantime I noted his appearance. Like Señor Garyzar he was dressed in clothes of American cut. I quickly decided that he was medium in every respect: age, height, weight, even nationality, for his dark pointed beard was more French than Mexican. Later,

I found that he was part French—and all courtesy and hospitality. His reading concluded, the Mayor invited me to his place of business, a general store facing the plaza. Office and sales-room opened upon the street, while at the rear there were store-rooms and a kitchen. After directing me to deposit my saddle-bags in the office, Señor Bouchet led the way up a flight of stairs to a suite of rooms where he resided. Later I found that all of the merchants lived thus in touch with their stores. As soon as he had apologized for appearances, explaining that his family was absent on a visit to Los Angeles, the Señor placed one of his rooms at my disposal. The extent of his hospitality dawning upon me, I protested that there was a hotel on the plaza and that I could not impose on his good nature. Protestations, however, were waved aside and I became a guest, a particularly agreeable position, as my host proved to be widely informed and a well read gentleman, at home in the English, French, German and Spanish languages.

After luncheon I enjoyed a short visit with the two Italian priests who were in charge of the parish and then passing through a gateway in a large enclosure, ascended a broad highway leading to the French quarters on the northern bluff, immediately overlooking the lower town. Anxious to obtain data for historic work, I directed my steps toward the office building of El Boleo, the French copper mining company, and sent in my card. After a short delay I was ushered through a hall-way and a succession of rooms into an inner office, where the clerk left me in the presence of a keen eyed French official, whom I soon found to be a polished and educated gentleman, well qualified to relieve a stranger of embarassment. The purpose of my call briefly explained, I retired from the offices of the notedly uncommunicative officials of El Boleo, with an assurance that my request would be given consideration. Twenty-four hours

later there was delivered to me a concise report in crisp
English, setting forth all the data which I desired.

On my return to the lower town I met on the plaza an
'American, a traveling dentist, who seemed nearly as glad
to meet me as I was to see him. He explained that although there were a few Germans, a couple of hundred
French and seven thousand Mexicans, Japanese and Yaquis
in Santa Rosalia, we were the only Anglo-Saxons. In the
usual unusual happening of coincidences it developed that
my countryman and I had been born in adjoining counties.
I entered his office, which of course faced the plaza—in
Mexico everybody seeks the plaza—and we were soon deep
in the novel exercise of speaking English. Presently we
heard childish voices in the adjoining yard singing in chorus,

"Cuan- do sa- li de la Ha-ba-na val-ga me Dios!
"Na-die me ha vis-to sa-lir si no fui yo
"Yu-na lin-da Guachi-nanga sa-lla voy yo
"Que se vi no tras de mi que si se-nor
"Si a tu ven-ta-na lle-ga u-na Pa-lo-ma."

Through the open doorway I could see the singers, a group
of small girls, hands clasped and moving from right to left
in time with the music. My companion's face had clouded,
and abruptly excusing himself, he rushed out and quieted
the children.

"What's up?" I inquired on his return, "the youngsters
were merely singing *"La Paloma"* (The Dove), which, by
the way, I've heard the *muchachitas* singing all the way
down from our Border. The air and soft syllables are decidedly pretty."

"I can't abide that song," replied the dentist, testily.
Recalling the pathos of the verses and that many Americans
in Mexico have painful home memories, I jumped at my
own conclusions and was silent. "Come," exclaimed my
companion, changing the subject, "let's find the good mayor

and indulge in a chat over there on the hotel veranda."

Again crossing the plaza, we found Señor Bouchet and were soon seated around a small table before the hotel. A passerby, the captain of a German vessel at anchor in the harbor, made a fourth to our party. Glasses were promptly filled.

"Herr Cap," I remarked, "you have sailed these waters for years, what do you think of Mexico?"

"Mexico! Ah, the Senoritas are *sehr schön*—but always chaperoned, always, always." He shook his grizzled head mournfully and then inquired of me:

"How do you get on with the *lingua?*"

I hesitated a moment. "Do you recall as a child hopping from stone to stone in crossing a stream—" "*Ja, ja,*" he interrupted, chuckling reminiscently. "Well, that's the way I *habla Espagnol*. Of nouns, adjectives, swear-words and adverbs I have a liberal supply, but as for the verb— Well, I hop over verbs. When I slip among them there's the deuce of a splash and I flounder shamefully."

The dentist nodded encouragingly. "Don't be disheartened, said he, "remember that even though your Spanish grammar be weak you have always your hands and shoulders. Which reminds me. The other day I heard a Mexican, in complimenting an American *amigo's* Spanish, say, 'Why, he could *habla* though his hands were tied.' "

"Where is the flavor of a conversation devoid of shrugs and gesticulations?" queried Señor Bouchet, in quick rejoinder. Then, leaving the subject instantly, for the rest of us were smiling appreciation of the yarn, he continued, with eyes twinkling merrily, "I, too, have a little story. Last week I saw an American tabulating English equivalents for Mexican words. Consider my feelings when I observed that he had our *now* set opposite your *tomorrow* and our *tomorrow* made an equivalent of your *never*."

This sally was thoroughly appreciated, for every man of us had suffered from Mexican procrastination. On regular polyglot tongues conversation sped forward.

The ensuing day I boarded a steamer for Guaymas. After spending nearly a fortnight in Sonora, I was again in Santa Rosalia, however, once more the guest of the hospitable Mayor. For four interesting days I remained under his roof. In odd moments he would pore over my books on ancient California history, pointing out in return modern characteristics of his people. In common with all in touch with Mexican affairs he was an ardent admirer of President Diaz.

"The General has given stability to our finances," the Señor remarked one day, "he has invited capital to develop our resources, he has enforced our laws. The next step, and the one toward which every patriotic Mexican must do his part, is to teach thrift to our lower classes. Have you noticed these small packages the people throng this store to buy?"

I nodded affirmatively.

"Well, those are one cent packages of beans, *panoche,* coffee, cheese, etc. On pay-day these people splurge; at other times they purchase necessaries in minimum lots, which, while giving the merchant a substantial retail profit, is a heavy drain on the purchaser. Such a habit merely typifies the lack of thrift which I deplore."

Through the days Santa Rosalia was supremely quiet, undisturbed save by the occasional entry of some pack train from the interior. Twilight, however, released the men from labor and brought forth bevies of feminine shoppers. Until ten o'clock the streets were thronged and in the store my host and his clerks were rushed with work.

The Señor introduced me to one of his customers, the daughter of his friend, Señor Garyzar. An extremely pretty señorita and a charming member of the Mexican *Primera Clase,* or high social class, she spoke English fluently. Though we found much in common to discuss, she was promptly whisked away by her inexorable duenna the instant shopping was concluded. Later I met her two particular friends, one of whom, Señorita Cuca P——, spoke English, French and German in addition to Castilian, quite essential accomplishments, according to the teasing Mayor, because of her American, English, French, German and Spanish admirers. Furthermore, she was a fearless horsewoman; and in Lower California, at least, Mexican girls rarely share their brothers' expertness in the saddle.

One day, while enjoying a stroll on the southern bluff where the officers of the Port and other Federal officials resided, I met two young señoritas as attractive as the trio whose acquaintance I had made through Señor Bouchet. As my dentist friend who was with me had been formally presented to the young Mexicans, he introduced me to them in due form. The younger, a fair girl with the blue eyes of Old Spain, was the sister of an official with a roving commission. She had just arrived with him at Santa Rosalia.

"I am bad company, Señor," said she, "I am feeling *triste.* I miss beautiful Guadalajara and the dear City of Mexico. You, too, have lately arrived; and by way of San Ignacio, as I understand. That is a pretty place, is it not?"

"*Sí, Señorita,*" I replied, "at San Ignacio there are green palms, beautiful gardens, a stream of water, an old mission and an atmosphere of the medieval."

The girl sighed. "Ah me, how I wish I were in San Ignacio." She glanced at me, wistfully. "What is there here? Tell me, American, what can you, a stranger, see before us?"

She waved a hand gracefully toward the town. I an-

swered slowly, "I see a deep sea harbor, protected by a
stone jetty out on which a train is carrying carloads of
broken stone. The Customs buildings are near the water
and from them wharves jut out into the harbor. An arroyo
debouches at the water's edge, immediately below us, forming the town site. The width of this arroyo may be three
hundred metres; at the upper end of the town it is even
more narrow. I see a plaza, faced by an hotel, a school
building, a most creditable structure, and several stores."

As I paused in my cataloguing, the girl exclaimed, impul-
sively, "Oh, you are as precise as my brother. Let me conclude: The whole lower town is mathematical—and, therefore, horrid. Those fussy French engineers laid it out,
doubtless, with a metre rule and a surveyor's chain. The
school house is the only painted building below us. There
is a complete system of electric lighting—and no balconies,
anywhere. There is a theater where at times plays are
given, tiresome ones. Annually there is a delightful ball—
dressy, *en masque* and well arranged by the French officials,
who, for the evening, are charming."

She paused, breathless, and I ventured, "In its appearance the town does rather resemble a combination of a deserted Arizona mining camp and a frontier military post.
Cold, barrack-like——"

"Yes, a thousand times yes. And unhomelike—un-Mexi-
can. No shaded promenades, no historic mission cathedral,
not even a patio with its garden retirement. The engineers
have banked the arroyo and not planted a single palm. Yet
the French are supposed to be creators of the beautiful
only; their Paris is almost as delightful as Madrid. Oh,
how I wish I were back in Guadalajara!" She turned away
quickly, her voice breaking.

Accepting our dismissal, my companion and I sauntered
on down toward the lower town. "Poor children! It must

be frightfully dull here for them," he remarked, sympathetically. "What is there to know concerning Santa Rosalia, past or otherwise?" he inquired, suddenly, changing the subject.

I shrugged my shoulders. "No traditions, a brief history, a busy present and doubtless a big future." Nor could I sum up the situation more accurately now. Thirty years ago there was a rancho and some slight surface mining done at Santa Rosalia. A German company was in control. A decade later a powerful French syndicate bought out the Germans. Favored by liberal governmental concessions, the syndicate made substantial improvements, enlarged their holdings to a million and a half acres, made a superb harbor and their copper mines are now credited as being among the world's greatest producers. But these facts are not advertised to the public. The office of the syndicate is in Paris.

The following morning, the second after my return from Guaymas, I accompanied my host to a session of the Municipal Court, which convened daily in a small frame structure situated on the high bluff at the north of the lower town. The proceedings proved decidedly interesting. One by one the offenders of the preceding twenty-four hours were ushered in by the Assistant Chief of Police, a good looking, athletic chap, in white sweater, belted trousers, tan shoes and the regulation peaked white straw sombrero of the southern Rurales. Standing at attention, this official would salute the Mayor, then twirl his cane and twist his mustachios while his chief, a middle aged Mexican of serious mien and white linen garb, would state the particulars of the offense. The well-groomed Mayor, seated behind a desk, would peer through his gold rimmed glasses at the prisoner and inquire why he had broken the laws. The accused, for the most part, were ragged and extremely dark of complexion; they would enter noiselessly, shod, as they were, with *guarachas* or *teguas,* and in soft, persuasive voices reply to the questionings, each making his own defense. No oaths were administered. The usual sentence, the offenses being misdemeanors, was *two dollars or two days.* Sentences were accepted in a most extraordinary manner. Thus, in one case, the complaining witness paid the fine; in another, a widow, fined a dollar for failing to send her eight-year-old to school, found herself released from prison, the Court advancing the *peso;* in a third instance, a father, whose son had been imprisoned, entered the room, openly thanking the Mayor for the sentence imposed. Indeed, not even the magistrate of a Juvenile Court could have shown a greater paternal interest in his charges than did this big-hearted Señor with his child-like people.

Later I learned that His Honor was not only a Solomon but a veritable Haroun Al Raschid as well; for that evening I found him wandering about the town, accompanied by the Assistant Chief, looking after the peace of the community and conversing with all possible malefactors. This was his nightly habit. He kept in close touch, moreover, with his fourteen Rurales, the mounted police apportioned to Santa Rosalia. Small wonder that even the cosmopolitan population of the mining community, including in its numbers many Yaquis, the fiercest, save the Seri, of the Indian tribes of Mexico, was kept within bounds.

This Assistant Chief of Police was a most obliging man. The day after my return from Guaymas I engaged through his assistance an old Mexican to assist Jesús in camp work. He gave his name as Praemundi Marron and stated that, as he had once resided in San José del Cabo, he would be ready to start southward with me within twenty-four hours.

But a new tangle had arisen, the solution of which put

the time of my departure more than twenty-four hours into the future.

On entering Lower California the question of how to carry funds on the long journey before me had been a puzzler. A bag of cash and currency seemed dangerous. Indeed, so recent has been the passing of the Mexican bandit that his reputation still shadows the camino, and it is difficult for an American to realize that, thanks to the ever ready Rurales, the traveler is as safe from molestation on the highways of Mexico, save in certain remote or Border sections, as he would be in the United States. Finally, I decided upon drafts and checks of small denominations as the safest financial supply. Doubtless, considering that I was alone with natives the greater part of the time, this was the best solution of the problem. Now, however, I learned that for the first five hundred miles before me I would require more change than I had on hand and would pass through no place where checks could be cashed. Indeed, there was no bank even in Santa Rosalia with its considerable population. Moreover, my drafts were used up and I did not care to presume so far on the hospitality of the merchants whom I had met as to ask them to cash a check for the amount I desired. In this dilemma I wired for money. After four days of exasperating delays I received this satisfying message from the obliging operator of the wireless office:

"Operator on other coast say he have two messages for some one, but his bread in oven—wife she away—and might burn if he leave it long. After lunch he transmit message."

Surely, in Mexico even the electric service has become impregnated with the spirit of *mañana,* of *poco tiempo,* and its *ahora* is translated "tomorrow" and its *mañana* "never."

▲   El Pilón (La Purísima)

Visita La Presentación   ▼

▲ Pozo Grande

Mission San Luis Gonzaga ▼

Thanking the kindly local operator, I strode out of the office, boiling with indignation. My vexation passed away, however, as soon as I repeated the message to my compatriot, the dentist.

"Now wouldn't that jar you!" he exclaimed. "One must become accustomed to such things, here, however," he added, grimly. "You can't measure by home standards. For instance, the commercial and mining laws of Mexico are far ahead of ours; their criminal laws have a certainty of enforcement unknown in the States; the courtesy of the men is delightful, the natural modesty of the women remarkable: these are items on the credit side. Range on the debit side lack of thrift, procrastination, such puerile methods of business as just experienced by you——. But come to my office. You are anxious to journey southward. I have seventy-five pesos, if they will suffice you."

And thus, through the kindly confidence of my fellow-countryman, I was enabled to start forth without further delay. That evening, therefore, I despatched Praemundi to Sant' Agueda. The ensuing morning I bade good-bye to Santa Rosalia. As it was Good Friday and all places of business were closed, Señor Bouchet accompanied me to El Providencia, where a fair was being held. We had seen its beginning the evening of the previous day—Holy Thursday—when a group of fantastically garbed Yaqui Indians, led by a masked musician decked out as a Chief Devil, had entered Santa Rosalia, disporting themselves hilariously. At the same time numerous vendors of preserved cacti fruit—some of it not half bad—and of sweet cookies had sprung up most unexpectedly. We now found several groups of these masked Yaquis dancing frantically in and out the gaily decked booths of the El Providencia fair. Their movements were timed to strains of wild music. They were muscular men of stocky build and some of their contortions were little short of fiendish. All the Lower California Yaquis are importations from Sonora, where they are continually on the warpath. In Lower California they develop into excellent miners.

Crowds of Mexican children were gathered about the booths, while a number of well dressed and distinguished appearing Frenchmen, mounted on horseback, were watching the performances of the Indians. The eagle-eyed Rurales were also in evidence, riding quietly in and out of the crowd. As I was anxious to return to my outfit, I soon bade the kindly Mayor good-bye and walked the two leagues to Sant' Agueda, where I found my Mexican boy and Praemundi awaiting me.

Though my burros were improved by their long rest, I found it necessary to purchase an additional one, and was thereby detained thirty-six hours. The time passed most delightfully, however, for Sant' Agueda is not only the garden of Santa Rosalia but the playground of the French officials of El Boleo. A gay party of these mercurial Frenchmen soon swooped down upon the Rosands, reining up their steeds at the very threshold of the house. There were over a dozen in the party, young and middle aged, including the wives of two of the older men. Madame Rosand immediately began the preparation of a sumptuous dinner to which I was invited.

Two of the party were on the eve of departure for France; one, a mere boy, was to enter the army; the other, after fourteen years' service with El Boleo, was about to retire, and, in company with his wife, enjoy a prolonged hunting expedition in Algiers; he examined my carbine with great interest, questioned me concerning calibers, and fairly bubbled over with enthusiasm over the lions he expected to shoot and the boars he would spear.

At seven in the evening we sat down to a long, rough

Yaqui Indians at SantaRosalia

board table, placed under an arbor in the open air. At one
the following morning I escaped to my blankets, though my
companions were still enjoying themselves. A better spirited company could not be imagined. The repast was
delightful and all were hungry, for few of them were good
horsemen and their ride had given the men effective appetite. There was an abundance of red wine. We drank the
healths of the ladies; we drank that of the men who were
about to depart. I was toasted, and on my proposing,
"The Three Republics: France, Mexico and the United
States: May they always progress in harmony," my hosts,
not to be outdone, rose cheering, and sang in French and
English the opening verse of "The Star Spangled Banner."
At my right hand sat a M. Cailliatte, who kindly translated
for me; at my left a musical chap from the south of France.
All the party possessed good voices and their universal
courtesy was charming. At my request my left hand neighbor scribbled down a verse from a little *chanson* of southern
France, which he sang to every one's delight, though he
persisted in explaining that it was a mere recollection from
his boyhood days near the Pyrenees. Here it is:

> "*Et celui qui le fait*
> "*Il' est de son village*
> "*O madame voila de bon fromage*
> "*Voila du bon fromage au lait*
> "*Il' est du pays de celui qui la fait.*"

Saturday morning we had breakfast together, after which
the Frenchmen hunted doves and rabbits, while I searched
for a burro. As we were assembling at luncheon, a new
Frenchman rode up for a brief visit. One of the physicians
of the Company, he was deeply interested in a new serum,
calculated to overcome the rattle-snake's venom. Luncheon
concluded, the majority of those assembled departed, many

of them, to the great dissatisfaction of their steeds, riding double.

Later I enjoyed supper with those who remained, and then, mounting my riding burro, rode out into the starlight at the head of my small cavalcade, southward bound along *El Camino Real* for the distant pueblo of Loreto, the ancient capital of the Californias. Turning in my saddle, I saw the flickering candles on the rough table and heard the kindly French voices calling after me, *"Bon voyage, Monsieur. Bon voyage."*

CHAPTER XV

TO LORETO!

FROM Santa Rosalia, via the Purísima camino, Loreto lies distant sixty-seven leagues, or slightly over two hundred miles. The natives, however, reckon this distance at one hundred leagues, attaining their figures by adding the hours consumed in journeying between the intermediary places and allowing two leagues to the hour of mule travel. But over the rocky sierra caminos of Lower California even four miles per hour is a high average gait for a mule train. Traveling with burros I made the distance, and several leagues extra, in fifteen days. Had I the time and opportunity I would gladly spend fifty days in going over the same ground!

Two months earlier I had revelled in the poppies and the other California wild flowers of La Frontera. Now, day by day, a riotous wealth of deep colors burst forth from the myriad varieties of cacti, glorifying the flower petals of the swelling buds, while the sober mesquit and verdant palo verde suddenly decked themselves in golden hues. Of soft pink, yellow, deep red or still deeper green, a hundred chalices caught the eye, whenever I looked aside from the camino, until my heart softened even toward the vicious cholla which constantly opposes the traveler with its needles and strews its bristling sections in his way. With its rosaries of lovely blossoms, even this hated cactus could momentarily banish memory of its evil fame and exact homage from the vision.

In the thirsty wastes between Santa Gertrudis, Oje Liebre and San Ignacio there had been a dearth of birds, but as we rode southward toward Loreto, gallant cock quails called out challengingly, and from the occasional thickets beautiful red cardinals piped forth with gentle tenderness, "Sweet, sweet—ah, dear, dear; sweet, sweet—ah, dear, dear," a tender refrain most unexpected in the wilderness. Nightingales, too, sang bravely, while doves flaunted forth their amorous notes, forgetting for the time their weird call. Morning after morning, out from the fading gray of the earliest light, the mountains would assume form, bold and dark against the clear sky, their outlines hewn and carved in stern sculptury. Then, stirring the trembling silence of the blushing morn with tuneful melody, doves, quail and cardinals would burst forth in triumphant chorus hailing the majestic and ever-wondrous coming of the day. As the east reddened and the chorus grew in fervor, a gentle breath of air would sweep across the land, a mellow radiance soften the rugged western heights and, welcomed by his songsters, the God of Day would spring forth in the east.

Surely, though in an age when the world itself was young, the noble lines of the Vedic *Hymn to the Dawn* must have been composed amid such surroundings as these.

> "   *   *   *   Thou art the breath and life
> Of all that breathes and lives, awaking day by day
> Myriads of prostrate sleepers, as from death,
> Causing the birds to flutter from their nests,
> And rousing men to ply with busy feet
> Their daily duties and appropriate tasks."

The doves were unlike those to be seen in the State of California. Like the cardinals, I had first observed them in the rugged Waist of the Peninsula, opposite Tiburon Island. There, late one afternoon, as I traveled down a wild gorge, an eerie call of three notes unexpectedly rang out with nerve-rending sharpness. Dismounting instantly, carbine in hand, I had peered anxiously ahead, and upon spying the offender, had called upon Jesús to bring it down with the small rifle. The poor bird had a bronzed head and back, long dark bill, blue eyelids and dark splash below the eyes, a white line across the wings and beneath the tail, and bright red legs. Except for the distinguishing white line, the doves along the way southward showed more subdued markings than this first specimen.

From Sant' Agueda to Loreto we passed three towns and a few ranchos. Throughout this two hundred miles of travel we met on the camino but three wayfarers! Of wild creatures we saw mountain sheep, coyotes, foxes, wild cats, ducks, quail and doves. Rattlesnakes were frequent. Those California roadside habitués, the jack rabbits, were daily to be seen ambling sociably about or considering us with long ears pointed questioningly forward. Within two leagues out from Sant' Agueda we were advised we were deep in the Land of the Padres by the sight of a large wayside cross made by placing boulders upon the ground in the conventional design. This may have been a first notice arranged in olden times to call the traveler's attention to his approach to sacred Loreto. Thereafter, ancient caminos, broken aqueducts, neglected cisterns, chapel ruins and enduring stone missions, attesting the tremendous energy of the Jesuits, advised us of our proximity to the earliest center of the missionary field in the Californias.

After our departure from Sant' Agueda I had a glimpse of a survival of the religious fervor which animated the past generations. Late Easter night we had spread our blankets on the edge of a stony arroyo by the site of the ancient Jesuit mission chapel of Santa Maria de la Magdalena.   In the small hours of Monday morning I had seen several horsemen in the moonlight; later, as the sun was rising, I heard the crunch, crunch of many hoofs, and looking down the arroyo, saw a cavalcade drawing near, gorgeously garbed—men, women and children mounted on richly caparisoned horses and mules.   They had been attending mid-day and evening Easter services at Mulege, some five and a half leagues distant, and in their anxiety to reach their distant *ranchos* had taken the camino long before daylight.   To be present at these services, they gladly rode from fifty to one hundred miles!

I had had some difficulty in locating these ruins of Magdalena.   From Sant' Agueda I had ridden direct to Santa Lucia, a diminutive settlement on the Gulf, and from there had followed the old Gulfo Camino down the coast a league and a half to San Bruno, another equally diminutive settlement, where symmetrical salt beds, a fine orchard of olive trees and a dignified white adobe, the residence of an English hermit, were clustered in close proximity.   Leaving San Bruno we bore away slightly west of south for over three leagues, picking a way through the cacti and brush or following a convenient arroyo until we came upon an ancient camino which brought us out at a spot where a large arroyo came forth from the sierras.   Here the remains of a substantial and extraordinarily well constructed stone and masonry aqueduct—apparently run several miles for the purpose of irrigating a very few acres—and heaps of grass grown ruins, marked the site of early missionary labors. In March, 1867, Professor Wm. M. Gabb, of the Ross Brown exploring party, evidently the only foreign visitors of modern times in this section, noted these ruins as the remains of the Jesuit Mission of Guadalupe.   Had the scientist been a trifle more conversant with early Peninsula history or had he visited the neighboring *rancho* of Magdalena, doubtless he would have avoided this error and placed Guadalupe Mission ten leagues to the west.

This Rancho of San José de Magdalena proved to be a small and truly delightful oasis with a field of grain, a thicket of sugar-cane, towering palms, enormous fig trees and a pool of clear water. The proprietress was a firm old Señora who despotically ordered about a numerous family of blooming *muchachas*. So overrun was the place with these wholesome looking girls and so lacking was it in males that I caused the old dame to relax her severity by renaming her property the *Rancho de las Muchachas*. From this point we rode across the desolate plains of Magdalena, once the site of some wildly visionary agricultural colony of American conception, into the hills. Coming down through a picturesque pass, we arrived at Mulege the afternoon of April the 16th.

The Mission of Santa Rosalia de Mulege, founded by the Jesuits in the year 1705, attained during the eighteenth century considerable prosperity. Of late years the stone church has been extensively repaired and is now in excellent condition. It stands upon a slight eminence above the town. Only two foreigners appear to have noted their impressions of Mulege. The first of these, Lieutenant Hardy of the British Navy, anchored in the offing while on a little pearl venture in 1828. Though he was delighted with the local port wine, he seemed to consider the village as a half deserted place in the grip of a shamefully profligate Friar. Thirty-nine years later, Professor Gabb, visiting Mulege, described it as "a straggling village of adobe houses with a population of, perhaps, two hundred persons." To his surprise he found a little coterie of accomplished gentlemen in the village, who made his stay with them most agreeable. As I entered Mulege I could but wonder whether the intervening thirty-nine years since Professor Gabb's visit had brought about many changes.

I quickly discovered that they had.

In place of a profligate Friar as in the days of Hardy, I found a scholarly, ascetic young Italian priest, Padre Marseliano. His clear cut, refined features, his deep interest in his people, in literature and in photography, won me instantly. So extensive, so rugged and so desert is the field of his labors—reaching from the mining camp of Calamajuet on the north to the Mission of San Luis Gonzaga on the south—that I doubt whether any soldier of the Gospel has in hand a task of greater severity. In place of a straggling village of two hundred, I found Mulege to be a prosperous town of full eight hundred inhabitants, with adobe houses, public buildings, narrow shaded streets, a tide-water stream, numerous irrigating ditches, fertile fields and acres of vegetables, sugar-cane, trellised vines, and orange, lemon, olive, fig, pomegranate and palm trees.

In the matter of the "agreeable coterie" of 1867, happily I found the only change was that of new generations. After conversing with the Padre, I visited the District Court where I met a handsome and affable young official, the Federal Attorney for the district. Later, on the plaza I came across one Señor Elias Bareno, merchant and surveyor, who introduced me to his "pupil in English," Don Mauricio Mexia. Thanks to Don Mauricio, I enjoyed a most delightful afternoon drive, for the genial fellow gathered into his commodious three-seater no less than six Señoritas of the *Primera Clase* and laughingly told me to squeeze in. To my pleased surprise one of the company was my recent acquaintance, Señorita Garyzar. She had come from Santa Rosalia on a Gulf steamer to spend Easter with relatives.

We drove along the stream for half a mile, then crossing

over through water to the hubs, entered a beautiful, shaded driveway leading to a picturesque sugar plantation, where we were given a great sheaf of cane stalks. The whole region was an Eden-like bower of green and flowers, the property, I believe, of some member of the party. Here we alighted, and as we strolled about under the great palms and amid the flowers, the girls began singing soft Spanish songs, until I seemed to be enjoying some delightful dream.

Foreigners have such a mistaken fashion of considering all Mexicans swarthy people that I cannot but note that there were only three brunettes in our little party: Don Mauricio and his baby daughter, who had joined us at the last moment, had the bluest of eyes, while his sister-in-law, a tall, statuesque beauty, was a decided blonde. Dark eyes were the exception. As we were roaming about the garden we came to a large vat where olives were pickling. The best lined the bottom. Desirous of obtaining these, each in turn, amid gay laughter, began reaching down into the brine. By rolling my right sleeve to the shoulder, I easily fished out a handful of fine black olives. As I passed the fruit, one of the girls, her gaze falling upon my bared arm, exclaimed in uncontrollable amazement, *"Jesu Christi, dos colores!"*

Having assumed from my tanned face and forearms that I was a dark-skinned individual, the *muchacha* had been completely taken aback by the unexpected whiteness of my upper arm. Her confusion was at once increased for "Jesusa, you must apologize to the gentleman for your expression," said pretty Señorita Garyzar, in a reproving aside in Spanish. "He will think you profane."

"Profane! I?" exclaimed the girl, deeply shocked.

"Certainly. In his country to use freely the expression 'Jesus Christ' is to blaspheme."

"Blaspheme! Victoria, it cannot be so. It is but an expression; it is my own name, even."

"I know," persisted the American travelled Señorita, "but, although we use the term as a given name and as a harmless by-word, in the United States—"

Here I hastened to the rescue of the embarrassed girl, but she was inconsolable, murmuring in blank distress, "I blaspheme—I could not so offend!"

Leaving the plantation we drove down to the water's edge and found the shade of a large palm, where we stopped to enjoy the sweet pith of our sugar-cane. As they held the straight, slender, reed-like stalks to their carmine lips, the girls looked quite like a group of pretty flute players. We were all in high spirits, applauding roundly the many gallant remarks of Don Mauricio. "Ah," said he, finally, chucking his little daughter playfully under the chin, and preparing to cross the stream, "it's doubtless the eating of so much sugar-cane that endows our Mulege *muchachas* with such rare sweetness." As I was seriously announcing my firm belief that the lasses surely lived half the year on honey, a bright-eyed miss inquired how many daughters I had at home. Making prompt answer that I was a single man, I produced, with mock formality, a Mexican passport describing me as *"un soltero"* (a bachelor), whereupon my inquisitress asked whether any Americans married. "Assuredly," she concluded, amid concurring nods from her mates, "all that have ever come here have stoutly averred that they were bachelors."

"I don't wonder," I replied, with an admiring glance at the pretty bevy. Certainly there might be compensations for being marooned at Mulege.

From Mulege there are two caminos to Purísima, one via the San Sebastian Arroyo, the other by way of Zapote and the Guadalupe Arroyo. As Professor Gabb had taken

Ancient Jesuit Mission at Mulege; Padre Marseliano
in foreground

▲   Puerto San Carlos, Magdalena Bay

Magdalena Bay   ▼

▲ Llanos de Jiray

La Paz ▼

the latter in 1867, I chose the San Sebastian camino. From my own observations the route a traveler does not select, he later decides was necessarily the better. Via the San Sebastian camino the distance is thirty-one leagues, the direction southwest.

As I left Mulege early the morning of April the 18th, the world seemed in perfect peace, the mission bells were ringing and there was no sympathetic sign of the great natural disturbance that was bringing disaster upon the busy metropolis of the State of California. That afternoon Coronado began to fail. The following morning, before breakfast, I endeavored to secure a new burro, a *vaquero* having one for sale. As he declined to execute a bill of sale, the transaction fell through. (Later, I ascertained that the man had no title to the burro.) When the animals were saddled I had Coronado's pack transferred to my riding burro and I proceeded on foot; such relief proved of no avail, and a few hours later, as we made our way upward toward a four-thousand-foot pass in the sierras, the poor beast sank upon the camino, unable to arise, urge him as we would. Unsheathing my carbine, I regretfully sighted for his heart, but as my eyes rested on the sturdy brown shoulders, I remembered how bravely they had borne my possessions for a thousand miles, I remembered our common sufferings on the *Llanos de Ojo Liebre*—and put aside the gun. "Is there a chance of his recuperating?" I asked of Praemundi who stood by.

"Perhaps. He had water this morning; there is feed here. Let him be, and by to-morrow he will be dead or up after feed and water."

Sheathing the carbine, I approached my poor dumb servant. "*Adiós,* Coronado," said I, feelingly, patting his bulky head the while. "You have done your level best for me. *Adiós.*" The old fellow looked up with great weary eyes, whereat I turned away with a lump in my throat. *"Vamunos"* (Onward), I shouted out roughly to my mozos. Forward we proceeded. Soon Cortez began to stagger, so I had Jesús dismount. The strain of a thousand miles of travel and of thirst on the *Llanos de Ojo Liebre* was telling.

On the 19th instant and the two days succeeding we proceeded on foot, no unpleasant exercise had it not been that my *teguas* were so worn that sharp stones and cacti continually wounded my feet. The third day of our walking we crossed over into the Purísima Arroyo and came to a rancho, then to another and another. In the afternoon we made camp on the banks of the Purísima Rio, a fine, clear stream, bordered by willows and sedge grass and running in a rock channel with precipitous walls rising close at either side and forming a magnificent gorge full a thousand feet in depth. Tired and footsore from over sixty miles of walking, I did not break camp for thirty-six hours, good, peaceful hours, in which I enjoyed four swims in a deep hole near by, let my blisters heal, philosophized with my old mozo, dipped into my two small volumes of Balzac and Kipling, and listened to the fascinating song of running waters, a song that carried me to scenes in the High Sierras of Upper California, then to my fevered hours on the *Llanos de Ojo Liebre* and, in prospect, to possible thirsty experiences to come on the deserts before me.

Jesús, for his part, slipped joyously away on a visit to the beehive and orange trees of a neighboring rancho, while Praemundi spent the major portion of his time laundering, the pot-holes in the rock flooring of our camp serving admirably for wash tubs. As he sat near me patiently awaiting the drying of the clothes, the old Mexican made an interesting study: A lean, wiry figure of sixty years or more, with long arms and bowed legs, with brown hands clasped and resting between his small knees, with dark eyes bent in somber study of the running water. A tawny straw hat, low-rounded of crown, with brim down in front and up behind, shaded his face, a kindly face, wrinkled, leather-colored, contrasting sharply with his white beard and iron gray mustache; a soft gray shirt, open at the throat, disclosing his brown neck and chest, the sleeves, rolled to the elbows, displayed his red undershirt carefully folded back at the wrists; a blue scarf, fringed at the ends and tied in the small of the back, belted in his faded gray trousers and held a long knife ready to his hand; worn sandals, loosely bound, protected the soles of his small brown feet. Kindly, genial and willing, a respectful servant, half philosopher, half child, and wholly typical of an earlier Mexican generation, such was the *paisano* seated before me. To bathe in the stream was something that neither Praemundi or Jesús would consider. Did they not wash their hands before mixing tortillas? why risk a cold by immersing their bodies?

The 23rd instant we proceeded forward and shortly came to a rancho, where I secured a stout riding burro, which Jesús promptly named "Colon" (Columbus). This burro was an excellent animal. For him and a leather bound water-bottle I gave five *pesos,* cash, an order for Coronado, if found alive, and Cortez. Both parties to this bargain were well satisfied, for while Cortez had become a dead weight for me, after a month's rest he would serve the *ranchero* as well as Colon. Another league brought us to a second rancho where for fourteen *pesos* I purchased a second burro, named "Vapor" (Steamboat).

In the acquisition of Vapor I experienced some delay. First it was necessary to heat an iron, throw the animal and give him a mark, for he was unbranded; and after this operation was completed the vendor discovered that he must send a messenger to secure requisite revenue stamps for his bill of sale. In bargaining Mexicans are regular

Yankees, and in dealing with them the traveler must examine his nutmegs and safeguard his purchases as closely as in Connecticut. During this delay the *rancheros* proceeded with their spirituous ambition of draining a generous number of bottles of mescal. The leader of the party, a comic opera bandit in appearance—flashing black eyes, twirling mustachios, ornamented sombrero, brilliant plush small jacket, tasseled sash, long dagger, voluminous trousers and wide flapping red leggins bound below the knee with ornamented cords—in the exuberance of his hilarity swallowed a copious draught that was horribly unlike mescal. Crying out that he had been deliberately poisoned, the comic opera individual drew his dagger and rushed toward the man nearest him, who sprang aside, drawing a revolver as he avoided the descending steel. In an instant daggers were in the air and pandemonium turned loose. Six-shooter in hand, I was looking earnestly for a friendly tree, when the sufferer's better half appeared upon the scene in search of her kerosene bottle. It stood upon the table where her husband had placed it after his unsavory taste of its contents. All thought of murderous intent now removed from his mind, the Mexican embraced his wife, kissed a screaming baby, struck a heroic attitude and proclaimed that he would meet death like a man, while his friends crowded about me beseeching that I save his life. Although I promptly separated the tippler from the kerosene and some other things, almost immediately afterwards I half regretted having done so, for every man Jack in the company, fascinated by the appearance of my medicine chest, at once complained of some ailment and begged for drugs. All that saved my pills and vials was the chorus of howls and sputtering that followed my quick doses of clear Jamaica ginger and the bitterest powdered quinine.

As I rode away, finally possessed of the stamped bill of

sale, my bibulous friends, embracing one another and rhythmically waving their sombreros, sang almost tearfully, *"El Vapor,"* a Mexican farewell song. A short ride brought me to the central portion of Purísima, a small town which, counting the *racheros* up and down the stream, claims six hundred inhabitants. Purísima Rio, a succession of large water-holes, carries the largest body of any stream in Lower California, except the Hardy. It runs through a deep arroyo to the Boca de Purísima on the Pacific coast, a few leagues distant. In fertile spots along this stream sugar-cane, figs, grapes, etc., are grown extensively. The Mission of La Purísima de la Conceptión was established by the Jesuits in 1718. The building is rather a small stone structure, situated near the Rio and in the center of the town.

As I was possessed of a letter of introduction from Padre Marseliano to Don José Osuna, the principal resident of Purísima, my brief visit there was made exceedingly agreeable. Señorita Osuna, the Don's sweet faced and dignified daughter, showed me the mission, and her brother, Pablo, then explained to me the six steps in the making of mescal from the maguay plant. The ensuing day father and son made me their guest at a bounteous dinner, while my mozos were cared for at a second table. Both tables were spread in the Don's garden which, after the pleasant fashion of Mexico, occupied the patio around which the house was built. The Señoritas provided us with two frequent and most pleasing standard Baja California dishes, the one made by frying vegetables and pounded dried beef in butter, the other by frying in lard beans already boiled and crushed. In addition they served rich soup, steak, boiled potatoes, rice with wild honey, excellent *tortillas,* jellies and beaten egg *dulce,* or sweetmeat. To drink we had tea, coffee and wine. The Osuna family is typical of the highest class of courteous, well informed, dignified and hospitable native land owners of the Peninsula.

Eight and a half leagues slightly south of east of Purísima lies Comondú. A rocky, broken mesa intervenes; after attaining an increased elevation of nigh three thousand feet the camino from Purísima enters this mesa, leaving behind the impressive and majestic scenery of the Purísima Arroyo. Immediately after dinner we began this ascent. At nightfall we camped by the wayside, as usual scraping aside the larger stones before throwing down our blankets. While we were eating supper a large tarantula, an unbidden and most unwelomce guest, came marching up to my plate. I yelled lustily and made a record jump, closely followed by Jesús. Praemundi, however, valiantly crushed the venomous creature with a stone; we had upset his tarantulaship's peace, of course, in scraping aside the stones. Reassembling, we discussed various snakes and insects of venomous nature, Praemundi describing native antidotes for practically all save what he called the "solecuate," a blunt tailed snake resembling in color the ordinary water variety, and the *mala zorea,* or small southern skunk. The bite of this latter creature—and in fear of it the travelling natives draw their serapas close about their faces at night — causes hydrophobia and death. Cheese and enlivening music were the remedies he suggested for the sting of the tarantula, certain varieties of which he considered fatal. After this cheerful discussion and before retiring to my blankets and bad dreams, I entered in my journal, after the style of the mighty Cæsar, "All Baja California is divided into three parts, of which one is all barren sierras, parched deserts and thirst, another is inhabited by snakes, scorpions, centipedes, tarantulas, *salamankasers* and *mala zoreas,* while the third is all palms, flowers, dates, oranges, sugar-cane, honey, running water and pretty *muchachas.*

The Mission of La Púrisima

Trouble is, the boundaries on the parts are undefined."

The following day, just before noon, we came upon a runaway couple. From snakes to romance! But El Camino Real is full of just such contrasts. The young people—they were eighteen and twenty-two—were resting by the wayside when we came upon them. Their belongings, tucked in a sack, were swung across the swain's sturdy shoulders, a leather water-bottle and a pair of short, pointed shoes were tied to the girl's left arm. He was clad in tattered garments, she in a blue calico gown with red dots in the waist; an eminently becoming yellow *rebozo*, or native headdress, completed her costume. Although she seemed unconscious of her lack of stays and hosiery, she was plainly distressed at being found wearing *guarachas*, for, as soon as I devoted my attention to her companion, she quickly slipped them off and forced her feet into the shoes. But though her feet were small, the shoes were yet smaller, and under their pressure her face became so wofully drawn with pain that I charitably assured her that *guarachas* were the preferable footgear for a rocky camino. This cheered her. The young people were rather attractive looking, the man's face showing less of the Indian than the girl's. After persistent questioning I gathered their story. They were on their way to San José del Cabo, where some of her people lived and where they would find a home. They were slipping away because his parents had objected to the match. Yes, they know that the Cabo was far distant, but they had little to carry and were excellent walkers. His name was Ramon, hers Susana. With kindly memories of a certain Susan, I promptly gave Susana the use of my riding burro for ten miles. She was grateful and so was he. To think of two youngsters on a six-hundred-mile walk for their honeymoon trip entirely upset my gravity, and yet their frequent little love glances and the underlying pathos of the situation appealed to my heart, and I found myself respecting the wanderers for being capable of so fervent a devotion. At luncheon we were a happy wayside party, Susana preparing the tortillas, good ones, too, though in her ignorance of baking powder she dumped in an alarming amount. I caught her picture as she patted a tortilla, and then found that she had no idea of the nature or purpose of a camera. When we were advised by the waning day of our near approach to Comondú, Susana dismounted, and the last glimpse I had she was heroically working into the tight shoes required by her sense of the proprieties to be observed by a bride.

Ten minutes later my caravan paused abruptly upon the brink of a deep chasm. Seven hundred feet below us lay a semi-tropical park, well-watered and verdant with olive, fig, palm, cottonwood and orange trees. In width it might have measured two furlongs, the windings of the arroyo precluded any further estimate of its extent. Here and there thatch houses showed through the foliage, while in the midst of the arroyo a cluster of adobes stood forth like so many boulders tossed down by playful Titans. As I looked upon this superb vista, tropical with deep verdure, waving sugar-cane, trellised vines and tall palms, the sounds of lowing cattle, baaing sheep and soft-voiced Mexicans came floating gently upward, mellowed by the distance, and in an ecstasy of delight I wondered whether the Happy Valley of Rasselas could have had the charm of this beautiful Arroyo of Comondú.

As a poet has sung,

> "There is no sun like the sun that shines
>   In the Valley of Comondú,
> There are palms and olives and figs and vines
>   In the Valley of Comondú."

Hugging close to the winding camino we made the dizzy descent into the valley, where a letter which I possessed admitted me to a substantial sky-blue adobe, the home of a kindly Don, who proved to be an exceedingly gracious and widely informed gentleman. With him I spent the night, receiving the most hospitable treatment, though through a remark made by Praemundi concerning my performances as a *medico,* I soon found myself in an amusing but embarrassing position. In short, I was invited to aid in the arrival of an hourly expected addition to the population of Comondú!

The ensuing morning I continued my journey, following a shaded camino leading up the arroyo. About eight hundred—or eight hundred and one!—people reside in the Arroyo of Comondú, which, in physical appearance, greatly resembles that of San Ignacio. So many of the men of Comondú have been drawn away to the mines at Santa Rosailia, and such is the good fame of its *muchachas,* that down the Peninsula the arroyo is frequently referred to as the "Adamless Eden of Comondú." Some eighteen hundred acres of fertile soil are under cultivation. There are two main settlements, a league apart, the upper being clustered around the old mission. This is a truly ancient establishment, having been founded nearly two centuries ago. Here is its story, as told by the chroniclers: In the year 1707, one Padre Julian de Mayorga came to California from Spain. Though he was a deep scholar, his health was so delicate that he appeared utterly unfit for the rigors of missionary life. However, after a year's rest at Loreto, he sallied forth with Padres Salvatierra and Ugarte. Sixteen—only they considered it many more—leagues of rough travel, westerly, brought the worthy Padres to a valley known among the Indians as "Comondú," or the Valley of Stones. From the high cliffs at either side of the arroyo and the thick sprinkling of stones carpeting the mesa to the north and south, I think the Indians showed great sense in choosing this name. A stream watered this valley and for several leagues there was much fertile soil. Here the Padres paused and founded the Mission of San José de Comondú. The well disposed natives assisted in the work, while funds, to the extent of ten thousand *pesos,* were supplied by the Marquis de Villapuente, the most liberal of the many contributors to the famed Pious Fund which supported the missions for over a century. Just above the stream buildings of stone were erected, fruit trees and vines planted— flowers already were growing in profusion—and the conversion of the natives and the making of caminos were auspiciously begun. In these pleasing surroundings Padre Mayorga, regaining health, lived peacefully until death called twenty-eight years later. San José de Comondú long flourished. Crops were large and certain, much wine and brandy were made and live stock multiplied. The *iglesia* was richly furnished and had a library of over a hundred volumes. This is the sum of the historic data of the old chroniclers.

The mission was built with the usual *iglesia,* cll and patio design. With inspiring majesty its massive stone walls and substantial pillars stand sentinel above the inroads of time, earthquakes and vandalism. Though vandals, seeking for building stone, have made a breach in one wall and growing trees have ripped open the stone and cement roof above the altar, the somber walls, four feet in thickness, retain their solidity. Unshaken, too, are the eight Grecian pillars, each a metre in diameter, placed four on either side of the main aisle of the *iglesia* and supporting the arched roof, the keystones of which are so cunningly set as to defy the centuries. Narrow windows and low doorways admit the light. Above the main entrance there is a choir loft,

The walled-up doorway of the Mission of San José
de Comondú

reached by a narrow spiral stairway of thirty-three steps.
The roof is vaulted and, in places, still resplendent with
red frescoing.   Above the eaves stone torches flame upward, and stone cylinders, perhaps for the drainage of rain-
water from the roof, point outward like cannon.   The altar
has been destroyed; at its right and left there are small,
dark rooms.   In length the interior of the church measures
forty-five paces, in width, sixteen; its height must approxi-
mate ten metres.   I obtained an excellent view of the interior by climbing to the crest of the wall behind the ruined
altar and looking down through the wide rent made in the
roof by growing trees; from the outlook before me I might
have been gazing into some ancient crypt.

The wing, forming with the *iglesia* the ell, is in perfect
state of preservation and its two rooms are utilized, the one
as a chapel, the other as a storeroom.   In the latter there
are two large bells, one of which is sadly cracked; in view
of its inscription of "San Francisco, 1697," the latter presumably came from the Mission of San Francisco Xavier de
Vigge.   Another relic, of even greater interest, is a carved
wooden saint, *sans* arms, *sans* feet.   I found him thrust
aside in a dusty corner where warlike "yellow-jackets" were
engaged in building a mud house between his poor knees.
Charmed by the sweet, pathetic expression of the upturned
face, I carried the poor wooden child—St. Joseph of Ara-
mathea, like as not—into the sunshine of the April morning and placed him gently beside the silent old bell.   There
are ten oil paintings and an onyx font in this chapel.

Within the ell there is a pretty and well kept garden and
two bells are swung from a low wooden frame.   One of
these bells bears the date of 1708.   Back of the ell thus
formed by *iglesia* and chapel, there is a well-watered garden with flowers and trees.   This garden is forty paces
square and enclosed by stone buildings and ruins.

Though at Comondú, as at San Ignacio, quarries were convenient and labor at the wage of sustenance only, nevertheless, even under such favorable conditions, the construction of so imposing a mission must have required a far greater outlay than the ten thousand *pesos* mentioned by the chroniclers. Perhaps the generous Marquis de Villapuente visited his Mission of Comondú, and, enchanted by its surroundings, increased his benefaction. It is of record that in 1735 he gave to the Pious Fund an estate of several hundred thousand acres in Tamaulipas, together with flocks and herds, farming implements and appurtenances. May the Grandee rest in peace, doubly blessed by his endowment to San José de Comondú! Also, may better days be in store for the Mission and the crippled little Saint.

Out from Comondú as many as three different caminos lead over the famous Sierra Giganta, the local section of the cordilleras, to Loreto. In constructing these caminos industrious persons—unquestionably Indians in missionary days, for the residents do not initiate such laborious tasks nowadays—removed the stones, burrowing down to earth, so that for the first league or more the traveler is practically below the surface of the mesa. Two of these caminos are in frequent use by pack trains travelling out from the prosperous arroyo laden with cargoes for shipment across the Sea of Cortez. I chose to travel by the third and least known route. This I did because of certain strange information which I had received the evening after my arrival at Comondú. At that time my kindly host, looking up from an examination of game trophies, had exclaimed abruptly, "But, señor, how comes it that you have not killed an antelope of the sierras *(un berrendo de los sierras)?*"

"*Un berrendo de los sierras?*" I repeated, inquiringly, with some unplaced memory struggling back of my brain.

"Yes, señor. The *berrendo de los sierras* is not unlike

▲   La Trinchera

El Triunfo   ▼

▲　Church, San Antonio

Arroyo San Antonio　▼

the mountain sheep in habits, but he is thicker through the shoulders, his horns extend further outward. In color these animals are black."

"*Los hay negros*" (they are black), that gave clue to my unplaced memory, and later that evening I turned to my notes from Clavijero. "*La gamuza . . . es mas grande,*" wrote the old Jesuit in his chapter on the native California animals, "*mas agil y mas veloz que la cabra. Los animales de esta especia se justan en manadas, y trepan en los rocas con incredible facilidad: los hay blancos y negros; su piel es apeciada y su carne buena para comer.*" Translating *gamuza* into antelope, the passage becomes, "The antelope is larger, more agile and swifter than the goat. This class of animals travel in flocks, and they leap among the rocks with marvelous ease: they are white and black; the hides are esteemed and the meat is good for eating."

Who ever heard of an American antelope that was black? and on the other hand, who ever observed one at a distance without thinking of its being white? Clavijero's white antelopes must be the ordinary variety, his *gamuzos negros* must be my host's *antelopes of the sierras;* having come to this conclusion I went to sleep with the firm intention of hunting the strange animal.

Two days later, therefore, having in the meantime followed the little known route heretofore mentioned, I made camp in an eerie spot high up in the Sierra Giganta, where a goat-herd had erected a poor adobe and a corral in the shadow of frightful precipices, above which towered a threatening black *picacho*. Early the next morning I started forth with Manuel, the goat-herd's eighteen-year-old son. The climbing abilities of this untutored youth were so superb as to be worthy of notice. Striking a gait which was a jog, varied with goat-like leaps, he calmly attained the summit of that peak without so much as getting out of breath, though my aneroid showed its elevation to be 3,650 feet above our sierra camp. For my own part I was nearly exhausted, though I had merely followed in his wake, while he, searching out the one break in the precipices where ascent was possible, had sturdily hacked with his keen machete a passageway through the thickets of *tunas, palo Adan, una de gato, garabatillo* and other thorny shrubs that hindered our advance. According to Manuel, we were the first to take the trouble to ascend the *picacho,* though one of his goats had twice made the ascent, *hobbled.*

When we were at an elevation of 4,000 feet above sea-level, Manuel suddenly pointing toward the east, exclaimed, "There, Señor, *dos berrendos de los sierras!*" Looking in the direction indicated, I saw two dark animals, one far larger than any mountain sheep I had ever seen, with great head and immense ram's horns extending far outward and of extreme bulk about the shoulders. The smaller animal slipped into the brush before I had a good view of it. The ram was jumping leisurely along among some rocks not over two hundred yards away, but as I drew down upon him the rising sun glinted over the sights, obstructing my aim. In another instant the *berrendo* disappeared in the brush, and although we found his great tracks we had no further sight of the creature throughout the day. Manuel explained that usually these *berrendos* were less wild, not being hunted, and that they kept aloof from the *borregos* which also ranged on the *picacho.*

Late that afternoon while tracking I became separated from Manuel, and, descending from the heights, reached camp, alone, at night. As I lay on a pile of hides, dressing a bad ankle and extracting thorns from my arms and shoulders, wondering the while whether two days' rest would fit me for another try at the *berrendos,* into camp rode a Mexican, the bearer of such news concerning San

The carved wooden Saint of San José de Comondú

Francisco, the home of those nearest to me, that breaking camp hastily the following morning I pressed onward without further search for game.

To me, perturbed in mind, how endless that day seemed! Finally, after sixteen hours of rugged travel, we made camp, halting beneath a group of ancient palms hard by the sea. The faint light of a late moon picked out silver spots beneath the boughs, it made shadow pictures of somber buildings, it glistened on the rippling waters of the Sea of Cortez. A dog ceased baying the moon to challenge us entering the sleeping village. Completely exhausted, torn by haunting anxieties, I threw myself upon my blankets. After over a thousand miles of *El Camino Real* I had come to sacred Loreto, the Mother of Missions, the ancient Capital of the Californias, but my thoughts were far away in Alta California.

CHAPTER XVI

THE PEARL MISSIONS OF THE JESUITS

UNDER a canopy of fluttering palms and spreading eighteenth century shade trees, her poor shoulders pressed close against the thorny thickets of a treacherous arroyo, the bereft Mother of the Missions sleeps the southern sleep of forgetfulness while the crooning voices of the Vermilion Sea whisper wistfully about her. They are telling of the days when the admirals of Cortez sought the Island of California, they are singing of the knightly Salvatierra, first of the Jesuits, of the earnest Franciscan, Junipero Serra, of cowled Dominicans, of haughty Dons, earliest Governors of the Californias, who here held court. They are murmuring of *armadores de perlas* who delved deep for brilliant pearls. With plaintive sadness they are whispering of storms that rocked the Mother Mission, of corsairs who bore away her wreaths of pearls, of the passing of the Padres, of glories lost, of oppression, of neglect and of dreams.

As I passed through the fringe of thatched houses and entered the plaza with its eighteenth century buildings of adobe and of stone, I felt that perchance the magic of the south had traced its finger tips across my brain, that perhaps the sharp imagery in my agitated mind would fade could I but silence the voices of the sea. It is easy for him who is far removed by distance to imagine, unreasoningly, disaster and death—and yet it is difficult for such a one to realize their actuality when they come in fact. Were my thoughts mere fantastic dreams? was I sleeping? was I waking? was my reason perchance disturbed by some fever? Insidiously, then clamorously, these questions arose, challenging consideration. In my native language, from the one American in the village I had just heard the unbelievable northern catastrophe verified, with merely a lessening of the loss of life first related, and had had thrust into my hands a Los Angeles paper that, by illustrations and headlines, certified to the destruction and burning of San Francisco.

From a merchant on the plaza I learned that Loreto had no communication with the world either by telephone or by telegraph; that a Gulf steamer had come in on the 28th instant and another might touch in a week, though perhaps not for two weeks; that the American steamer, the *Curacao* from San Francisco might stop at Magdalena Bay on the 9th of May, it certainly would touch at La Paz on the 17th of May. How far distant was Magdalena Bay? *Quien sabe,* probably seventy-five leagues; La Paz was one hundred and ten. My course I outlined even as he spoke: Magdalena Bay, then back across the Peninsula to La Paz. I consulted with Praemundi. The burros were a trifle tired after their hard trip from Sant' Agueda, but *pasada mañana* (day after to-morrow) he thought they would be ready for the camino. Could they start to-morrow afternoon? *"Si, señor, listo mañana tardes,"* (Yes, sir, ready to-morrow afternoon) was his reply.

Half wishing myself a devout Roman Catholic, able to forget all troubles in prostration before the Cross, I strolled over to the mission, mechanically noting its detail. A large church it was, built of stone, the rough and cut cemented together, flat roofed, with bells swung above the northeast corner. Off at the right were a cemetery and an ell forming a chapel; to the left extended a goodly patio. At the main entrance, facing the sea, there were doors, double and ancient. Pausing before them I searched in vain for the inscription mentioned by the historian Bancroft as being upon the casement. Entering, I noticed above me a projecting gallery, perhaps a choir loft, with a high carved railing. So long and narrow was the interior of the church that I had an impression not unlike that received upon entering a deep, high vaulted cave. Thinking of the early days when the altar was decked with golden ornaments and the shrines and images with ropes of pearls, I could easily imagine that on holy days the flickering candles made a scene as effective as when twinkling lights call forth a brilliant resplendency among the myriad stalactites in some deep and lofty cavern. By pacing I found the width of the interior but twenty feet while its length was nearly nine times as great; the height I estimated at thirty-five feet. With walls five feet in thickness the windows and doors of the church are deeply indented; shutters and rounded wooden bars protect the windows. The flooring is part stone cubes, part earth—and the footprints in the dust are all of women. Though made of stone the altar has been sadly dismantled. About it there are several one-piece onyx fonts, beautiful even in their fractured state. Above the altar hang three large oil paintings and five empty frames; above and back of the shrines—of which there are several—there are immense torn tapestries, sadly faded from the rain that has come through the leaky roof. At the left of the altar there is a closed room, used to store what has escaped the cupidity of vandals. From the patio a broken stairway leads through the choir loft and upwards to the roof and the bells, five in number. Dating back as they do to the close of the seventeenth century, it is not surprising that the rim surfaces of these bells have been worn smooth, the outer surfaces, too, for the usual method of sounding them seems to have been for a man to strike them

in quick succession with an iron bar.   The mission has suffered so severely from earthquakes and neglect that only a
suggestion of its pristine beauty and majesty now remains—
and unless repairs are promptly made the main building
will shortly fall asunder.

Though the Padre comes but once a year the women of
Loreto are constant in their visits to the church. Even while
I loitered within its precincts a sound of deep sobbing advertised the presence of a worshiper. She had thrown herself
down at the right of the altar before a latticed door through
which she could look upon the image of the Virgin in the
adjoining chapel. A more forlorn figure I never saw.
Absorbed, unconscious of my presence, she poured forth her
grief in doleful cadence, confessing such transgressions that
I fled in embarrassment.

In Loreto there are half a thousand residents, varied and
numerous varieties of fruits and vegetables grow readily
and there is a considerable export trade, much of it being
the produce of Comondú. Off shore a league or so lies
Carmen Island where there is a supply of salt so inexhaust-
ible as to remind one of the fairy tale of a salt mill that
supplied the ocean. To the west of the town rise the majestic heights of the Sierra Giganta. But I gave small heed
to surroundings, scenery or people, though I do remember
that it was the first settlement in Lower California where
I found the word *"Gringo"* in use in place of the more gracious *"Americano."* Also, and with pleasure, I recall a
young Mexican of twenty-five or six, Don Amadeo Romero,
who introduced himself and his brother to me: they were
the most thorough gentlemen and the most progressive men
of their age whom I had met upon the Peninsula. "Sir,"
said Don Amadeo, "you presented a *carta de recommen-
dación* to a gentleman in Santa Rosalia to whose daughter
I have the honor to be affianced. It is my privilege, there-

Ancient Mission Bells at Loreto; Sea of Cortez in the distance

fore, to be at your service and it will be a pleasure for me to give you *cartas* to my friends further south." Did I want to write? Yes, it would be fitting for me to write from Loreto, the early capital of old California, to the Governor of the new California at Sacramento; furthermore, I would write to my brother. Then the office was at my disposal, the library, too, the home. Ah, how can the traveler fully express his appreciation of that gracious courtesy of Mexico, inherited from the ancient Dons, that expansive hospitality which, upon the slightest demand, blossoms out, flower-like.

I spent the evening leaning against a *lancha* down by the shore, looking abstractedly out across the moonlit waves. Disturbed at length by two drunken Yaqui Indians, I tapped my revolver significantly and strode away to my blankets. The ensuing morning I revisited the Mission in time to witness an interesting little scene in the chapel. The mother of five daughters had come to give tardy thanks to Our Lady of Loreto—the special patroness, apparently, of mothers, for an infant son. Kneeling before the image, the naked child in her arms, the mother poured forth her prayers of gratitude and thanksgiving. From the walls twenty paintings of sacred characters looked down upon the scene, while flowers decked the altar, making fragrant the air. Soon the father and *muchachas* entered and I was given permission to take a picture of the mother and babe.

"He is a man-child, a man-child," cried the woman, fondling the chubby infant, happily.

"I have a son," said the father, proudly. Then in his expansive joy he inquired whether I had sons. "What, *un soltero!*" he exclaimed aghast. Quickly recovering himself, he added, with a gay laugh, "Ah, our first born, Carmen"— or Maria, Lolita, Josefa—I have unromantically forgotten just which—"is twelve, in three years return, she will then

be a Señorita. You may wed her, Señor." Carmen—or
Maria, Lolita, Josefa—her father's arm on her shoulder,
nodded smilingly while I, placing my hand upon my heart,
bowed in acknowledgment of the honor.

That afternoon, May the first, I was again on the camino.
Departing from Loreto by the Los Parros trail, we soon
escaped from the cactus clad plains and entered a long winding arroyo from which a steep trail ascends into the Sierra
Giganta, passing through the precipitous gorge of Los Parros. Here, turning in the saddle, I obtained a superb view
in which the distant Gulf, the sloping plains, the lofty cliffs,
the pinnacled picachos, the ferns, wild grape vines and mesquit were before the eye at a single glance. By the upper
end of the gorge and beyond a sudden turn in the trail snug-
gles the Rancho of Los Parros, a few verdant acres of rich
soil drawing life from a tiny network of irrigating ditches
and rich in lofty olive trees, fluttering palms, ancient orange
trees—full ten metres in height—trellised vines and deep
green garden. On the 2nd instant we crossed a divide byond
Los Parros and soon came to another rancho, the Watering
Place of Doves, a name typical of many of the euphonious
and delightful designations to be found among the Peninsula ranchos. The name of this rancho, however, proved
more attractive than its people, whose ranching, by the way,
consisted in making mescal.

A league and half southeast from this rancho brought
us to a sharp bend in the arroyo, passing which we arrived
unexpectedly before the Mission of San Xavier. Although
I had heard extravagant tales from the natives concerning
the beauty of this mission I was in no wise prepared for the
splendor of the structure that now arose before me. Crossing a small brooklet, we entered the village—a few Indian
shacks and half a dozen low Mexican adobes—and rode
down its single street, guarded on our right by a stone wall

that seemed to admit the futility of endeavoring to screen
the immense orange, lemon, olive and pomegranate trees
which even generations ago must have overtopped its highest points. At the north end of the street there stood a substantial stone monument surmounted by an ancient stone
cross. Down at the farther end of the street, a hundred
paces distant, rose the Mission of San Francisco Xavier de
Vigge, a splendid stone structure, rich in the noble elegance
of Moorish and Romanesque architecture, and worthy of
the name of the most beautiful mission church on the Pacific
coast. Since the halcyon days of the missions when noble
prelates and armored grandees made stated visits to the
Peninsula, doubtless no Bishop's eyes have seen this glorious
church of the wilderness. Once only, in each year, does a
Padre cross the threshold. A dozen, possibly fifteen, families, Indian and Mexican, constitute the village: they are the
sole worshipers before the rich altar of San Xavier; they are
the sole guardians of its precincts, the faithful custodians of
its secrets. Close around *iglesia,* adobes, and shacks, rise
the lofty peaks and ridges of the Sierra Giganta, grimly
watching, protecting.

From the southwest corner of the *iglesia* there juts out an
ell within which dwells a kindly Mexican family. Here,
doubtless, in olden times the Padres lived and received
chance travelers; here, until my departure the following
day, I was lodged, for, as I bore a letter to the Señor of
the household from Don Amadeo, a hospitable welcome
was accorded me. The few hours at my disposal, excepting the time I spent in chatting with my hosts and paying
visits to a sick boy in the principal adobe, I passed with
delighted interest within the church.

One entered by a great double doorway at the west. Similar doorways open out at the north and east. Once there
was a patio into which the western doorway opened. Pre-

sumably, those at the north constitute the main entrance, for cut in the stone archway above, are the figures 1751, being, I assume, the date of completion of the structure. By the eastern doorway there is a cemetery. A well-built wall of cut stone protects the churchyard at the north and east; to the south there are stone cisterns and aqueducts, the ruins of an earlier church, and perhaps fifteen acres of irrigable land. The interior of the church is spacious and well lighted. In length it measures forty paces, in width, seven; the height must be above twelve metres. The broad doorways indent the sides. High aloft, on either side, four windows—deep set for the solid walls are five feet in thickness—admit the light. The altar is of stone and wood, and on either side doors open into lofty rooms wherein are stored what remains of the ancient and costly altar trappings. Eight paces below the altar there is a carved altar rail, and on either side of and below this rail there are alcoves, seven paces by five, floor dimensions. Each alcove has its saintly shrines. The floor of the *iglesia* is level and marvelously smooth, the blocks of stone with which it was constructed having been cunningly welded together with a rare cement, the secret of which is said to be lost. The walls are whitened, the roof is vaulted and in places there are frescos. Bending forward slightly, back and above the altar, stands a life size image of San Francisco, skillfully carved out of hard wood. Against the wall, above the image, there are two full length oil paintings of saints, ranged one above the other, while two other tiers of paintings with three canvases to the tier, are arranged one on either side of the center tier. Each shrine, moreover, has similar sets of paintings, together with many smaller ones. At the east shrine there is a small canvas with a masterly representation of the Last Supper. From each of the shrines some paintings have been abstracted, so, also, have some of the jewels from the

▲   Santiago

Church, Miraflores   ▼

▲   San José del Cabo

Church, San José del Cabo   ▼

The mother and child in the chapel at Loreto

Communion Service and from the halo of San Francisco.

Within and just above the main entrance to the church there is a choir loft, with a spiral stairway leading to it and upward to the dome-shaped belfry above, where once eight great bells chimed forth their peals. The upper portion of this stairway is of palm wood and shows signs of decay, the lower portion is of stone. Six of the bells have been removed: one to the City of Mexico, one to Loreto and the others to La Paz and Comondú. Roof and belfry, alike, are of stone and cement and there is no evidence of tiling about the structure. So magnificent was the workmanship of the builders of San Xavier that the passage of time, neglect and the convulsions of the earth, alike, have failed to mar their handiwork and the mission stands to-day in a perfect state of preservation.

The history of the mission dates back to the seventeenth century, for it was in the fall of 1697 that Padre Francisco Maria Piccolo, a highly educated native of Sicily and a staunch friend of Salvatierra, joined the latter at Loreto with a firm purpose of establishing a mission. Two years later he successfully laid the foundations of the Mission of San Francisco Xavier de Vigge. San Xavier was located in the midst of an Indian settlement, situated eight leagues southwest of Loreto. With a stream of water and a plot of fertile soil near by, crops were abundant; the Indians, however, were turbulent and to curb them required much muscular Christianity.

The site was thrice changed. This data and a mass of miraculous details are provided by the old chroniclers. Tradition adds that over two million pesos, a portion of the Virgin's share in the pearl fisheries of the Gulf, were expended on the *iglesia,* the service and paintings, that the work of construction continued over thirty years and that buried treasure lies within ninety-nine metres of the altar.

Were San Xavier in the path of the sight-seer its beauty would be heralded universally. In the closing days of the eighteenth century there were over thirty mission establishments in Baja California. To-day ten secular Italian priests, volunteers sent by his Holiness the Pope, minister to the Californians. To the three most beautiful Missions, San Ignacio, Comondú and San Xavier, a Padre comes but once a year. Rarely, indeed, are these missions visited by travelers from the outer world. Ignorant eyes gaze sleepily upon massive architecture in which Grecian, Moorish and Spanish types are strangely blended. Paintings over which Italian masters labored, look down upon unappreciative clods. When the Anglo-Saxon visitor comes, he usually comes as a despoiler, seeking for buried treasure which exists frequently in tradition, only, or in fable.

Although the sierras tower above the *iglesia* of San Xavier in all the somber grandeur of repellent cliffs, its shadows fall upon lovely gardens where sweet-scented flowers bloom in the midst of alfalfa, corn, garabanzas and grain, where delicate tendrils from trellised vines cling to white limbs of mammoth fig trees and where olive, pomegranate, orange and lemon trees rival one another in their unusual size. The oranges are juicy and of excellent flavor. The lemons are large, rounded like an orange and in taste resemble grape fruit rather than the lemons produced in more northerly climes. When we made our departure from San Xavier, we were overwhelmed with these golden fruits, tokens of a mother's grateful appreciation of the medicines which I had gladly administered to her sick boy.

CHAPTER XVII

A LONG FORCED MARCH

BEFORE leaving San Xavier I gave serious consideration to the journey immediately before us. According to local authority, La Paz, via the shortest
trail, the San Luis Camino, lay distant one hundred leagues.
As local authority could safely be depended upon for an
exaggeration of sierra distances, I reduced the hundred to
sixty-five. From this route, however, it would be necessary for us to deviate many leagues in order to carry out
my plan of making inquiry for news at Matancital, near the
great Bay of Magdalena on the Pacific. How many leagues
of deviation, I could only indefinitely surmise, for I had been
unable to find anyone who had ever traveled to La Paz,
via Matancital. I knew that San Luis lay in the sierras.
Praemundi was certain that the barren sweep of the dread
Llanos de Magdalena measured full twenty-five leagues
from the ocean to the sierras. If this proved correct, crossing the Llanos de Magdalena and then swinging back to San
Luis would increase the distance to La Paz by fifty leagues.
Realizing that on the plains a mule might approach his two
leagues per hour, I merely struck off one-sixth from Praemundi's figures, leaving the aggregate distance at one hundred and seven leagues, an accurate approximation for the
Matancital route, as I learned later. To reach La Paz
the night before the arrival of the steamer *Curacao,* it
would be necessary to cover this distance in fourteen days,
inclusive. This meant an average of twenty-three miles a

day, over rough and unknown trails and with no allowance for rests.

Possessed by anxiety concerning the consequences of the northern disaster, I cared for no rests, and realizing the possibility of the steamer's bringing me such personal ill news that I would wish to dispose of my outfit and take passage for its return trip on the 20th instant, I felt that I simply must undertake, and, within the fourteen days, must complete the impressively long march to Matancital and thence to La Paz. My mozos appreciating my anxiety stood ready to push on, although they both feared the dread Llanos de Magdalena. In deliberating I gave serious thought to my animals. My outfit consisted of two large pack burros, Vapor and Cabrillo, and two riding burros, Colon and Serrano. Of these Cabrillo and Serrano had just covered two hundred and forty miles from Sant' Agueda in eighteen days, during six of which they had been at rest. Prior to this and with but a fortnight's rest intervening, Cabrillo, the finest burro I ever knew of, had come in ten weeks through eight hundred and fifty miles of sierras and deserts, bearing a cargo at times weighing two hundred pounds. He now carried one hundred and thirty pounds and Vapor about ninety. With my one hundred and sixty pounds of avoirdupois, my saddle, canteen, cantinas, carbine, revolver and camera, Colon had two hundred and twenty pounds to carry. Serrano, an active stocky burro, had an easy time with Jesús, a slender boy sitting a light saddle. Finally, my animals, my mozos and I were in perfect physical condition.

Midday of the third of May bidding the kindly people of San Xavier "Adiós," we entered the camino southward bound. Following the course of the arroyo for three and a half leagues we came to a grove of superb fan palms growing in the mouth of an intersecting arroyo down which we

Mission of San Xavier, Mission de Vigge, showing west entrance (to the left)

turned. Half a league further I discovered in a thicket of brush and cacti, just off the camino, the ruins of an extremely ancient mission. The *iglesia* had been well constructed of cut stone and its walls were still standing. Near at hand were the remains of other buildings made of rough stone; also, and in excellent state of preservation, a magnificent cistern, seventy feet square and six feet in depth, and a large corral with high substantial stone walls. Two sets of stone stairways descended into the cistern and aqueducts led to and from it. In response to inquiries which I put to him, a passing *ranchero* stated that this was the site and these were the ruins of La Presentación, a mission far antedating San Xavier. As no such mission is mentioned by the chroniclers, La Presentación was doubtless the first foundation of San Xavier and as the earliest structures at Loreto were temporary, this *iglesia* is probably the oldest mission church in the Californias, the one survival, indeed, from the seventeenth century.

Early the morning of the 4th instant we were under way and thereafter the journey became a feverish, restless march. Weeks before I had read those lines in which Kipling describes the impatience that seizes upon the hunter and now into my mind again and again came the second stanza,

> "He must go-go-go away from here!
> On the other side the world he's overdue,
> 'Send your road is clear before you
> When the old Spring fret comes o'er you
> And the Red Gods call for you!"

I seemed unable to escape the first three lines and over and over with personal application I would repeat,

> "—go-go-go away from here!
> On the other side the world you're overdue,
> 'Send the road is clear before you—
> —go-go-go away from here!" etc.

For a time I fretted constantly over the slow advance of my burros and chafed because, not daring to assume that the San Francisco banks had weathered the storm, I could not, by recourse to my check book, purchase horses. But when the caminos were at their worst and grazing scant I realized that the horse has his limitations and the burro his advantages. For the humbler beast no sierra trail is too fearful, no provender too poor; browsing on cacti he can exist without water; he survives or avoids the eating of poisonous herbs; he outlasts all other beasts of the sierra caminos. Though his pace is deadly slow, it is steady, continuous; it goes on, on, monotonously on perhaps, but ever on, unswervingly on, on, cutting away and wearing down distance until the goal is attained. And yet when one is in a hurry this perfect mountaineer, this faithful, slow moving, unhastening servant rarely receives his due.

There is a fascination in such a steady continued onward march. As I fell into the swing of it I began to imagine myself a mere cog of locomotion, finally becoming so feverishly impatient of any break in the advance as to permit only the imperative halts at noon and night—and to postpone them. My camera swung in its unopened case, my carbine remained sheathed, leaving the camino to shoot with the small rifle was forbidden. Our manner of life becoming fixed, fell into systematized grooves. With the break of day we would awake. Wrapping his serapa close about his shivering shoulders, Praemundi would start forth in search of the grazing burros leaving Jesús to make a small fire and prepare breakfast. After dressing myself, performing my ablutions and rolling my blankets away in a dunnage bag, I would proceed to transfer the preceding day's entries from pocket notebook to journal. Soon Praemundi would appear with the burros, and while he put the pack-saddles on Cabrillo and Vapor, Jesús and I would saddle our riding animals. Then sitting together, cross-legged by the fire, we would eat a plain breakfast of broiled doves or "cotton-tail" rabbit, stewed prunes, boiled rice, hard-tack, or flour and water *tortillas,* and wild honey. My mozos drank strong coffee, water sufficed for me. On the Llanos de Magdalena and in such other localities as we found dense morning mists, Praemundi took his coffee before going in search of the burros. In fact he lived at all times princi-pally upon coffee. Breakfast concluded, the boy would rinse the tin dishes while Praemundi and I stowed the sup-plies in the *alforcas.* Then the two would pack Cabrillo and Vapor, employing a sort of "old squaw" hitch with the rope. Meantime I would strap on my revolver, slip the *cantinas* over my saddle pommel and continue my journal work.

"Listo caminando" (Ready for marching), Praemundi would sing out, presently. With a responsive *"Bueno,"* I would mount my burro, and slipping my journal into the *cantinas,* ride to the head of the little caravan. The animals once in their gait, I would dismount and walk ahead for sev-eral hours. These walks were bracing and I expect Colon appreciated my taking them. They certainly kept me in revolver practice; for I would invariably find a rattlesnake or two stretched across the camino. Halting at midday, we would have lunch, first, however, unsaddling and turn-ing loose the animals. Our menu would be dried slabs of beef broiled on the coals, hard-tack, boiled rice and wild honey. After an hour's nooning the Mexicans would round up the burros while I wrote in my journal. These midday halts would occupy between one and two hours' time. Again on the march we would travel until six or eight o'clock at night, camping in the vicinity of feed or water, or both, if possible. Each afternoon I walked a league or more but Praemundi, my walking mozo, was the springy, easy-gaited,

high class pedestrian of our party. That man could walk a horse to death.

As soon as we halted for the night, packs and saddles would be quickly removed from the burros and the weary creatures would slip away, unhobbled and untied. From the necks of two of them ropes would be left to drag and accentuate their trail. In grazing they kept well together. We would now be hungry and deadly tired. Again we would eat broiled dried beef, boiled rice, honey and *tortillas,* with strong coffee for the Mexicans. Supper concluded, we would clear of stones and cactus thorns places large enough for our bodies and then throw down our blankets. For two months I had rarely pitched my tent. During the day Jesús or I would have shot half a dozen doves, or perhaps a "cottontail," with my short-barreled, single shot .22 calibre rifle which, for the most part he carried swung by a strap from his saddle. These he would now dress while Praemundi and I discussed directions for the following day. Neither of us had ever been through the country, though he had traveled along the Gulfo Camino years before and I had an ancient map, that was fairly accurate, and two modern maps that partook of the wonted unreliability of Peninsula California interior charts. Soon we would all stretch out, each man swathed by himself like a mummy. Though I was too anxious to rest well, my companions slept soundly. We always took care to spread our blankets off the camino itself, for at night it would become the highway for "side-winders," *mala zoreas,* and I know not what other evil creatures and insects.

Except when we were upon the Llanos de Magdalena, all the trails—and many of them were ancient caminos of the Padres—were clogged with stones. Even on these plains bristling sections of *cholla* and swaying branches of *pithaya amarga* retarded travel. Moreover, we were in a cattle country where cross trails and by-paths made the question of which was the main camino a matter of frequent debate. Early one morning we met the most rapid pedestrian I ever saw, a gaunt Italian, outward bound from La Paz. Save for a long dagger and a canteen, he carried no luggage or accoutrement. His haste, his business or his lack of outfit were no affairs of ours, but his tracks served to advise us of the camino. Later in the day two incidents occurred illustrative of the farcical Peninsula misuse of the word *camino*, which is supposed to signify a roadway. Wondering which to follow, we had halted at the junction of half a dozen narrow cow paths, when Praemundi pointing to the least used trail exclaimed, *"Alli, los rastros del Italiano"* (There, the tracks of the Italian.) Jesús at once dismounted for a close examination. *"Si, Señor,"* he announced quietly, *"aqui el camino"* (Yes, sir, here is the highway.) We followed the "highway." Presently a young "cottontail" rabbit darted across our path, some rods before us. When we arrived at the spot where the little fellow had crossed, Praemundi paused and looked critically about. "Ah," he whispered pointing earnestly toward the tiny tracks leading off into the cacti, *"alli caminito de conejito. Conejito muy bueno carne."* (Ah, there is the little highway of the baby rabbit. Baby rabbit excellent meat.)

Twice we fell in with Rurales. The second party consisted of an officer and two men. After giving his name and rank—Carlos Gonzales, Captain of the Gendarmes Federal—the officer inquired, in excellent English and in the most courteous manner, by what authority I carried a carbine and side-arms.

"Captain," I replied, formally, for I realized that he was acting in accord with the regulations, "I am in your country as a traveler and a hunter after big game. I am traveling under the protection of a Mexican passport and of one from

Washington.   Moreover, I have a formal Mexican permit
to carry arms."

"I assumed as much, sir," he replied, "but it was my duty
to make inquiry.   I trust your travels have been pleasant."

"Thank you, Captain Gonzales, they have indeed been
pleasant," I replied.   "As for my passports and permit
they are here in my *cantinas.*"

"Further examination is needless.   I have your word and
I do not wish to hinder you further," he replied.   Then,
while I persistently produced the documents, he addressed
Praemundi in Spanish, saying, "Señor you may meet some of
my men along the camino.   We are searching for an
offender.   Tell them that I have said that your patron is
not to be molested."

I especially appreciated the courtesy of the Captain, for
having been upon the trail so long I looked more like a
contrabandista or a desperado than a peaceable traveler.
Fortunately for me Captain Gonzales was too keen an officer to judge by appearances. Had he officiously detained me
as a suspicious character or allowed his men the opportunity
of delaying me, my plans would have been upset entirely.

Each day we came to some well or water-hole close by
which would be the house of a *ranchero.*   Although these
rancheros controlled all the way from a thousand to a hundred thousand acres—the area of one grant ran into the mil-
lions—their houses were usually mere *jacales,* or huts with
thatched roofs and stake-and-mud walls.   The limitations
of their larders accorded with the poverty of their homes.
With cheese, dried beef, milk, beans, *tortillas,* wild honey,
coffee and salt on hand they considered themselves well pro-
visioned.   Many of them were without coffee or *panoche,*
while flour and rice were luxuries.   Their *tortillas* they
made from flour crushed on metates.   Though big horn
were to be had in the sierras and deer and countless doves in

Burros on the march

both sierras and on the plains, the men were frequently without ammunition and absolutely ignorant of the art of trapping. Every *rancho* would support flocks of goats and herds of cattle and stock. The goats were held at two and three pesos each, burros from ten to twenty pesos, cows from thirty to thirty-five, horses from twenty-five to sixty-five, and mules from thirty to seventy-five pesos.

The *rancheros* and their sons usually wore leather leggins and in riding were further protected from thorns by immense flaring leather *chaparejos*. The Señoras were extremely religious and many of the younger Señoritas decidedly pretty. Upon one *rancho* I found a widow living alone with three little daughters, the guardians of her flock of goats. Noting the clear complexions, graceful bearing and clear-cut features of these poor, bare-footed little lassies, I wished that some pastoral poet might appear, for surely their beauty would awaken the Muse. The *vaqueros* reported lions extremely troublesome in the sierras, and we saw any number of coyotes, foxes and large hawks. At one *rancho* a burly, good-natured Mexican showed me the heads of three lions which he had recently slain with the assistance of his *perros grandes* (big dogs). With keen regret I declined his hearty invitation to delay and hunt with him. Notwithstanding their impoverished condition, these people were universally cordial, selling me dried beef and honey at moderate prices and expressing deep sympathy with my anxiety concerning the northern disaster. With the *"adiós"* of parting they would invariably couple a wish that I find my *"familia y dinero"* (family and money) safe.

In the sierras our route followed the course of immense cañons, the San Xavier, Las Palmas, Santa Lucia, Santa Cruz, Guadalupe and Los Reyes Arroyos, which twisted about until I again and again put aside my compass in absolute despair of keeping accurate record of directions. Down upon the Llanos de Magdalena, likewise, our course was continually placed in doubt by the multitude of cattle trails. Though these extensive plains are arid and overgrown with cacti, were they cleared and watered their soil would prove productive.   The appearance of this country is desolate and forlorn.   The nights are foggy and the days stifling hot. It was along the shores of the great Bay of Magdalena which indents these plains that a company of which General Butler was the president, attempted to plant a colony back in the early seventies.   Hostility of the local government, coupled with mismanagement, lack of water, over-booming and general misrepresentation, made the scheme a failure. A Boston and New York concern now controls the coast line along the Pacific from latitude twenty-three degrees thirty minutes north, to the twenty-ninth parallel of north latitude, with an inland extension of fourteen miles.   This barren principality contains over four million acres, quite a farm.

We arrived at the Rancho of Matancital, the local head-quarters of this company, the evening of the 9th of May. The moon was shining brightly as I halted before a high fence within which stood a well lighted frame house, the home of the resident manager, W. J. Heney, Esq.   Finding a doorway in the wall, I entered and strode along a board walk to the porch.   Pausing before an open doorway, I saw within a decidedly blond, wide-awake looking man of thirty-two or three engaged in conversation with a handsome middle-aged matron.   I knocked on the casing.   The two looked up, the lady at once withdrawing.

"*Buenos noches, Señor,*" I began, unconsciously employing the Spanish greeting.

"*Buenos noches,*" replied the blond man, surveying me listlessly.

"*¿Ista casa se de Señor Heney?*"   (Is this the house of Mr. Heney?)   I continued, suddenly possessed with a curiosity to see whether an American would accept me as a Mexican.

"*Si, Señor,*" was the response, in a deeply bored tone.

"*¿Señor Heney aqui?*" (Mr. Heney here?)

"*Si, Señor.*"

"*Ta bueno, Señor Heney. Yo tengo una carta de recomendación por V'd,*" I continued. Then, unable to keep up the farce, I laughed outright and added, "When my burro train comes up, I'll yank the letter out of my *cantinas*. Meantime, North is my name—I am an American. What news have you from San Francisco?"

"Ah," he muttered, with a quickly drawn breath of readjustment. "I thought you were a Mexican official come to arrest me for the violation of some new stamp act of the existence of which I had not as yet been advised. It is some little time since my last arrest." This final remark he made in a musing tone. "Come in," he added.

I entered, mightily glad to confer with a fellow countryman. We chatted together until midnight. Of the northern situation he knew little more than I, though he had a notion that the banks in San Francisco had gone under. The following day I saw something of Matancital. Trees, vines and vegetables were flourishing under irrigation from a twenty thousand gallon cistern, kept overflowing by a steam pump which forced a large stream from a well in a neighboring arroyo. Heney presented me to his aunt—the matron whom I had observed—and her daughter. The latter, as his secretary and the company's bookkeeper—accounts are required to be kept both in Spanish and English—has her time well occupied. In place of bemoaning her exile, this young lady has so won the respectful esteem of the *Rancheros* and Señoras in the vicinity that for days I had heard praise of her knowledge of Spanish, her graciousness and her bravery.

Complimenting her upon her spirit, I said, "I am told that you have spent ten days at a time, alone, down at the island residence, a revolver strapped to your waist." She smiled. "Had you seen me one noon crouching in the shadow of a cardon on the Tepetates Camino, weakly crying because I was tired, you would not have thought me a heroine." Knowing that modesty and spirit are close friends, I ceased my compliments. I was to hear, again, however, of these "weak tears." They were shed from sheer exhaustion in the midst of a one hundred and eighty mile ride which she made in three days and a half—and made in the interest of others!

At noon on the 10th of May, the Heneys drove down to Magdalena Bay, a few miles distant, while I, enriched by gifts of eggs and Mexican hard-tack, took the trail for La Paz, fifty-six leagues distant. When twenty leagues slightly south of east of Matancital, we arrived at the old Jesuit Mission of San Luis Gonzaga, founded in 1740. Though small the *iglesia* is well ornamented and in excellent state of repair. The subsidiary mission buildings are used by Don Benigno de la Toba, a descendant of one of the old California Spanish governors and the proprietor of the *Hacienda* or Plantation of San Luis. Near the mission we observed an extensive red brick store, the most imposing modern private building in Lower California. In the absence of the Don, we were cared for by his major domo, an old Mexican of methodical ways.

At dusk, two days later, we met Don Benigno on the camino. He was mounted upon a splendid animal and his dress and accoutrement were well chosen. Perhaps he was forty-five years of age, perhaps a trifle more. In build he was rather portly. His manners and bearing were those of a gentleman accustomed to the company of gentlemen. After reading a letter which I presented to him, he answered my

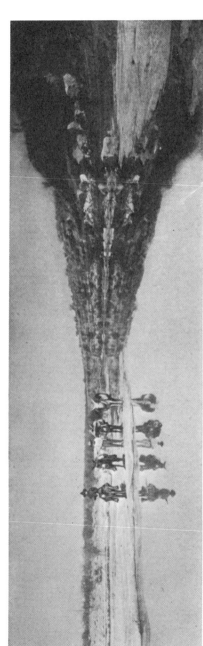

A rare stream of water

The Pithaya Pulse or "Organ Pipe" Cactus and native cavaliers

numerous questions with extreme affability.   His *hacienda*
contains over one hundred thousand acres of land and
twenty families are employed in its care.   Barring droughts
that at times afflict the country, good rains can be counted
upon every other year.   On his property he has had over
twenty wells dug, water being found at an average depth of
thirty metres.

Though no hint of the subject was given by either of the
principals, *rancheros* assured me of the existence of a bitter
feud between Heney and Don Benigno, a feud which has increased with the continuance of legal differences.   The
situation is simple enough.   Both men are cattle barons and
their lands adjoin.   It is a case of worthy foemen.   Heney
is a fighting American, of the same blood as a certain noted
prosecutor; the Don comes of an ancient and illustrious
Spanish family.

Out from San Luis I had taken the Salto Los Reyes
Camino, a trail enriched by beautiful scenery.   Deep in an
arroyo we found the *Salto Los Reyes,* the Kings' Leap, a
high bluff, crowned with a pile of stones, quarried in bygone
days, and frowning down upon two shimmering pools of
water where swallows, doves and hawks, side by side, slack
their thirst.   It is a royal spot.   Out from the very heart of
the cliff comes the water, clear and limpid. Down from this
sheer cliff, in ancient days, 'tis said, a king of the Guiacuras
leaped, close followed by a king of the Pericues.   'Twas a
mighty leap.

As the sun was sinking on the 16th day of May, a weary
little party made camp close against the Gulf shore, just beyond the Rancho of Arripaz and within sight of the capital
of the *Distrito Sur.*   Before us spread the lovely Bay of La
Paz, calm as on that day, nigh four centuries gone by, when
Cortez there found shelter.   Whether the traditional and
published tables of distances were correct and our round-

about route from San Xavier had taken us over four hundred miles or whether my lesser figures were more accurate, I did not consider.   We had completed a long forced march on time.   Another day would end suspense.

CHAPTER XVIII

A S the sun was gilding the heights of the Cacachilas, I took an invigorating plunge into the Bay of La Paz; three hours later, my outfit corralled hard by the outskirts of the pueblo, I was striding along the wide streets inquiring the way to the Government House. A child, an aged woman and a muleteer successively and indefinitely informed me that it faced the plaza; then a soldier, clad in a white linen uniform, obligingly accompanied me to the very portals of the building. At the proper department I made inquiry, of a courteous and stately old gentleman, for Sr. Coronel Agustin de Sanginés, the *Jefe Político* of the District. His Excellency was not in, I was informed. Would I see his Secretary? I would. After a brief delay another most affable official, Sr. Arcadio Villegras, Secretary to the Jefe Político, entered from an adjoining office and, greeting me in English, said: "I regret exceedingly that His Excellency, Coronel Sanginés, is not in. If you will be so gracious as to accompany me, however, you will find mail which you are doubtless anxious to peruse."

In another moment I was seated at a desk in a private office deep in a packet of letters. Though I have read since then many graphic accounts of San Francisco's fire and earthquake, no one of them has meant as much to me as did the first lines of a brief note which I read at La Paz. It was from my brother, dated at San Francisco, April 21st, 1907. "Yours of the 4th instant duly received," it began.

Even an earthquake could not upset his methodical acknowledgment of a letter. "None of us are injured. I should have wired you but lines down and your whereabouts unknown. This city looks like Hell. Banks are closed. Hope you are well and that quake didn't reach you. Better come home for a month."

Stuffing the other letters into my pocket, I strode out into the open air, smiling and at peace with the world. After seventeen days of continual anxiety, after repeated visions of those nearest and dearest engulfed in flames or lying crushed, "None of us are injured" was a message that made life worth while again. My eyes once more noted surroundings.

As the capital of the Southern District, a prominent shipping port and the seat of the Gulf pearl industry, La Paz has long enjoyed a certain prestige. For many years it was the most populous place in all Lower California. Even now its numbers are on the increase, exceeding, in the aggregate, five thousand. It aspires after the ways of larger cities, however, and loses, thereby, the quaint medievalism that makes delightful such pueblos as San Ignacio and Comondú. I will not express an opinion as to whether or not La Paz has acquired due compensation for her loss. Indeed, I am not qualified to render an expert opinion on the subject. To my way of thinking man was absurdly stupid when he invented cities. I could enjoy being marooned on a million acre *rancho* and invariably suffocate when I am thrown into one of those mighty artificial tread-mills where a million mortals irritably rub shoulders against one another, dully thinking their fretful race to the grave is living. Therefore, I may as well hold my peace on the subject of cities.

However, the hundreds of tall palm trees, the blossoming gardens, the streets lined with red-flowered trees—the *arbol de fuego*—and the low, flat-roofed adobes give to La

Paz a delightful picturesqueness, lying, as it does, hard by the beautiful harbor.   In this and in its historic associations lay, for me, the greatest charm of the little city.   Here whites first set foot in the Californias; here Cortez attempted to plant a settlement full seventy-five years ere the foundation of Jamestown; here swaggering buccaneers congregated; here landed Alexander Selkirk, the inspiration for Robinson Crusoe; here were quartered American troops during the Mexican war; here came Walker with his tall young filibusters.

After my early call on officialdom, I strolled about the town, admiring the gardens, meeting several Americans and finally locating an excellent hotel.   The welcome *Curacao* having already nosed into the harbor, a ship's boat brought its chief officers ashore.   The purser, a big, broad-shouldered, handsome chap, Byrd by name, smiled upon me rather quizzically.   "Guess you're my man," he exclaimed, heartily.   "We're just in from San Francisco.   I've got letters and instructions to cash a check for a traveler of your description.   Banks at home all closed so you couldn't draw on 'em here.   Call on me.   We return on the twenty-second."

After this encouraging greeting I continued my tour of the town with increased good spirits.   In a very brief time I discovered that the community was in the throes of intense excitement over charges preferred against one of the resident foreign consuls.   As he was a man of means and a native of La Paz, feeling ran high and I had a difficult time explaining that a possible game of tennis and an inspection of the local pearl fisheries appealed to me more than discussing a consular matter in which I had no concern.   To give the official credit, he made no mention of the absorbing topic.   After two sets at the nets I visited a factory where buttons were being made from pearl oyster shells.   The pearl fishery regions of the Gulf are divided among three concessionists, one English and two Mexican. Yaqui Indians do the diving and the pearls are marketed in Europe. According to public rumor, one of the Mexican concessionists was far away in durance vile all through forgetting some ten thousand dollars' worth of pearls when making his declaration at the Customs House in San Francisco. It's strange how the atmosphere of a custom house does affect the memory!

As I was returning to the hotel, after my stroll, I met a burly individual hurrying along with an immense revolver protruding belligerently from his inside coat-pocket. He explained to a resident with whom I chanced to be walking that he was avoiding the shedding of official blood by keeping away from the Governor. When I met the latter, as I did upon calling at the Government House later in the day, I decided that there might be two sides to the blood-letting operation. Sr. Coronel Sanginés, Territorial Chief, or "Governor," is a swarthy, keen-eyed, middle-aged officer, well able to take care of himself and perform the duties of his office. Both he and his Secretary treated me, a visiting stranger, with extreme civility. The latter even undertook a wearisome amount of research to place at my disposal certain historical data.

As Lower California is merely a territory, each of its two districts are in charge of a chief executive and military officer, a federal appointee, formally styled the *Jefe Político y Militar*. The majority of the local federal officials have offices in the Government House, an imposing structure built around a court where soldiers lounge at ease. It occupies a block facing a plaza made attractive with flowers and shrubbery. Upon the opposite side of this plaza there is a large church with adjacent parochial buildings. On visiting the church I had the pleasure of meeting Padre Rosse, an agreeable and well educated Italian, the Superior of the Peninsula Fathers.

As I was recrossing the plaza, bound hotelwards, a carriage with three occupants passed slowly by. One of the three I recognized instantly as a classmate of university days. "Hi, there!" I called out.

"Hello. Who is it?" he answered. "Why, Great Scott, old man! Say, get in here and ride with us. Heard you were somewhere on the Peninsula. This is my wife—we are running a mine down at Triunfo. Come visit us."

As the sequel of this pleasant meeting, I threw my saddle on a horse the following day and rode southward eleven leagues over a good road which wound gradually up into the hills, bringing me to Triunfo, a pueblo of three thousand inhabitants, which has grown up about the "Triunfo," or, as they are now termed, the "Progresso" gold and silver mines. Like Santa Rosalia, Triunfo is essentially a mining town, quickened by foreign capital and supervised by foreign brains. There all similarity ends, however, for Triunfo is less cosmopolitan, less ready-made and far more attractive than Santa Rosalia. Also, it is older and smaller. In addition to the mining plant, with its tall brick chimneys, chugging stamps, cosy residence—"The Hacienda"—and high protecting stone wall, grim relic of revolutionary days, Triunfo boasts a rakish looking church, intended, primarily as a stable for the racing stud of a sporting mine superintendent. I spent two enjoyable days at Triunfo and the neighboring pueblo of San Antonio Real. Not being technically versed in mining, however, I was more interested in the remarkable precociousness of the superintendent's baby daughter than in the completeness of the noisy mills. Ultimately the little toddler, climbing into a small engine used to haul ore cars, signified her intention of taking us "for a long ride, fast'r than burro."

The ancient village of San Antonio Real lies deep down in a cañon a league to the southwest of Triunfo. Here, early in the eighteenth century, was begun the first mining, so far as is known, ever done in the Californias. In the still more distant days of Sir Francis Drake and Sir Thomas Cavendish—the merry English rover who sailed blithely up the Thames with plundered silk spread forth for sails— doughty buccaneers were wont to harbor at Ventana Bay, a few leagues distant, eastward from the pueblo site. How imperiously the old sea gallants must have strutted about in their flapping jack-boots; how their sharp eyes must have glittered as their swift barks swooped down upon some luckless and richly laden Manila galleon! Even during the nineteenth century, southern corsairs, prowling inland from Ventana Bay, rifled the old stone mission chapel at San Antonio of its ancient golden altar ornaments and long strings of pearls.

Making the trip on horseback, I visited San Antonio Real in company with a genial young giant, Hughes by name, a veteran of the Philippine War. We returned to Triunfo by a steep road which opend about us a magnificent view of the Cacachilas. These sierras, sharp and rugged in their outline, attain a maximum height of 4,700 feet. On our arrival at "The Hacienda" we found Mrs. Nahl, my classmate's wife, in the garden with a college flag.

"Let us rejoice in our colors, gathering together the alumni," she laughingly exclaimed.

"Everywhere the American collegian," answered Hughes, responsively. "Think of four of us with the same Alma Mater being down here under the Southern Cross! Why, if the Pole is ever discovered and an ice fence built about it, there'll be a bunch of collegians sitting on the top rail in no time, a-smoking away as cool as you please."

"My new engineer is a California man, too," interposed

Porch of the ancient house of the Hidalgos at
San Antonio Real

Nahl, who had joined us. "My predecessor, also, came from Berkeley; Brookes, first manager of these mines, had a son who went to New Haven, becoming Yale's fleetest Mott Haven sprinter. We must certainly have a picture here under the bananas."

The ensuing day I returned to La Paz. Before visiting Triunfo I had paid my mozos the amount due them, whereupon Praemundi had immediately hied himself to a *cantino,* or drinking saloon. In appreciation of his marvelous pedestrianism, I had also presented him with Vapor. The other burro I had necessarily sold, though parting with plucky Cabrillo had proven a truly sharp wrench. Now Praemundi appeared before me in a state of cheerful inebriation, begging for a written ratification of my gift. He was penniless. Indeed, between liquor and thieving companions his first twenty-four hours in La Paz had cost him forty dollars. Without giving thought to his purpose, I gave him the desired formal bill to Vapor; possessed of this instrument, he sold the faithful animal forthwith, then proceeded to spend the proceeds, his entire worldly capital, for more mescal.

So much for the sober burros and their unfortunate packer. Jesús, for his part, had blossomed out in new apparel from head to foot. Indeed, though I had at no time given especial thought to his looks, I now laughingly realized that my youthful mozo was a handsome young dandy.

That evening four of us—two Americans, an Englishman and a German—dined together at the hotel. As my companions were men of education and had spent years on the mainland, I listened with keen interest to their expressions concerning the vulnerable characteristics of the natives. Crystallized, their opinions were that the Mexican lacks appreciation, is improvident, a hard bargainer and unreliable. At the same time they were in accord in admitting that these traits might be subdued by a continuation of the present enlightened and progressive administration of government. In reaching their conclusions they eliminated the higher classes from their reckonings and referred to the brief period in which education has been within general reach and to the comparatively recent cessation of successive civil wars as extenuating circumstances to be considered.

After supper, to enjoy the twilight, we sought a balcony, overlooking the Bay. "See those couples, trios and quartettes of girls promenading up and down the long wharf," remarked the American, between puffs of his cigar.

"Yes," I assented. "I've been admiring their graceful, easy carriage."

"They belong to the *Primera Clase* of La Paz. It is a good object lesson for us *Gringos* to reflect on their freedom. In our country, in England, on the Continent a dozen men would obtrude upon such attractive, unescorted girls. Here no one would think of addressing them without a formal presentation."

The German chuckled. "There's a man famine in local high circles," he remarked. "A dozen charming Señoritas of the first class; only two eligible men—and of the two one is a woman-hating Judge, the other a stripling."

"La Paz must occasionally produce men children of the same social class as these girls," I demurred.

"Certainly," interjected the Englishman, "but they leave for the larger business fields of the mainland. These proud Señoritas then await their return, preferring spinsterhood to accepting men socially in a lower strata."

The following morning I embarked on the *Curacao* for San Francisco. Two leagues down the Bay of La Paz we passed the sheltered harbor of Pichilingue where Uncle Sam maintains a coal station with ten or twelve thousand

tons of coal for his war ships.   A fine, deep harbor, well
sheltered by San Juan Nepomucino Island, it derives its
name from having been a pirate cove in early days.   Swinging off across the Gulf we visited Topolobampo, Mazatlan
and other mainland ports, at each of which we took on English and American mining and sugar people, most of them
intent on looking after their northern bank accounts, for San
Francisco is the Mecca and supply point for the entire west
coast of Mexico.   Recrossing the Gulf we cast anchor off
San José del Cabo.

Here, in company with a Scotch traveler, I landed on a
freighter and visited the pueblo, a mile inland.   As we found
two rentable mules, the distance was easily covered.   San
José del Cabo is a charming and picturesque pueblo, with
the inevitable mission and plaza, many sky-blue, flat-roofed
adobe residences, attractive gardens, rich soil, much running
water, and every tropical and semi-tropical fruit conceiva-
ble.   It has a population of sixteen hundred and enjoys a
wonderful climate.   Leaving the town behind us, we rode
through fields of sugar-cane toward Santa Anita, a garden
spot, presumably the site of the early eighteenth century
Jesuit Mission of San José.   It is a frequent saying down
the Peninsula that if a man stops a week at San José del
Cabo he becomes a "lotus eater" and only ropes can haul
him away.   It certainly is a dreamy garden.   The small
boys who crowded about us demanding *centavos* were an
evidence of foreign visitors for, at Rosario, when I had offered to toss pennies for several small children who had
showed me the mission ruins, the youngsters had no idea of
the meaning of a penny scramble, seeming well content to
hold my hand and walk beside me.

Leaving San José del Cabo and rounding Cabo San Lucas,
we bore away toward San Francisco, 1,160 miles distant.   At
Magdalena Bay we made a brief halt; at Ensenada we spent

a day; and then we steamed northward toward the Golden Gate.

And now, before proceeding any further with my adventures, let me accord a full chapter to the strange story of that superb harbor, Magdalena Bay.

At anchor off San José del Cabo

CHAPTER XIX

TO an American looking forward to the completion of the Isthmian Canal, the location of Magdalena Bay is startlingly strategic. Indenting the southwest coast of the California Peninsula, distant a full thousand nautical miles from San Francisco on the north and over twice that distance from Panama on the southeast, this infrequently considered port is the only great anchorage between the Golden Gate and the Isthmus. To conceive of its vastness, picture a landlocked sheet of water fifteen miles in length and over twelve in breadth! But even then the conception is incomplete, for the actual length of the roadstead is nearer forty miles than fifteen, although points reaching shorewards from the adjacent Island of Santa Margarita, a long, narrow strip of land, barren and of volcanic origin, divide this mighty stretch of water into two bays of which only the northerly one is properly referred to as Magdalena Bay, the southerly division being usually called Almaca, or Almejas, Bay. The old-time whalers termed these divisions Weather and Lee Bays.

The formation of Magdelena Bay is peculiar. From the peninsula coast at the north headlands jut out into the sea; at the west a long narrow strip of land, sometimes called Man-of-War Island, parallels the inequalities of the shore line, while to the south and southwest lies the Island of Santa Margarita. By practically hemming in a portion of the

---

* Reproduced, in part, from "Sunset Magazine," March, 1908.

247

sea these successive lands form the harbor, for Magdalena Bay does not deeply indent the coast.   As these protective girders are lofty enough to shelter the harbor from gales, they served in older days to conceal buccaneers and smuggling craft from chance ships of the Crown.   The formal gateway to the ocean lies betwen the northern extremity of Santa Margarita Island and Punta Entrada, the southernmost point of the so-called Man-of-War Island.   There are additional passages, however, for lagoons, fringed with mangrove shrubs, run northward finally opening into the Pacific—others extend inland—while to the south there is easy egress through Almaca Bay.

Pictured in an earlier chapter, the country inland from Magdalena Bay is desolate in the extreme.   First, reaching from the shore eastward for twenty miles, comes a barren, undulating waste of sand and cactus.   Next the plains sweep inland with an upward swell for another twenty miles, finally wedding with the hills and plains which stretch down from the eastern cordillera of the Peninsula.   Save for the mesquite, which line the broad, shallow arroyos—occasional scaro on the interminable desert—the face of the country is veiled entirely with cacti.   It is not a pleasant region.   The ground is parched.   The days are stifling hot. Great waves of fog roll in during the nights, effectually shrouding the country in the mornings.   Until he has proceeded inland from one hundred and seventy-five to two hundred and seventy-five miles from the bay, the chance wayfarer need have no thought of finding the fertile district along which, strung out in the form of a crescent, lies the historic mission sites of Todos Santos, La Paz, Dolores del Sur, San Xavier, Comondú and Purísima.

The history of Magdalena Bay, a story never yet knit together, is dashed with the wild flavor of the romance of centuries.   Its theme is ever thirst, *thirst*.   First visited by

Europeans in the days of Cortez, in various centuries the gathering place of voyagers from the Spanish Main, galleons from the Philippines, buccaneers from England and the Netherlands, American filibusters and whalers from a dozen ports, less than forty years ago the favored property of a powerful New York syndicate presided over by General John A. Logan and financed by Belmont and Jerome, to-day the magnificent harbor looks out upon desolate shores unknown to the world. With few shoals, sheltered from gales, this noble expanse of water, spacious enough to accommodate the navies of all nations and be heedless of their presence, this grim bay of the southwest nevertheless counts an incoming sail an event. The explanation is thirst, *thirst*. For every man who has ever visited the shores of this superb, ill-starred bay has felt the want of water, *water*.

First came Francisco de Ulloa, a resolute Spanish admiral outfitted by Cortez. In serious search for the rich pearl island of Ciguatan where charming Amazons were supposed to live in sovereign state, de Ulloa coasted along the shores of peninsula California, discovering successively the Colorado River and Magdalena Bay. To the port he came at Christmas time in the year 1539, but though he fell a-foul of warlike savages he could get no sight of pearl-bedecked Amazons or of living springs of water. And for lack of the last he mourned the deepest.

In the wake of de Ulloa sailed Juan Cabrillo. In his ship's log, under date of July 18, 1542, appears this early notice concerning Magdalena Bay, "this is a good port and it is sheltered from west winds; but *it has not water or wood*." Later came the restless pilot Viscaino. But he, too, found little water. "They could get no intelligence of any water," wrote his chronicler, "except in a cavity among the rocks, and what they had there was excessively bad."

After Viscaino's visit occasional Spanish galleons, Isth-

mus bound from the Philippines, sought the shelter of the
great harbor, and graceless Dutch and English buccaneers
followed close at their heels.   In the sands southward toward Cape San Lucas lie buried the surplus riches of many
a ravished treasure ship.

Thus passed the sixteenth and seventeenth centuries.   In
the eighteenth the fearless Jesuit padres sought a mission site
overlooking Magdalena Bay.   But even these intrepid explorers retreated from its thirsty shores, content, perforce,
with the foundation of San Luis Gonzaga, nigh fifty miles
inland and the nearest of the links of their extensive mission
chain.

Finally with the opening of the nineteenth century, the
bay region experienced surprising prosperity in consequence
of becoming the center of an active smuggling trade between
the dwellers by the missions and voyagers from Europe and
the United States.   This free trade was the outgrowth of a
commercial embargo enacted by Spain during the Na-
poleonic wars.   With mules and donkeys laden with hides,
occasional furs and pearls, fruits and honey, the natives
wended their way from the missions toward Magdalena
Bay.   In the lagoons they would find expectant sailors awaiting them with long boats freighted with woven stuffs, trink-
ets and the like, acceptable articles for exchange.   It was a
thirsty business.   The Californians prepared for it by bringing with them well filled leather water-bottles, while the
sailors supplied themselves with an inferior quality of the
liquid by sinking barrels in the sand, then stoving in the barrel heads and waiting for the seepage.   The proceedings
were enlivened by cordial exchange of native mescal and
ship's grog.

For a third of a century this contraband trade flourished
to the great joy of the natives and the immense advantage of
shipping houses engaged in Pacific commerce.   Finally,

with the diversion of the famous Pious Fund, and the achievement of Mexican independence and the passage of the Secularization Acts, came the decadence of the missions and the consequent ending of the halycon days of the Magdalena Bay *contrabandistas*.

But visitors of higher repute began shortly to frequent the great harbor, for nations were not blind to its possible strategic importance. In the late thirties and early forties Admiral Du Petit-Thouars, Captain Sir Edward Belcher and Captain Kellett successively investigated Magdalena Bay. They reported it accursed by thirst.

Shortly before the middle of the nineteenth century the bay region experienced its second period of prosperity for a veritable fleet of whalers, sealers and guano gatherers made it the center of their operations. New England whalers, alone, were soon coining over a quarter of a million dollars annually, from whales taken along the shores of the Peninsula. Magdalena Bay rejoiced in the doubtful honor of being the favorite spot for "trying out" the oil.

In the midst of these doings came the Mexican War. This was in 1847-48. Upon its outbreak Commodore Selfridge landed a body of marines and two companies of New York volunteers at La Paz, one hundred and seventy miles to the southeast of the great harbor. Late in 1848 these troops were withdrawn.

Five years later Filibuster Walker anchored with his bark the *Caroline,* in Magdalena Bay; subsequently he passed the same harbor while en route to Nicaragua and the culmination of his career.

Undisturbed by these various historic events the whalers and sealers continued to make the bay their general headquarters. But, despite its remoteness even this region was destined to become a pawn in the political game. The first move was made in the early sixties, when General Juarez, hard pressed by Maximilian, shrewdly conveyed to an American syndicate a large slice of Lower California territory, including the section about Magdalena Bay. In 1867 the syndicate engaged the late J. Ross Browne to examine its bargain.

In the course of his work Browne made this entry in his journal: "Proceeding close along the shore of Magdalena Bay some two or three miles toward the heads, we came to a plateau or mesa, apparently formed by nature as the site for a town. The extent of the mesa is about two miles in depth by three in width. Probably a better point could not be selected for a naval depot."

But though impressed by the magnificence of the bay and its availability for naval purposes and charmed by the salubrity of its climate, Browne reported adversely as to adaptability of the adjacent lands for agricultural purposes. "Until within two weeks of our visit," he wrote, "it was said by one person near the bay that rain had not visited this region for fourteen years." Thirst, thirst, always thirst!

However, August Belmont, Leonard W. Jerome, Ben Butler, Wm. G. Fargo, Ben Holladay, Caleb Cushing, John A. Garland and John A. Logan, the active spirits of the syndicate, were not men of a type to be deterred by a mere report. Accordingly Baron Philippe de Rougemont, a noted French engineer, was engaged to map and survey the country about Magdalena Bay while a large party of pioneers were sent into the interior to dig wells, build roads and clear the ground. By May, 1871, it was reported that there were five hundred settlers located about Browne's "town-site." But these newcomers were oppressed by their surroundings, the fear of thirst came upon them and they fled the country.

Meantime the Mexican government had annulled the grant and its officials had pounced upon the colony, dispos-

Magdalena Bay

sessing its local agent. These latter proceedings caused the U. S. S. *Saranac* to hasten to the rescue. By this time General Butler, who had become president of the syndicate, began complaining after his own peculiar fashion. So alarming was his roar that the Mexican government offered a compromise by which, as a salve to his injured feelings, the syndicate was accorded the privilege of gathering *orchilla* for a period of six years. This orchilla is a lichen which grows on the stems and branches of the shrubs and cacti along the coast of the Magdalena Bay region. In appearance it resembles drooping tufts of gray moss. Dyes of valuable properties are produced from orchilla.

In 1874, and prior to the expiration of the Butler extension, there appeared in Magdalena Bay the U. S. S. *Narragansett,* a vessel engaged in the survey of the west coast of Mexico. This important undertaking had been confided to the commander of the *Narragansett,* a quiet young naval officer by the name of George Dewey. According to the 1880 report of the U. S. Hydrographic Office, compiled from data gathered by Commander Dewey, it would appear that the American Jackies found the water problem at Magdalena Bay as vexing as it was in the days of the Spanish navigators. Says this report:

"In the summer season the only regular supply of fresh water is obtained about 40 miles from the bay, near one of the northern lagoons. Small vessels make regular trips for the express purpose of bringing it to the settlement. . . . At the time of the *Narragansett's* visit there were about ten houses near the beach on the west side of Man-of-War Cove, one of which was used as a Custom House and the others chiefly occupied by men engaged in collecting and shipping orchilla. . . Magdalena Bay is one of the most spacious and safe harbors in the world."

A decade after the visit of these naval surveyors, a California company secured a grant of land adjoining the bay. Probably to their own surprise as much as any one's, these new speculators made a fortune from the concession.   This came through unusually large crops of orchilla which brought to the bay region a third period of prosperity. Subsequently the concessionists transferred to a Boston and New York syndicate the Magdalena Bay grant which may be described as a four million acre farm embracing a belt of land reaching fourteen miles inland from the bay and extending along the coast north and south some hundreds of miles.   Though this grantee, at least in 1906, gave small heed to orchilla, it developed a fine well at Matancita, with a cistern and a steam pump capable of supplying many thousand gallons per day.   Matancita, the local headquarters of this immense *rancho,* lies immediately to the north of one of the northern lagoons.

Though these commercial matters have been mere incidents to Magdalena Bay, bringing with them no steady rush of settlers, they have had their immediate bearing on recent events.   Commander Dewey, become an Admiral, was thoroughly conversant with the entire west coast of Mexico; he knew that with abundant water at Matancita Magdalena Bay was useful.   Presently, therefore, through the courtesy of Mexico, the United States was accorded the privilege of sending her men-of-war to the great harbor for target practice.   Since then, at periodic intervals, the resplendent fighting machines of the White Navy have glided into Magdalena Bay, their grim cannon breaking the calm of the silent waters and rousing the echoes above the rugged shore. Thus again the bay has awakened to such life as it had not known since the passing of the *contrabandistas* and whalers; only now it is a less continuous and more superb manner of living.

Though the modern visitor to this ancient harbor is impressed by the magnificent expanse of its waters, the clearness of the atmosphere and the absence of commerce, he finds its shores practically deserted. The only settlement is at Man-of-War Cove where there are some seventy-five Mexicans, a handful of them port officials, the others engaged in turtle fishing and the gathering of abalone shells. Immediately inland there are no residents, except the local manager of the American grant with his *vaqueros* and their families, forming the small cluster of houses at Matancita.

Magdalena Bay has little inland intercourse. In fact the region is not rich in roads. From Matancita trails run north to the beautiful valley of prosperous Comondú, and south to the gardens of Todos Santos and thence to La Paz or San José del Cabo. But on these *caminos* there are stretches where water-holes are forty miles apart. San Luis, to the east, is the junction of many of these trails, relics of mission days, which wind through the sierras and across the plains with springs or water-holes every twenty miles or so. Corrals and shacks of *rancheros* mark these oases.

Despite their impoverishment the *rancheros* are an hospitable, kindly people. But though careless of the mountain lions that deplete their flocks, and heedless of rattlesnakes and tarantulas, they have an inherent dread of the Plains of Magdalena. "The shores of the great bay are accursed by God," they say, "and therefore many men have died in the region after the Devil's favorite fashion of taking them off, and that is by thirst, *thirst*, THIRST."

I believe this dread is contagious. And yet, after ascertaining what slight labor has sufficed to develop the verdant *huertas*, or gardens and orchards, at Matancita and about the wells on Don Benigno's Hacienda, the traveler is disposed to conclude that the curse might have been lifted these many moons, except for the glaring lack of system and energy which seems to have characterized the various schemes to develop the Magdalena Bay region.

PART III

LA FRONTERA AGAIN

CHAPTER XX

A FRONTIER BALL AND AGAIN THE SIERRAS

EARLY in July I was again in Ensenada, having had, in the meantime, a glimpse of San Francisco. Ensenada is a rather recent American-Mexican-English built town with a population of fifteen hundred, a delightful climate and a beautiful situation above the curved white beach of Todos Santos Bay. It is at once the headquarters of an English colonization company and the seat of government of the Northern District of Lower California. Six months earlier, on Christmas evening, just before entering the country of the Catarina Yumas, Juan, my two American friends and I had reached the town in time for a late and well appreciated dinner at the foreign hotel. We had at that time come overland from Tia Juana. The next day I had observed two usual signs of English occupation, golf links—rather neglected—and a portable tub!

After leaving Magdalena Bay in the *Curacao,* I had visited Ensenada a second time and been introduced to the "Governor" of the District, Sr. Coronel Celsa Vega, a courteous, well groomed, rather good looking individual. Now, in July, my list of local acquaintances was extended to the Post Master, to Sr. Luis Fernandez, of the Customs House, and his associate, the Collector, to Sr. Oymart, a most obliging local merchant, and to various other gentlemen. Without exception they showed me most generous consideration.

Indeed, whatever his shortcomings, the civility of the

average Mexican is superb. He inherits it from his Spanish forefathers, he acquires it at his mother's knee, he learns
it at school. In January, Eloisa, the pretty child of the
Señor of San Vicente, showed me her Mexican primer and
this was the first lesson therein: "Albert's mamma gave Albert a piece of cake. Albert, greedy boy, without a word
began eating the cake. Albert's mamma took the cake
away and gave it to the cat. The cat said '*Meow, meow*'
(Thank you, thank you.) Albert's mamma thereupon gave
the cat a second piece of cake."

With such training is it at all surprising that the Mexican
is an individual of rare politeness?

The evening of the ninth of July, after bidding my new
acquaintances good-bye, I returned to the *St. Denis,* a small
coasting steamer on which I had come to Ensenada, and the
anchor hoisted, we turned southward. The following afternoon I disembarked at San Quintin, possessed of vividly
amusing recollections of previous adventures in the little
pueblo—and with liberal expectancies of additional experiences to be had. I was not disappointed. After dispatch-
ing a messenger southward for my former mozo, Timoteo,
and for the now recuperated Pedro Ximenez—having given
out months before, he had been left at Rosario—I took
notice of the people about me.

Some fifteen or sixteen men had landed from the steamer,
two of them being accompanied by their wives, plucky, un-
obtrusive women. The entire company seemed interested
in mining, either as promoters or investors. For the most
part they were wide-awake Americans, with just a leavening
of well-bred young Englishmen. Immediately after our
landing, activities focussed about a frame building, part
Customs House, part hotel and altogether the largest structure in San Quintin. Here I again met Sr. Victoria, now in
charge of the Customs, here I found two hustling, agreeable

Ensenada

Reproduced from "The Mother of California," by
courtesy of the publishers, Paul Elder & Company.

Americans, sometime whalers and, according to ever uncertain rumor, smugglers as well, now peaceful storekeepers and proprietors of the hotel.

But the first individuals that I especially noted, as I grew observant, were two swarthy fellows with the treading-high air of those homeward bound and well pleased thereat. I made their acquaintance forthwith. They were scientific men, just in from Cedros Island where they had been collecting for Harvard University and the John Thayer Institute. Until their departure, via the northward bound *St. Denis* on the 12th instant, we passed the time pleasantly, even enjoying several close bridge games with one of the Englishmen as fourth man. My attention was also early drawn toward an elderly, quiet-mannered wanderer. As he proved to be a miner just in from four months' prospecting on San Pedro Mártir Sierra, whither I was bound, I questioned him freely. He was a kindly old hermit, ready to laugh heartily over the recollection of his chilly spring near the snow line and his panic in March when awakened by a severe earthquake. Of the general topography of the sierra he was frankly ignorant. In fact, though the storekeepers and several of the local residents had hunted or mined on its southern and western slopes none of them knew it as a whole. Moreover, as it was unsurveyed and uncharted, people who ventured upon it would surely get lost. So insistently did they make this declaration that my interest in the not infrequently visited Sierra was increased immediately. If there was a fair chance of getting lost in such a region of game and water, I was anxious for my chance, for to be lost under such circumstances would surely be fascinating.

On the *St. Denis* I had met an energetic, vivacious promoter, Brown by name, a man long associated with the Northern District, and one whose very vitality made him

interesting. Through his initiative, keenly seconded by one
of the proprietors of the store, a *baile grande,* or grand ball,
was given the evening of the 10th. The scene of the func-
tion was the hotel dining-room. At San Ignacio and other
southerly pueblos I had attended *bailes,* but this one was a
more cosmopolitan affair, not unlike an American frontier
social event. The dancers consisted of eight Señoritas, two
American women, wives of San Francisco "refugees"
stranded, Heaven knows how, at San Quintin; a dozen
American and English mining men, five Mexicans, the scientists and myself. A wheezy phonograph provided music,
while beer and mescal were on hand for the thirsty. A native audience of mothers and babies, grandmothers and little children, sat on chairs and benches close against the wall
and in blissful content silently enjoyed the succeeding hours.

The women dancers were dressed in simple, attractive
gowns, but the English and American men were laughable
to behold. A stocky, middle-aged mine owner, wearing
great goggles over his small, near-sighted eyes, presented
himself attired in a black frock coat, very baggy khaki riding bags, gaiters—and no stockings! Two of the Englishmen wore dark green puttees, swathed close about their
bulging calves, while three of us Americans appeared in riding clothes with leather leggins and heavy shoes. It was a
bizarre scene. Here a handsome young mining engineer glid-
ing over the floor with a swaying, graceful little *muchaha,*
his thoughts perhaps harking back to some collegiate cotil-
lon; there an erect young Britisher, with Oxford yet fresh
in mind, soberly footing the mazes of a rollicking waltz
and primly holding at arm's length a brown little *muchacha,*
all a-fire with the excitement of her first *baile grande;* here a
sturdy American miner galloping with a swarthy Señorita,
her flashing eyes and striking features betokening Apache
ancestry; there a Harvard scientist, bravely seeking to de-

spoil a native dandy of half a dance. One of the American refugees and three of the little Señoritas—mere girls of fourteen—were really excellent dancers, far and away above the others, and for their favors there sprang up a gay rivalry between a young English mine owner, an American mining expert, one of the scientists and myself. Furthermore, each of the little Señoritas had a particular native cavalier, vainly claiming monopoly and effervescing with frenzied jealousy at sight of our attentions.

At midnight heaping baskets of *cascarones* (blown eggs, stuffed with many colored confetti) suddenly and mysteriously appeared, and in an instant eggs were cracking on dark and fair heads alike and the room was a-glitter with a shower of brilliant confetti. In another hour some of the miners grew uproarious and in wild glee and with most uncertain aim began shying bottles at a serious beetle, leisurly intent on promenading across the ceiling. Even amid this excitement the shy little Señoritas would venture upon no more extensive conversation than *"Si, Señor,"* or *"No, Señor."* By two A. M. the men were growing weary. Three of us, however, doffing our coats heroically kept on. An hour later a thoughtful miner jammed a mescal bottle in the phonograph. That ended the *baile grande*.

For two days thereafter San Quintin was agog with the bustle of departing outfits. Then, with much shouting of mozos and sharp tinkling of bells, a long line of riders and pack trains swung out upon *El Camino Real* en route for the southern mines, while the balance of the prospectors, under the leadership of Brown, embarked on a schooner bound for Cedros Island. Meantime the *St. Denis* had departed for the north, leaving San Quintin to slumber once again and its hungry hordes of accursed fleas to devote their exclusive attention to me. Fortunately for my peace, my temper and my soul, I had an invitation from one of the outward bound passengers* to visit his mines at Valledaras on the west slope of San Pedro Mártir Sierra. Accordingly, goaded to desperation by the greedy tormenters, I hastily loaded my camp equipage and supplies on the Valledaras four-mule freighter and upon the arrival of Timoteo, the two of us climbed up beside the Indian driver, thankful to escape from San Quintin without further delay. At the same time mounting a Mexican boy on Pedro, I dispatched him northward with instructions to secure five burros at the Rancho of San Antonio del Mar, where my faithful Cabrillo had been reared, and to bring them to Valledaras.

The first evening out, after having covered twenty-one miles, we made camp beside a stream near the Dominican Mission of Santo Domingo. As two of their friars resided here as late as 1854, this establishment may be regarded as the last stronghold of the Dominicans in Lower California. Moreover, as the ruins even yet boast standing walls and one room intact, Santo Domingo may be looked upon as the best preserved of the Dominican foundations on the Peninsula. An Indian showed me the contents of the one room: some candle-sticks, figures of Our Lady, of Santo Domingo —quite a dandy—of San Rafael, of San Antonio and of San Pedro Mártir. This last image had suffered special martyrdom of its own, having been pierced by a rifle ball. In the earliest days of Santo Domingo Mission, the worthy friars said Mass in the caves of a lofty red cliff, a mile below the mission site, and this cliff the natives still refer to as the Old Mission.

Almost in the shadow of this *Misión Viejo* there is a pretty flower- and vine-clad cottage, surrounded by orange trees. Here two elderly Canadians, a brother and widowed sister, make their peaceful home. As this gentle couple had shown me extreme kindness in February, I now called

---

* The lamented C. J. Young, since then foully murdered.

to express my appreciation, telling them that I had not forgotten their homelike attentions given at a time when I was sick and dispirited. Vigorous in the aggressive health of continued outdoor life, I was distressed to find the sister's daughter suffering with erysipelas. Concerning the gravity of her misfortune—there was no physician to be had—the young invalid was silent. She made eager inquiries, however, about various portions of the Southern District and then spoke with sweet enthusiasm concerning her "neighbor," an American born girl residing at San Antonio del Mar, forty-five miles to the north.

"In January you visited San Antonio del Mar and Miss Bertie was then at Socorro," said she. "Now you are going to Socorro and she is down by the sea. It's a shame!"

"It is too bad," I replied, smiling at her ardor. "She must be a marvelous young woman to win the praise that natives and foreigners alike lavish upon her very name."

"You must not laugh," said the invalid, in a hurt tone. "She's the most interesting personality in all this countryside—and yet I can't describe her. Though she has lived in these wilds since babyhood, she has the gentle traits you may find in the girls at home. And I must tell you about her pluck. Once during the absence of her men folks, she heard that some marauding Indians and Mexicans were about to make off with a bunch of her father's range cattle. Without pausing for rest or giving thought to the risk, she rode for thirteen hours; indeed, using up two saddle horses, the range riding was so rough. She saved all the cattle. Another time she was in San Diego with her father. A man of considerable means, he coolly pointed out a magnificent eastern residence to her, saying, "Bertie, you girls mustn't remain Amazons. I think I'll buy that place for you." She knew that he might be in earnest. "Oh, you wouldn't make us live in a city," she cried. "Town life must be so crowded. Can't we always live in the sierras? There we can breathe."

"Good for her," I cried, applauding. "I am converted, without even having seen your heroine."

The ensuing day we passed the rancho of Camalú, camping in the foothills at Burro Spring. Early the following morning we were awakened by a wild yell from our stalwart Indian driver. A gopher had rubbed against the powerful chief's spear hand! The sixteenth found us up among the spurs of San Pedro Mártir Sierra, where quail, coyotes and rabbits were plentiful, the air crisp and the nights dewy. The seventeenth we attained an elevation of over four thousand feet, then, with squeaking wheels and brakes and dragging chains, slid down into a deep arroyo by the sheerest pitch I have ever heard termed a wagon grade. Crossing a clear, willow-bordered stream, we followed a good road which shortly brought us to the gold placers of Valledaras. Here, set in an amphitheater of the mountains, was a swaying field of green alfalfa, bordered by fine oaks, a water ditch, hydraulic rams, miners' cabins and picturesque Indian shacks. Well up among the mountain spurs, we were now at the end of the wagon road and in the very shadow of the heights of San Pedro Mártir Sierra, the "Top of the Peninsula."

CHAPTER XXI.

THE TOP OF THE PENINSULA*

THE day after our arrival at Valledaras I rode northward through the sierras ten miles to a giant scoop amid the ridges where a water ditch, reservoirs, gold placers, adobes and miners' cabins stood out in sharp contrast against the unchanging olive green of the surrounding chemise brush. This was Socorro, the mining property of an American family, the proprietors of Rancho San Antonio del Mar. Certain of these good people I had met in January at their rancho, quickly recognizing in them the highest type of American frontiersmen and women. Now, with added pleasure, I made the acquaintance of the remaining members of this sturdy family, including a dark-eyed fine spirited young girl of barely twenty. This latter was "Miss Bertie." Possessed of quiet dignity and a certain direct manner quite in accord with the strong character written in her face, she seemed worthy of the characterization, given her by the invalid at Santo Domingo, of being "the most interesting personality in all the countryside."

Twenty-four hours after my arrival at Socorro, Timoteo rode in from Valledaras with news that the Mexican boy, unsuccessful in his mission, had arrived with Pedro Ximenes.

Accordingly, accepting four burros proffered by my kindly host, early the ensuing morning Timoteo and I returned with them to Valledaras where we loaded on our sup-

---

* Republished, in part, from the *Bulletin* of the American Geographical Society for September, 1907.

plies. Then we traveled easterly until we arrived at the rancho of Santa Cruz.

The real ascent of San Pedro Mártir Sierra was now before us. This was the 20th of July. Thereafter, and until the 13th of August, we traveled steadily up and down and about the craggy mountain. No chart or complete description of this magnificent sierra has ever been published, a rather surprising circumstance in view of the fact that in recent years its inviting glades have become the most frequent goal for visitors to the interior of Lower California. Perhaps the very grandeur of the views off the eastern slope, defying description as they do, may, in part, explain this seeming neglect.

San Pedro Mártir Sierra is not an isolated peak, essentially distinct from the mountain chain of the Peninsula. On the contrary, it is a plateau section of that chain, a lofty region where the mighty back-bone of the Lower California cordilleras have attained to their supreme height. Doubtless some of the admirals of the brilliant Conquistador, Cortez, in their voyages up the Vermilion Sea in search of a Northwest Passage, were the first civilized men to behold the mighty mountain hulk, while Cabrillo, sailing northward along the Pacific coast, perhaps first studied its white outlines from the west. In the year 1702, Padre Kino, the famous Jesuit explorer, made note in his journal of seeing the Sierra, and sixty-three years later Padre Link, the founder of San Borja Mission, came within a few leagues of its southern spurs. If I have read correctly one of the old chronicles of San Borja, he was only saved from death at the hands of a vast multitude of mountain Indians by the intervention of a woman who, although she accompanied the savages, was decently clothed, of regal bearing and keen understanding. After founding his Lower California Mission of San Fernando, good Padre Junipero Serra traveled

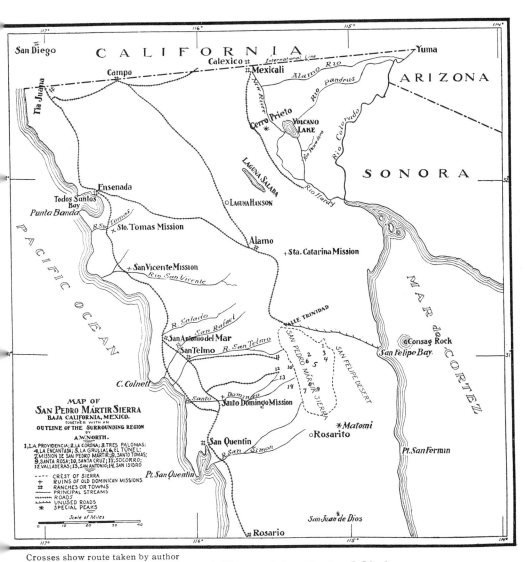

Crosses show route taken by author

The uncharted Sierra of San Pedro Mártir

around the southern and western spurs of the Sierra on his
historic journey northward to San Diego and the field of
his famed mission work in Upper California. Later Padre
Cayetano Pallas established the Dominican Mission of San
Pedro Mártir de Verona on the southwestern crest of the
Sierra and twelve leagues east of the Mission of Santo Domingo. Two years thereafter, in 1796, Lieutenant Governor Arrilliga made an official visit to the new mission, only
to find that the neophytes had fled in a body and were unwilling to return until a new Padre was conceded to them.
So much for history.

The trend of the California peninsula is southeast and
northwest and so, also, is the trend of its greatest sierra.
Approximating from the coast line charting of the little
known territory, the geographical bounds of San Pedro
Mártir Sierra are as follows, viz.: at the north, 31° 5′ latitude, north, and 115° 40′ and 115° 5′ longitude, west; at
the south, 30° 25′ latitude, north, and 115° 20′ and 115°
longitude, west. Out in long sweeps from the western crest
of the Sierra, reach a series of rugged spurs, some of them
only breaking against the shore line of the Pacific Ocean
over fifty miles distant; to the east, with appalling sublim-
ity, sheer precipices and sharp granite ridges bridge the im-
mensity of space between the crest and the San Felipe Desert
reaching back from the barren hills down against the Gulf;
to the south the main ridge breaks, merging into hills only
to rise again, later, in the vicinity of the heights of Matomi
and San Juan de Dios. To the north, also, the sierra range
lessens until at *Valle Trinidad* (Trinity Valley) it loses its
identity.

The main crest of the Sierra is approximately fifteen
leagues in length by three and a half in breadth. This lofty
area is occupied by grassy meadows, timber covered swales,
cross ridges and *picachos*. There are perennial springs,

cold streams, and at the meadow of *La Grulla* (the Crane) a small lake. The sierra is snow clad in winter and early spring, while summer thunder storms feed its hurrying streams.

Beginning at the south and passing northward along the crest the successive meadows are known as Sant' Eulalia, Santa Rosa and Santo Tomás, El Misión or San Mártir, *La Grulla, L'Encentata* (the Enchanted, so called on account of the ease with which, owing to its secluded position, it seemingly eludes the traveler), and *Vallecitos* (Little Valley.) These meadows, each containing from one to two thousand acres of verdant plain, are connected by indistinct and broken cattle trails which criss-cross the sierra.

Scattered broadcast along the crest lie massive white and gray granite boulders, while here and there stately white granite picachos loom upward spurning haughtily the level of their surroundings. To the immediate north of L'Encentata three of these picachos, the *Tres Palomas* (Three Doves), are ranged side by side. Farther north a mighty peak, *El Providencia* (The Divinity, Providence)—also known as *El Picacho Blanco* (The White Peak) —rises high above the clouds, the jagged summit of all Baja California, the unchallenged retreat of lions and mountain sheep, the unscaled lookout of eagles and mighty condors. The glittering granite sides of this majestic peak glisten in the sun as though robed in purest snow and even from the banks of the Colorado, a hundred miles away, its jagged white pinnacle juts boldly above the sky line. *La Corona* (The Crown), a high, timber-capped ridge to the southwest of El Providencia, vies with the latter in height, attaining an altitude slightly in excess of ten thousand feet. A third, and almost equally lofty ridge, lies to the north of Corona and is unnamed. A small, rock-bound meadow is concealed below the summit of this ridge and here the ruins of an old shack with a stone foundation indicate the one-time retreat of a notorious gang of horse thieves who occupied the sierra some years ago, their operations extending from Baja California over into California and Sonora.

Pines are a rarity on the peninsula. On the crest, however, of San Pedro Mártir—from a distance apparently a gigantic mass of barren white cliffs—spruce, cypress, tamarack, fir, incense cedar, yellow pine and sugar pine, the pitch pine and the pine that bears the piñons beloved by the Indians, flourish and fearlessly invade the meadows and the granite ridges. About the streams the aspen and the willow, ferns and wild flowers cluster, forming cool enticing nooks, and yet the awful chasm which primeval forces gashed into the northern and western sides of the sierra, shaping courses for these same streams to rush down and lose themselves in the San Felipe Desert, are grim and forbidding.

In making an ascent of the sierra, either from Valledaras or Socorro, the traveler rises slowly for a league, then, with a sharp upward pitch, the trail zigzags nerve-rackingly skyward two or three thousand feet, winding in and out of the white granite boulders and cliffs and leaving behind the mines and the Mexican and Indian ranchos of Santa Cruz, San Antonio, and San Isidro. Finally, mountain benches, six or seven thousand feet above the sea level are reached, pines and grass bound streams appear unexpectedly, the lower world becomes a vista of distant peaks—and the crest of San Pedro Mártir Sierra is attained. The traveler now finds himself in a new world, totally unlike the balance of Baja California, a world where he may wander at will; for condors and eagles, wild ducks, mountain quail, deer, wild cats, lions, coyotes, half wild horses and cattle—descendants of the herds of the Frailes—alone dwell on the crest. During short periods native vaqueros occupy shacks at the meadows of Santo Tomás and La Grulla, but the crisp nights and mornings, most invigorating to northern blood, are little relished by the Mexicans.

Throughout Lower California the deer are rapidly disappearing. On San Pedro Mártir Sierra they will soon be a tradition; and yet, in the open forest glades, they add wonderfully to the charm. They are too easily killed, however, to long survive professional hunters and amateur butchers. Until the middle of the nineteenth century large gray wolves roamed over the great sierra; the last one seen was killed in 1903. In the early eighties a lone bear took up his temporary abode on the mountain crest, doubtless enjoying himself hugely, for the native hunters fled in dismay before his tracks, reporting that the Devil was at large on the Sierra. In even the most remote regions of the peninsula bears are unknown. The mountain sheep is the best protected variety of game on San Pedro Mártir Sierra. Among the barren crags along the well nigh inaccessible eastern and southeastern sections of the sierra, numbers of these magnificent creatures live almost in undisturbed content, lending an additional picturesqueness to the majestic scenery.

In prehistoric times a race of people drew petroglyphs on cliffs in the deep cañons about San Pedro Mártir Sierra —and drew them where men of modern stature may not reach. They were succeeded by a tribe of Indians who were also of magnificent physique, for six feet is but an ordinary height among the Kaliwas, the descendants of these old-time red men. The Kaliwas are stalwart, dark-skinned, people. They live in the *rancherias* of Arroyo Leon, Janook and San Antonio, small clusters of thatch and pole shacks situated upon the northern slope of the sierra and within easy journeying of the piñon trees. Mixed bloods from this tribe are found at many of the Mexican ranchos

north and west of the sierra. According to the old Jesuit
Link, the Indians on the southern slopes of the mighty sierra
that blocked his northern explorations lived in houses of
wood, but he may have used "houses" relatively, referring
merely to shacks.

The Dominican Mission of San Pedro Mártir de Verona
was erected on rising ground at the northern edge of a well
watered meadow. The walls are now nearly level with the
ground. The buildings were of adobe, built around the
usual court. They faced slightly east of south and covered
a space eighty-five paces by fifty-seven, with entrances at the
north and south. From the outline of the ruins there were
apparently two small forts near the southwest corner of the
mission, and a stock enclosure, with an area of eighty-five
by twenty-nine paces, adjoined the walls at the north. There
was also a defensive wall of some sort extending southeasterly from the northeast corner of the main court. As I found
pieces of old red tiling about the ruins, I assume that tile
roofs were in use at San Pedro Mártir Mission, although the
Lower California establishments were usually roofed with
cement and gravel, or with thatch.

According to tradition, three-quarters of a century ago
this mission suffered so frequently at the hands of the Kaliwas that soldiers and armed Indian converts from the missions of San Vicente and Santo Domingo were sent forth to
subdue the troublesome ones. As the Indians all delighted
in warfare and as each tribe considered the others its enemies, one may imagine the holy joy with which the Indian
converts (?) entered upon the pursuit of the *"broncos."* Before the dread firearms the latter eventually capitulated and,
bound hand and foot, they were carried down from the
mountain crest, tied behind their mounted conquerors.
Later, the captives were put to work at the Missions of
Santo Tomás, San Vicente and Santo Domingo, where lung

infirmities shortly decimated their numbers. At this time brief visits to the crest of the sierra in search of piñons or venison mark the utmost extent of any Kaliwa's interest in the old haunts of his tribe.

Written references to San Pedro Mártir Sierra have been so rare during the past century that one might count them upon the fingers of one hand. In the "Historical Summary of Lower California History", written by the early California historian, A. S. Taylor, and brought out forty years ago by J. Ross Browne, a lone paragraph appeared concerning a lofty, snow covered peak lying between the Missions of San Fernando and Santa Catarina. In 1894, Mr. George Gould hunted mountain sheep along the northern spurs of the sierra and his experiences are recorded in a publication of the Boone and Crockett Club, brought forth in the nineties by Colonel Theodore Roosevelt. Eight years later, Mr. Edmund Heller, of the Field Columbian Museum of Chicago, collected mammals along the western half of the sierra and a report of his doings is on file in the archives of the museum. The ensuing account of San Pedro Mártir Sierra, giving it an unwonted name, is quoted from the "West Coast of Mexico," prepared by the Hydrographic Office of the United States Navy from data furnished during the seventies by Commander George Dewey of the U. S. S. *Narragansett*. This book was published in 1880 and in subsequent reprints the same improper designation has been given the sierra; moreover, in consequence of this governmental error, recent French and Mexican writers have committed the same blunder.

"Calamahue Mountain," says the account, "sometimes called Santa Catalina Mountain, from the Mission of that name near its foot, lies 28½ miles S. 84 W. (W. by S. ¾ mag.) from Point San Felipe. It has a whitish appearance with a jagged top, and is the highest mountain in Lower

California, having an elevation of 10,126 feet above the sea level, and can be seen in clear weather a distance of over 100 miles. Strange as it may appear it was never set down on any chart until those of the *Narragansett's* survey, 1873 to 1875, were published. Father Kino speaks of it, in 1702, as being covered with snow during the winter and spring.

"There is said to be in the vicinity of Mount Calamahue, a large mountain lake, which feeds the various small streams that flow toward the Pacific coast.

"The Cocupa Indians, who inhabit some parts of this region, report the existence of gold there, and they occasionally come to the Colorado River bringing nuggets of pure gold with them, which they trade off. They do not permit white men to enter that part of the country which they inhabit, and thus far have succeeded in keeping undisputed possession of their treasure, . . .

"The coast from San Felipe Point to the mouth of the Colorado River, a distance of about thirty miles, trends nearly due north."

To my numerous inquiries made throughout Lower California concerning the mountain's name, San Pedro Mártir Sierra has ever been the unfailing response. Survivors of the once numerous tribes of the Pais, Kaliwas, Santa Catarina Yumas and Cocupa Indians, who, from time immemorial, have visited the mountain in war and for game, piñons or gold, invariably say that San Pedro Mártir has been the sierra's title for a long, long time and that they have never known the names of Calamahue or Santa Catalina to be associated with it. In this the Mexican and foreign residents concur. Moreover, the Mission of San Pedro Mártir de Verona was established upon the crest in the year 1794, and this was full three years prior to the foundation of the Mission of Santa Catarina, or Catalina—which, by the way, is fifty miles to the north of and not "near the foot" of the mountain. Unquestionably the sierra derived its name from the Mission of San Pedro Mártir. "Calamahue

Mountain" is a misnomer, a name entirely without authority.

In the days of the *Frailes,* as the Dominican Friars were termed by the Indians, mountain crest and mission were reached by four different caminos. The Sierra Camino Real passed directly through the mission grounds, coming in from *Agua Dulce,* San Fernando and the Ranchos of San Juan de Dios and Rosarito at the south and continuing along the sierra crest and down its northern slope whence it crossed Valle Trinidad making straight for Santa Catarina Mission. A branch trail of the Gulfo Camino crossed a dozen leagues of arid hills and desert swale from the Bay of San Felipe to the mouth of the Santa Rosa Arroyo, thence by an ascent rapidly increasing in dizziness, bore upward to the crest whence it wore along nearly due west to the mission. A third trail—and an excellent one—approached the mission from the west, heading at Santo Domingo Mission, down on the Pacifico Camino.

By this last trail Timoteo and I reached the mountain crest on the 25th of July. From the mission ruins—in recent years even the ghostly walls were put through the gold pans of treasure hunters vainly searching for the traditional buried wealth of the Frailes—we crossed and criss-crossed the crest, following old trails which invariably died out and left us to the guidance of my compass. Finally, the magnetic needle was put out of commission by a fall which I had. Thereafter we roamed at will. But while this method of traveling was giving me an absolute familiarity with the sierra, it was wearing upon the nerves of my mozo. I had engaged him not only because he was a good packer but more especially because he was a good packer who had never been on the San Pedro Mártir Sierra, for to my mind when one really wishes to explore any section of country the ordinary guide is an abomination, being ever ready to cook up most alarming stories in opposition to any route other than the cut and dried one with which he chances to be familiar. On the evening of the 29th of July, we made camp in a particularly eerie gorge and my man lost his nerve.

"Señor, where are we?" he asked, in trepidation.

"On top of San Pedro Mártir Sierra."

This simple response failed to calm him. "Señor, are not you afraid?"

I laughed. "What is there to fear?" And as elements of security I pointed successively to my fire-arms, the provision packs, two freshly killed deer, my outfit and the clear stream flowing not ten feet away.

"We are alone, Señor, in a wild place which neither of us has ever before seen!"

Had I told him that these very elements doubled the interest of our camp, he would not have understood me. I therefore asked, "Do you not know that until our time comes, nothing can injure us? that when it comes there will be no escape? that there is only one death?"

The Mexican pondered a moment over this fatalistic view that is so quieting for those who venture into dangerous places. Then, as a lion screeched inanely in the crags above, he made response, "Señor, that may be well for a single man. I have a family to consider."

Certainly there is an uncalled for dread of the recesses of San Pedro Mártir Sierra, and with equal certainty the proper companion for the mountains is hard to find. Finally, Timoteo expressed a willingness to travel about the Sierra, provided there was a third man in my party; but he would not follow me on my proposed trip across the deserts to the Colorado River.

Two days later we left the crest by the Santa Cruz Camino, a steep but plain trail leading westward from La Grulla, and returned to Socorro. In vain, however, did I inquire among the Mexicans and Indians about the mines for a mozo willing to cross the deserts to the Colorado. They did not know the way, they said; one man knew the route but considered such a trip in August certain death. Ultimately, when I stated my determination of continuing though I went alone, even the good Americans remonstrated, advising me to reconsider my course.

Then upon the scene appeared the "Colonel." We had met in January at San Antonio del Mar. Of long locks and matted beard, sharp-eyed, slight, wiry and agile, part and parcel of his steed: such is my friend the "Colonel." An orphan early thrown on the world, he entered, at the age of twelve the Confederate Secret Service. As a Rebel spy, his sense of duty to his cause became so a part of his nature that deep contrition marked his confession to me that, on one occasion, he had let slip a clear opportunity of bagging a Union cavalryman—merely because he feared, the trooper being a sister's husband, that the man's death might bring tears to her eyes! The feeling that this unsportsmanlike omission savored of treason and mawkish susceptibility still rankles in the mind of the Colonel; indeed, as he naively explained, except for this most regrettable case of youthful weakness, he has always made a point of never allowing his sentiment to interfere with his shootings. The war over, he drifted to the cow trail in Texas; later, Indian fighting in Colorado claimed his attention; for a time, gambling at Deadwood enthralled him. Eventually, however, the south and the west alike became too tranquil for a man accustomed to an active life and, in 1887, the Colonel crossed the Border. Though he carries over fifty years and has, at various times, gone down before pistol bullet or rolling mustang, his energy is unimpaired, as I early discovered when he held me even in a sprint after runaway burros, notwithstanding certain and numerous hours which I had devoted to the cinder path in the nineties.

The Colonel

My New Year's experiences with the Catarinas had reached the Colonel's ears and he pined to be with me now that I had planned revisiting that predatory tribe. I did not deny him the pleasure. In fact, had there been occasion for urging, I would willingly have drawn upon my entire reserve of persuasion.

"―― ―― it," he began, greeting my invitation with sulphurous sincerity, "if none of the ―― ―― ―― Mexs and Indians 'll go with you, an' you're so Hell-fired set on goin', I'll make the trip. ―― ―― ―― me, if I'll see a white man tackle a ―― ―― ―― ride like that alone. An' from what I hear there's like to be somethin' doin' when we meet them Yumas."

"Colonel," said I, warmly, "you're a gentleman."

"An' no offense, but you're a ―― ―― fool, that's what you are, goin' onto them deserts in August. An' you're a man of my own kind. An' before we start, I'd appreciate your fixin' up my will for me for those deserts 'll be ―― ―― thirsty."

That evening Lettie and Lollie, the youngest members of the pioneer family, besought me to write down for them the words of some song. To their delight I immediately gave them the lines:

"I went to the animals' fair,
"The birds and the beasts were there," etc., etc.,

the monkey refrain of which had served many times to put life into my depressed or wearied mozos. I then wrote out for them that classic, the "Spider Song," the one that runs thus:

"Oh, the blooming, bloody spider went up the water spout,
The blooming, bloody rain came down and washed the
    spider out,

The blooming, bloody sun came out and dried up all the rain,
And the blooming, bloody spider came up the spout again."

This so delighted Lollie that as a reciprocal favor she volunteered to visit certain old Indian friends of hers and obtain for me specimens of their songs.

The following morning, reinforced by the Colonel and an American mining man from South America, Timoteo and I reascended the sierra by the Socorro Camino. This time we found camped at Vallecitos a plucky American woman, surrounded by her boys and girls. I invited one of the young fellows, a sturdy looking chap, keen for a good shoot, to accompany us to the Colorado, but either my rough appearance or the statement of his alarmed San Quintin guide (?) that the Cocupas would scalp us, caused him to decline.

On this trip I completed my examination of the sources of the various immense cañons that swing out from the sides of San Pedro Mártir Sierra. Beginning at the southeast and continuing to the east these arroyos are known as Agua Caliente, Santa Rosa, Providencia and Arroyo Diablo—in its fearful majesty well earning this name; Arroyo Copal, Arroyo Esperancia and Arroyo San Mattias which trend northward; Arroyo Leon, Arroyo Wecks (Lizard), Arroyo San Rafael and Arroyo San Pedro take westerly courses, while Valledaras and San Antonio Arroyos at the west and southwest ultimately unite, forming Santo Domingo Arroyo, which empties into the Pacific leagues distant. San Antonio Arroyo, formed by the junction of the water courses from the old mission and from La Grulla—which, at its headwaters, is called *La Zanca* (The Shank)—is the one trout stream in Lower California.

Well supplied with venison, we shortly returned to Socorro, following the Corona and Concepción Caminos

that we might leave at the Concepción Rancho a supply of
fresh meat with a married sister of Miss Bertie. This
energetic matron was busily looking after a ranch while her
husband was managing a mine leagues distant. Except for
her three little children and a faithful Mexican girl, she
was alone and unprotected in the mountain wilderness.

"Madam, are you not in continual fear?" I ventured.

"I and my little people are in continual good health," she
answered, amused at my amazed expression. Then, becoming serious, she added, "I was born in the States. There
I would not have dared live so alone. Here, there are few
wanderers and no tramps. The Indian and Mexican women
consider me their friend—I give them medicines and treat
them kindly. The men keep their distance. They know
that my hound would notify me of their approach, and that
I am armed. They realize that while father has taught my
brothers to be slow in using arms mother has always cautioned us girls to shoot at the first provocation. Moreover,
they know that even though they escaped my revolver, they
could not escape such indefatigable trackers as my husband,
my father, my brothers, the Colonel and my native friends
who would follow them down and shoot them like dogs.
No, here I am safe from insult."

At Socorro I returned the borrowed burros and bought
three in their places. These I named "Padre Hernando
Consag", after the great Jesuit explorer; "Guillermo
Walker", after the American filibuster, and "James O.
Pattie," in honor of the early American trapper. Having
approved of this christening, Lollie confided to me her store
of original Indian philology which she had acquired from
certain ancient native friends. "I had quite a time, at first,"
said she, "they wanted to show me that they understood
Spanish, but I held them down to their own lingo."

Spelling the words phonetically, I submit the following

as examples of Pais and Kaliwa words, *à la* Lollie, viz.:

> "*Hu-pa ma hup; sing ye, a mi wai-sa,*" (repeat).
> "*A no-che, cheu spili pow-wow, cheu spili pow-wow,*
> "*Yu-i, myu-mai, chi-wamai ka-ka, chi-wami kaka.*"

The first line constitutes the old war song of the Pais, the second and third an ancient love song, still in use among that tribe. From the Kaliwas come these jaw breaking words: *Pahamehamakaipa* (An American); *Marashree-pahachahamakaipa* (An American Girl); *Chibiskwi-kwiro* (wire); *Mezai* (Good), and *Mahâ* (Meat).

With my new burros, together with three of the Colonel's picked broncos—one of which, Winnie, I soon purchased—the Colonel and I were now prepared for our venturesome trip. After some hesitancy my mozo decided to accompany us as far as Valle Trinidad. Poor fellow, the Mexicans and Indians had told him such terrifying yarns that his fears were not surprising! Immediately prior to our departure Miss Bertie baked for us a choice batch of biscuits and an entire haunch of venison. Lettie and Lollie, meantime, introduced me to a nest of "yellow-jackets" from which I fled, ingloriously; their father cautioned us to keep our canteens and barrel filled against thirst and their mother privately instructed the Colonel, and later on admonished me, to be kind to the stock and good-tempered to each other.

As I bade the kindly matron good-bye, I said, "Let me take back to civilization your receipt for bringing up sons and daughters. I've met seven of your children and more industrious or happier young people I have yet to see. Here, for instance, at the end of the world, you have three attractive young girls. They cook, milk cows, round up cattle, sew, wash dishes and clothing, iron, "break" stock, 'tend store, look after the mining reservoirs; they work from daylight to darkness; they are always running or trotting, they never drag listlessly about. They sing at their work; they find odd minutes in which to read books and magazines; they are happy without company and retire early without complaining. Such contented girls I never have seen elsewhere. How have you done it?"

At first surprised, then amused, the mother listened to my long inquiry. "Well," said she, "I was married at sixteen. Some of the women in my family—my father was a minister of the gospel—suffered from ill health. Upon marrying I decided to live an out-door life. Only twice since then have doctors entered my home. I have borne ten children. Nine live. I have taught them to respect the law, be honest, avoid going into debt, be industrious and be thoughtful of each other. In childhood each one of them at some one time thwarted my will; in each case, first carefully explaining why I was right, I have absolutely insisted on my stand. Every one of them has been given his chance to make some money individually. That's all. I guess they've just come up in the fresh air."

Reascending the sierra by an unnamed suggestion of a trail, I quickly crossed the crest with my outfit and came to a halt at the head of the Santa Rosa Arroyo. The Camino Real at the south, and the Agua Caliente Camino at the southeast, were so distinct as not to require exploration; here, however, was the beginning of the ancient and forgotten Santa Rosa Camino. Taking a brace on ourselves, we started downwards. The Santa Rosa is one of the two most diabolical caminos in all Lower California! Moreover, and with my compliments, the San Felipe Desert is a mighty bad place to visit in summer. Thus after a frosty morning on the crest we found ourselves at night stretched out on burning sand with the thermometer registering 112 degrees.

CHAPTER XXII

WITH August now well advanced, the Lower California deserts were vast, broiling sand-spits, catching the fullness of the sun's rays and sullenly holding their heat during the short, breathless nights. Even the craggy sierras glistened and baked under the great, glaring, unveiled eye of fire. Those who venture into such an atmosphere grow chary of words, bowing before the heat by day, and cursing it and their own foolhardiness when the horizon puts away the sun for the night.

Thus had the day passed with the Colonel and myself, descending the sierra slope, and thus, as we sought rest in the evening, he burst forth, "Curse it, curse it, curse this heat," he cried, wildly, "the cursed earth is a-fire burning through my blanket. With nothin' over me I'm burnin' up. The near way down's been the way of the sun to-day. How damn hot is it, anyway?"

"It's 112 dgrees, and 7:45 P. M.," I replied shortly, after consulting both thermometer and watch.

"Don't wonder your *mozo* didn't want to tackle the San Felipe and Colorado Deserts this time o' year."

We were silent a few minutes.

"Colonel," I then queried, "my head's bad. Do you suppose this heat has phased me?"

The old frontiersman grunted. "Dunno, it's main queer for a man to see things. Better git some sleep. I'll bet that desert 'll be hell-fired hot to-morrow."

Half an hour earlier, as we were unsaddling on the edge of a *tinaja* in the frightful arroyo down which we had come eastward out of San Pedro Mártir Sierra, I had vainly endeavored to point out to my companion what seemed to be a large black animal moving among the white boulders on the mountain side, half a mile distant. There are no bears in Baja California, and the Colonel was certain that there could be no such large dark animal as I described.

His sleeping advice was good. Nine hours later I sat up in my blankets, feeling much refreshed, hauled off the jacket of my pajamas, slipped on a thin undershirt, then seized my carbine and half a dozen extra cartridges, leaving the completion of my dressing until a later time; for there had come to my ears from up the mountain side a quick succession of snorts and pig-like grunts followed by a great crashing as of giant boulders falling upon one another. Again my eyes had seen the large dark animal. This time, however, there were two of them and each had bulky shoulders and great rams' horns extending outward. If the heat has affected both my sight and hearing, I thought, as I slipped on a pair of Mexican slippers and hurried down the arroyo, I may as well see what will come of a little shooting.

Fifty yards from camp I crouched down in the concealment of a mesquit and for fifteen minutes watched a knightly combat. High up on the steep granite mountain side two rams were fighting a desperate duel. Backing off ten or fifteen paces, they would rush forward grunting and snorting, their mighty heads bent low and when they crashed together their great horns resounded like rolling boulders. Doubtless, to a disinterested observer the scene would have been amusing: high among the cliffs the two big rams in

tournament engaged, butting each other, oblivious of all
else; and down in the trough of the arroyo, a wild-eyed
hunter in undershirt, pajamas and teguas, rubbing the sleep
out of his eyes and wishing the sun were on the mountain
so that he might see the game distinctly through his carbine
sights.

Finally, an ordinary sized ram, seemingly a referee or a
peacemaker, appeared on the scene and endeavored to separate the combatants. Then the shooting began. At the
second shot the "referee" dropped in his tracks. The others
scattered for the moment, then returned and renewed their
contest. By this time my cartridges were exhausted and I
called for more. The Colonel quickly appeared with an
unbroken box and I climbed upon a boulder and resumed
firing while my companion expostulated, saying that if the
sheep were allowed to fight I could creep closer. But, crude
though it may seem to the polite hunter, to me "shelling"
is far more interesting than stalking, and my carbine was
soon blistering my hands. One ram quickly rushed away to
the right, the other to the left. The latter, as he seemed to
be wounded received attention for full a dozen shots during
which time he fell three times.

We soon had the "referee" in camp though I didn't do
the carrying. He had a short mane and except for his light
rump and nose, was of the darkest mole color; perhaps he
was one of Clavijero's *berrendos negros,* certainly there are
no hides of like color in our museums, although that tireless
sheep hunter, Sheldon of New York, secured one, not unlike it, in Chihuahua.* By the time the ram was in camp
and the pack train ready, the thermometer registered 114
degrees in the shade with higher promises that did not en-
courage us to scramble after the wounded duellist, although
we were certain of his whereabouts owing to the devoted

* Note C: Appendix.

attendance of a ewe that appeared upon a cliff just above where he had fallen at the last shot. As we journeyed toward the mouth of the arroyo, she looked fearlessly down upon us and we, on our part, watched with keenest interest the ease with which she moved up and down the almost perpendicular sides of her lookout point, seeking the best vantage ground for observing our movements.

I left the arroyo realizing that I was losing a wonderful ram, but with the increasing heat and the necessity of hastening across the San Felipe Desert, not even a gold mine would have been an incentive for delay. Indeed, at 10 o'clock, A. M., as we crouched in the poor shade of a *palo verde* waiting for the distant night that might bring a temperature possible for traveling, the Colonel gave brusque expression to his thoughts, "There's no dyin' till your time comes, but ourn may not be just far off."

Even now as I write, the memory of the next ten days is a kaleidoscopic nightmare of privation and tense strain, of simmering deserts, tawny Indians and alluring treasure. Up the San Felipe Desert we fought our way, contending against frightful heat and the impending danger of yet more frightful thirst. Once around the northern spurs of the sierra, Timoteo turned homeward, taking an easy southwesterly trail and leaving the Colonel and me to venture by ourselves among the Catarina Yumas and the Cocupas.

Later as we two huddled close around a grouchy camp fire in the Valle Trinidad, drying out after the drenching of an unexpected thunder storm, an intelligent looking mestizo appeared before us. Receiving the usual invitation, he crouched beside our fire and, after accepting a proffered smoke, entered into friendly conversation in the course of which he met my inquiry about *jeroglificos* by asking whether I had ever seen *"las jarras viejas"* (the ancient jars)—as I understood him—in the Arroyo Grande. Then

our eager questioning brought out the statement that even
a century ago, in the days of his grandfather's youth, these
jarras were in a secluded niche in a high cliff which succeeding generations of Indians had vainly endeavored to
scale. With the advance of the tale the Colonel became as
breathlessly interested as I. Knowingly squinting one eye,
he whispered quietly to me, in English, "Aztec treasure! I
oncst made a great haul that way over in Arizona." The
same thought already possessed me. To our delight, upon
an offer of ten pesos, the mestizo readily agreed to show us
"*las jarras*."

Our minds instantly aflame with alluring mental pictures
of fantastic ancient jars overflowing with Aztec gold and
jewels, we brooked no delay. Pushing on rapidly to the
little mining pueblo of Alamo through which I had passed
seven months before, we halted there just long enough to
purchase such spikes and additional rope as might be useful
in cliff climbing—not forgetting a supply of lemons and an
extra canteen for use on the desert near the Rio Hardy—
then we had hurried back a few miles to the *Rancho Viejo*
where the mestizo awaited us. That name, Rancho Viejo,
looks and sounds excellently well, though it means, simply,
Old Ranch, a most frequent designation for premises on the
Peninsula.

From the rancho we followed an indistinct and ancient
Indian trail, once a part of *El Camino Real*. By nightfall
we were within a quarter of a mile of the ruins of the Santa
Catarina Mission, and near a green vale where a hill shut
us off from the Indians and where a brook of cold water ran
close by. Here we made camp. Though dogs were barking and we could see lights shining out from the shacks at
the further side of the valley, we refrained from making
any visits. After picketing the animals, in place of turning
them loose with hobbles, and throwing his blankets near the

more valuable portion of the outfit, the Colonel seemed to have no further concern about surroundings. For my own part I slept little that night. A cooling dew soon fell, and as we had just left the dry, burning desert, the dampness was refreshing. After over two thousand miles of travel in Lower California, I was ready to give the Mission of Santa Catarina the palm for cool weather.

Early the following morning, we left our outfit in camp and rode up to the *rancheria* where I observed more shacks than before. Two of the new ones were in front of an old oak cross, a relic of the days of the Frailes in whose time it had served to support the mission bells. From these shacks we received friendly greetings and the mestizo stopped for a chat while the Colonel and I rode on to the ex-chief's residence.

I found that the old fellow had not forgotten me. At sight of my camera, Anita, too, smiled in recognition. Of the incidents of New Year's day they seemed in ignorance and I made no mention of their tribe's misdoings but at once proceeded to show the family pictures which I had taken of their shack and of other Indians and of game. The ex-chief was much pleased at a picture of a mountain sheep while Anita and her sister gazed with interest at a picture of a Pais Indian girl. It was soon arranged that I should photograph the entire family, a blind patriarch—father of the ex-chief—the ex-chief himself and his squaw, Anita and her sister and Anita's parents. As a thunder shower was thinking seriously of breaking loose, I was dubious of results. After two snaps, I tried smaller groups and then asked Anita and her father, a big, dark, burly buck, in no way like her, to pose together; but no, Anita would be taken alone, but not with *"him"*.

She was not quite thirteen years of age and her youthful figure was as straight and slender as that of a boyish cadet captain. Her bright eyes were the modest eyes of a child. The sister had a stolid expression like the father's, but Anita's clear-cut features were more Gallic than Indian. Both girls, with their simple gowns, their conventional shoes and stockings, their air of fresh, wholesome neatness, seemed far removed from the wonted squalor of the rancheria.

The old man, the only beggar in the group, asked for tobacco. Later, in response to questioning, he told of the mission days, and, with a senile boast, stated that his tribe had always been "very fierce," that they had quarreled with the Frailes and with the Cocupas, Kaliwas, and neighboring Indian tribes. Rambling along, he related how he and his braves had fought first with and then against Filibuster *"Guillermo"* Walker, and how they had, at another time, joined their relatives, the Yumas, along the Gila, in harassing the caravans en route to the Sacramento Placers.

"I have killed many men," said he, with a grin on his toothless old visage, "but the best was when I killed women and children from those caravans—they had such fine, long scalps." Raising his wizened old arms, he imitated the drawing of a bowstring and the handling of a scalping knife, the meantime chuckling reminiscently. As I looked at the sputtering old villain and thought of the helpless women and children that had died to make up the "best time" of his life, I felt a most ardent desire to turn my six-shooter upon him.

Anita's father now volunteered to show me the old mission bell, though the grandfather seemed doubtful and made some remark which I could not understand. Following three of the Indians, the Colonel and I proceeded to a brush shack about a hundred paces distant. Our guides opened the door of the shack and we found within a large, heavy bell. It was inscribed, *"Santophe* 1757." As I was endeavoring to make a favorable impression on the Indians by raising the old relic from the ground, we heard guttural exclamations and quick hoof beats. I put down the bell and stepped out from the shack just in time to meet an angry Catarina Yuma.

He was the *Capitan,* or chief, it seemed, and as such he objected to a stranger's entering the precincts over which he was guardian. He was mounted on a fiery, black stallion. He carried a knife, which did not look friendly, rode bareback and wore no clothing save a breech-cloth and a *serapa.* My friends made some explanation, the Colonel offered cigarettes and we left the *Capitan* with his bell. As we returned to the other shack, Anita's father explained that this man had supplanted the old chief because the latter drank too much *mescal,* and now this fellow was drunk all the time while the ex-chief had become temperate. It would seem that the excitement of office goes to the head of even a Catarina Yuma. We observed as we rode away that the Indians had a field of over a hundred acres of fine corn and melons.

We traveled hard that day; late in the afternoon we rested a few minutes before the brush camp of a Mexican *vaquero.* Tanned hides were stretched about in wild confusion, and the Mexican, noting that they attracted my attention, remarked that he intended to have them made up into "shaps" and leather pantaloons.

"As you stopped down there by the Catarinas," he continued, "you doubtless saw the well dressed little squaw, Anita. She sews well, she cooks well. In a few days I go to the chief and get her. I am lonely and I have much sewing here to be done."

Somewhat astounded, I looked at him rather cynically. "She is but a child," I explained.

"The better," he answered, "the chief will sell her to me for half a beef."

Before leaving the *rancheria* we had endeavored to persuade the ex-chief to accompany us to the Colorado River. Vain our efforts. In August the Arroyo Grande was well nigh impossible, said the veteran, while, as for the deserts beyond, his people never had ventured upon them in midsummer. Then they were too much like *el Infierno!* Undeterred by these well-meant warnings, we three rode eastward over into the barren country about the spring of *El Tule,* known among the old Pais Indians as *Jacal* or Running Water, thence we hastened onward past Eagle Peak, across thirsty mesas and over rocky ridges. Finally, the third day after our departure from the *rancheria,* down in the narrow depths of the Arroyo Grande, where the slant red cliffs rise to dizzy heights skyward, three swarthy, rough appearing men, reining in their mules, stared upward at a niche fifty feet above the sandy arroyo bottom. The sweltering day was far advanced and in consequence of a vain scramble after an illusive band of mountain sheep two of the men were short of temper and reeking with perspiration.

"*Alli* (there) *las jaras!*" exclaimed one of the two, with an upward jerk of his right hand.

"*No lo veo las jarras*" (I don't see the jars), said the other, impatiently.

"*Alli, alli las jaras*" (There, there, *las jaras*), repeated the first speaker, emphasizing his final word.

"Hell, man, them aint *jarras*," cried the third rider, in a sudden blaze of anger. "—— —— y'u, have y'u bin play'n us?"

As I, the second speaker, caught sight of feathered arrow ends protruding from the rocky niche and realized that these were the "ancient jars" over which the Colonel and I had waxed enthusiastic, the indignation of the imposed took possession of me and I was ready to join the Colonel in roundly cursing the mestizo for "playin'" us.   Meantime the latter had become so astounded by our non-appreciation of his services that cooling down I paid him the agreed ten pesos.   I am glad that I did so, for, though *"la jarra"* means "the jar" and *flecha* is the usual Spanish word for "arrow," I have since learned that *"la jarra,"* Spanish for "the cistus," has an idiomatic meaning of "the dart."   The mestizo had been honest; we, however, had mistaken his *"las jaras"* for *"las jarras."*

Out of curiosity and a desire to show the fellow how much superior we were to Indians, we presently turned our energies toward reaching the arrows.   By placing a fallen mesquit upright against the cliff and by jamming horseshoes in cracks still higher up, I managed to climb to a considerable height.   Then, with a long pole made by splicing two maguay stalks together with raw-hide and affixing a fish-hook to the tapering end, I managed, after numerous wearisome failures, to yank out ten ancient war arrows, together with an old fashioned, twisted, fire-hardened spear shaft.

As soon as we had accomplished this feat, the mestizo remarked that he must leave immediately, for his mule was thirsty and he was satisfied that all *tinajas* east and north where we were going were dry.   Following this cheerful statement with a hearty *buenos tardes,* he spurred away in the direction of Valle Trinidad while we journeyed silently down the arroyo.   At eight o'clock that evening we found well-filled *tinajas.*   In the middle of the night a brown scorpion stung me above the right knee. The following day while I nursed my wound—the poison had spread out forming an angry red and yellow spot, as large as my hand and extremely painful—the Colonel rounded up our straying burros and killed a mountain sheep. That night we dislodged from our blankets an immense green scorpion over three inches long!

CHAPTER XXIII

L OATH to leave water and wondering what fate we were tempting, we broke camp the twenty-fifth, bound for the junction of the Hardy and Colorado Rivers. By one o'clock in the afternoon we found ourselves beyond the mouth of the Arroyo Grande and on the southeastern edge of a desert which seemed to extend for forty or fifty miles to the northwest. Halting at this point for lunch, we rested our heated animals. The sand-swept Sierra del Pinto was opposite us, distant, perhaps, ten miles. In these mountains there is no known water. Fortunately they seemed to break entirely away toward the northeast, leaving a desert sweep of ten or twelve miles intervening before the rise of the Cocupa Sierras, a northwesterly continuation of the range. For this gap we were bound. Somewhere beyond it lay the Hardy, a tributary of the Colorado River. Just *how* far beyond was a question for our personal solution, this being a region not exemplified on the maps and frankly dreaded by Mexicans and Indians, because of its extreme heat and absolute lack of water-holes.

Eight months earlier I had spent a night burning a signal fire to save the hunter lost on this very desert, and the ensuing afternoon had been advised by the *ranchero* Juan, an experienced guide, that it was so dangerous a region that he had never dared venture upon it; his friend Denton had, indeed, made the passage successfully, in four days' time, but Denton had been favored by rainy, wintry weather.

Although this four-day story had seemed fishy, I recollected that Pattie, the noted trapper, had nearly succumbed to thirst somewhere in this section, which he afterwards characterized as the most dangerous portion of his ten thousand mile ride from Kentucky to the Californias and return. On the other hand, across this desert in former times stretched the war trail by which the Catarina Yumas reached the Colorado and Gila River country; moreover, over these very sands Filibuster Walker and his tall warriors had marched in April, 1854, and sixty years earlier, Arrilliga, the adventurous Spanish Governor, had made the trip in safety. Furthermore, I was satisfied that native vaqueros had occasionally done the distance, and in less than four days.

The time of the year was all that really disturbed me, for we were thoroughly well prepared. The Colonel's life had been a succession of hardships that fitted him for such a venture as this. I was in superb condition. Our stock— two riding mules and five young pack burros—were fairly fresh, and with only two hundred and sixty pounds of cargo among them the burros had the lightest of packs; in fact, each day some one of them was permitted to travel without any load. Of water we had ten gallons, contained in three covered canteens and in one five gallon wine cask. Moreover, I had tucked away a yard and a half of rubber tubing with which, in case of supreme urgency, I hoped to be able to distil salt water. Of every drop of the ten gallons, we were most chary, however, for, doubtless, three days would elapse before we could replenish our supply. And without water? Well, south of the Imperial country they say that on an ordinary August day along the Colorado Desert a pedestrian can last perhaps eight hours without water—then come insane delusions, harbingers of death by thirst. In his deluded stage, the wretched sufferer, divesting himself of all clothing, seeks to plunge into splashing pools just beyond his reach.

After an hour's nooning we resumed our journey, traveling due north across the desert. Though four hours of this course brought us to the point of the Pintos, we found to our alarm that we could neither cross the ridge nor swing immediately around the point. We had come upon an encrusted bed of sand so completely undermined and so thoroughly honey-combed by burrowing creatures that our stock stumbled and sank to their bellies. Alarmed, unable to advance, they balked and floundered helplessly. Retreat, also, became difficult, for the sand had already begun to cave in about the deep trail which we had made. To add to the confusion, the obscurity of the twilight limited the range of our vision, while frequent angry whirrings from disturbed "side-winders" admonished us to avoid dismounting and searching too curiously. After floundering hopelessly about, we swung well out to the left, but even there the traveling was so heavy that by 8:30 in the evening we were forced to consider our animals and make camp as best we might in the scorching sand. This upset our plans for covering a goodly distance in the cooler temperature of the night.

After scratching over a level spot with our cleaning rods so as to dislodge any possible "side-winders," tarantulas, scorpions or other local residents whose company might prove undesirable, we stretched out with our blankets beneath us and had a light, non-thirst producing supper of hard tack, cold broiled mountain sheep and lemonade. Our poor beasts, meanwhile, were quick to sniff the water. Indeed, crowding about us they made such pitiable efforts to tell of their thirst that we had not the heart to carry out our intention of giving them no water until morning. During our journey across the San Felipe Desert, they had learned to drink from a sauce-pan and now, with glad subdued whinnies, each sought eagerly his small portion and then plead for more. We dared not humor them, however, for on the following day water would be more absolutely necessary for them and, careful though we had been, the Colonel and I had already consumed two gallons in the fourteen hours since leaving the *tinajas*. Truly, the dry heat on these southern deserts has a wonderful way of bringing the perspiration from a traveler, leaving him so parched that his whole system calls constantly for great gulps of water.

Though we found immediate sleep our slumbers were frequently disturbed. Winnie, a wayward, silver gray burro, at once the youngest and tallest in our train, was the offender. Again and again did she rub her soft nose against one or the other of us, pleading for a chance at the water cask which rested between us. About midnight a slight breeze sprang up. An hour later the air grew fresh enough for a thin blanket to be acceptable. Yet even in the last hours of the silent desert night the mighty waste of sand retained the heat of the evening as though the desert were some huge ash-covered bed of embers only waiting the first breath of a new day before breaking forth into flames.

We were in the saddle by 6 A. M. Even then the mercury registered 78 degrees, giving us grim warning of what to expect at mid-day. For the first league we traveled over a succession of sand dunes which were so honey-combed with underground run-ways of burrowing creatures that our animals again and again broke through the upper crust and became engulfed in the treacherous sand. Then the welcome sight of a lake dead ahead and extending far to the northwest gave us new life. Alas! on nearer approach the sheet of water receded and we rode upon damp salty flats, the scene of some recent overflow. To the northwest we could still see the glimmering sheen. Presently, close to our right, appeared a small pond. As a family of curlew were disporting along the shore, we concluded that this was no delusive water. Dismounting, therefore, I hurried over with the intention of having a long drink. A single taste sufficed. The pond was as salty as the ocean! While I stared about in disappointment, the curlew approached within a few feet, studying with every evidence of wonder.

After resuming our march, we shortly found the softness of the ground to be such that our animals could not travel over it. "Lordy," ejaculated the Colonel, as I led off on an easterly tack, "in figurin' on the *desert* I warn't countin' on *mud!*" More of these bogs soon made it necessary for us to change our course to the northeast. In this direction we continued until early afternoon.

The intervening hours were desperately trying. Nature, herself, seemed bent on our undoing. The fiery shafts of a relentless sun beat down upon our heads. The hot, saturated earth again and again gave way beneath our feet. The air was stifling, murky. Mirages concealed the true horizon. Thickets and strange weird objects arose at either hand only to disappear in the twinkling of an eye. The glassy surface of a broad lake glittered in the sunlight before us, its unstable shore-line ever receding, while a shimmering sea crept stealthily in our wake. Deceived by our eyes, hemmed in by the unreal, we came to doubt the stability of our minds.

For a day and a half the very heat had made us unwontedly uncommunicative. Now I felt an inclination to shriek out meaningless nothings, while the Colonel, who had over-taxed his strength in securing his last mountain sheep, began to voice half delirious recollections of the days when he rode with Moseby and Quantrell. As he was unconscious of his rambling, it is possible that I, too, talked queerly.

Splendid horseman though he was, several times my companion reeled in his saddle until I feared that he would fall. Once I inquired concerning his condition, but, though he admitted that his head and stomach were troubling him, he uttered no complaint, nor did he once blame me for bringing him into such a region. For my own part I slouched forward in my saddle and endeavored to keep control of my mind; for the hot air pressed close about my head like a tightly drawn iron band until I felt that the very sutures must soon fly apart.

The ground over which we were passing was thickly strewn with glittering salt. Save for pools of salty water, patches of salt grass, infrequent bushes and occasional heaps of driftwood, it was a barren, unbroken plain of sand and sediment. The natural situation was easy to comprehend. We were close on the heels of an overflow of the Hardy River, a stream usually impregnated with salt from the mud volcanoes at its source and from the tidewater running up from the Gulf of California. With the advancing hours I became alarmed, fearing that we might find our way blocked by a large body of this overflow, which would so delay us that our water supply might become exhausted ere we could discover more.

At noon we called a brief halt and, having broached the water cask, gave each animal a half pint drink from a saucepan. They whinnied and begged for more, but we had become sternly inexorable. An hour later the thirsty creatures, breaking from the line of march, rushed over toward a small pond a few rods distant. Their instinct was correct. The water was fresh, brackish certainly, but none the less acceptable to them. A thunder storm had passed that way. Finding a thicket of mesquit a league farther on, under its shade we rested until five o'clock—with the thermometer registering 120 degrees!

On resuming our march we pursued a northwesterly course which shortly brought us to a corral, a shack and a wire gauze frame house. Raised above the level of the ground both buildings were protected by a small levee. Beyond them flowed a sluggish, muddy stream a hundred yards in width. We had reached the Hardy, the largest river in all Lower California! Also, though no one was at hand to greet us, we had stumbled on the "Salada" cattle camp. With a feeling of relief we removed saddles and packs from our exhausted animals and prepared supper. Presently a vaquero appeared, and from him we gathered that the junction of the Hardy and the Colorado Rivers was but a league and a half to the southeast; that the last overflow of the Hardy was just receding, and that at the time of these periodic floods, *tidal bores* or waves from four to five feet in height came rolling *up* from the Gulf of California, inundating the entire country. Furthermore, he stated that he had come in from Yuma via Sonora and that we could not get out by any other way.

The ensuing morning, Sunday, August 27th, we left our outfit at the Salada and rode down to the junction of the rivers. Here we dismounted, and while the Colonel prowled about in search of an old boat of which the vaquero had told us, I contentedly seated myself on the high bank of the Colorado and enjoyed my surroundings.

Twenty feet below me flowed a muddy stream not over a hundred and fifty yards in breadth. Beyond this, on the Sonora side, glistened a wide stretch of mud flats reaching back to a low grass-grown bank, a quarter of a mile beyond. Over these flats, long-horned Mexican cattle and snorting mustangs were coming and going in continuous procession. One by one they would halt at the water's edge, drink deeply, then face about and flounder eastward again. Meanwhile, circling overhead and dotting the shore

line, myriads of raucous sea fowl and long-legged waders
were making a veritable Bedlam with their quarreling and
squawking, while leaping silver-hued fish incessantly disturbed the surface of the river. Heedless of the stock and
undisturbed by our presence, no less than nine coyotes pa-
trolled the flats, running in and out among the larger birds
in restless search for food. Frequently they would all
congregate in a snarling crowd about the remains of a half
grown whale. The vaquero had told us that this leviathan
had strayed up from the Gulf, lured on by the sweet voice
of a wild burro. In this story the Colonel expressed entire
belief. Said he, "That whale wanted a choice meal. Burro
meat is the sweetest flesh there is." On this statement I
can offer no comment, as yet having had no occasion to in-
vestigate the merits of burro steak.

To the south and southeast lay the Sierra del Pinto.
Early in January I had stood on a southerly point in these
mountains and looked down upon the mouth of the Colorado River with its broad, glistening, reddish-white shores.
Now, as then, I could but marvel over the fact that while
this was one of the first sections ever explored on the American continent, it is to-day one of the least known. In 1539,
centuries ago, Francisco de Ulloa, an admiral of Cortez,
discovered the mouth of the Colorado while searching for
the *Northwest Passage!* A year later Hernando de Alarcon, admiral to the Spanish Viceroy Mendoza and companion of Francis Vasquez de Coronado, arrived at the headwaters of the Gulf. "And when we were come," de Alarcon
wrote, "to the flats and shoals . . . the pilots and the
rest of the company would have had us do as Captain Ulloa
did, and have returned back again. But because your Lord-
ship commanded me that I should bring you the secret of
that Gulf, I resolved that I should not cease for anything.
. . . After this sort we came to the very bottom of

the bay, where we found a mighty river which ran with so great fury of a stream that we could hardly sail against it." And small wonder that the old rover found the sailing difficult, for the tide here ascends full twelve leagues up the river, battling—until the recent diversion of the Colorado into the Salton Sea—with the furious current of the mighty Colorado and producing a marvelous tidal bore, the lowest thereof being three feet and the highest some twenty.

In 1721, Juan Ugarte, the Jesuit Padre, sailed into these waters in his *Triunfo de la Cruz* and noted with awe the terrific velocity of the bores of the river. A quarter of a century later the illustrious Padre Consag passed close to certain reddish marshes, probably the ones which I observed in January, and continuing onward in canoes, ascended the river until forced back by the tidal bore, some seven leagues up stream. His report served the map makers until near the close of the *nineteenth* century!

In the month of January, 1826, the intrepid Pattie party, their horses stampeded by the Yumas, recklessly descended the Colorado in dugouts, trapping beaver on the way and setting the first fashions amongst the Cocupa squaws by offering them their hunting shirts and modestly intimating that it was not good form for woman to go unadorned! Finally, their camp was flooded by "a high ridge of water over which came the sea current combing down like water over a mill dam. . . The fierce billows shut us in from below, the river current from above, and murderous savages on either hand on shore." About the same time Lieutenant R. W. Hardy of the English Navy discovered the False, or Hardy's, Colorado. Thirty years later Lieutenant Ives, an American officer, passed up the Colorado on a voyage of exploration, giving no attention, however, to the Hardy. If I have correctly welded together Indian tales and old records, the California and Sonora filibustering expedition of William Walker went to pieces in April, 1854, immediately after its disastrous attempt to cross the Colorado just below its junction with the Hardy.

Notwithstanding this list of noted visitors with its hall mark of olden days, modern knowledge of the lower delta region of the Colorado is so limited that the Hardy River is rarely found on even the more complete maps. Indeed, it does not appear even on the recent charts of Lower California prepared by the Hydrographic Office of the United States Navy. As a matter of fact the Hardy carries a large body of water and winds along a tortuous course over fifty leagues in length. The distance from its junction with the Colorado River to the mouth of the latter is—the meanderings of the river considered—full fifteen miles. The air line distance is vastly less.

After the Colonel had found the boat and a long limb, a drift-wood board and a tin can, we boldly embarked upon the turgid Colorado. While I paddled vigorously with the board, he alternately bailed and poled. In this manner we attained the Sonora shore in safety. Our landing, however, so annoyed the coyotes that three of them *waded*—a possibility consequent upon the diversion of the Colorado at this point—across the river just above its junction with the Hardy! Amazed at this sight my companion suddenly decided that it would suit him to be able to say that he had waded the Colorado. Unfortunately for his ambition, he chose a place below the junction of the rivers where midstream developed a seven-foot depth that called for the exercise of his swimming abilities.

In the afternoon we returned to the Salada and, after packing our burros, set forth for the Cocupa Indian settlements up the Hardy. The remainder of the day and the major portion of the ensuing forenoon—nine hours, in fact, of steady travel—wore away, however, before we had so much as reached the Indian trail along the high lands off the northeastern slope of the Cocupa Sierras. The distance covered amounted, perhaps, to fifteen miles! Ordinarily we would have had an easy wagon road every rod of the way. As it was we had a close shave getting through at all. Again and again our animals bogged. Here thickets of thorny mesquit barred the way, there tangled weeds and stinging nettles defied us; now we strode through dense masses of *tules* growing five and ten feet above our heads, and again we found ourselves compelled sullenly to make a wide detour to avoid some swamp or lagoon. Riding was out of the question after the first few miles, but our animals followed our lead right gamely, even when called upon to wade in water to their shoulders.

Monday afternoon tried our endurance to the limit. Gradually, under the oppressive, stifling heat of the biting, tropical sun, our minds ceased to consider poise and proportion and to exercise self-control. Sullen, overheated, lacerated by thorns, we were quite ready to see a malignant personal animosity in each tangled growth that opposed our passage. From querulous ill-temper, we passed to smouldering anger that lent a viciousness to every slashing, brush-cutting blow of our long Mexican blades. Vindictively we hacked and tore through the thickets with the savagery that marks the advance of the wounded tiger as he malevolently rips and tears each vine and shrub that bars retreat to the jungle. Finally, at 11 o'clock we came out upon a plain trail at the base of and paralleling the sierras. For a moment we paused and stared at one another. We were plastered with mud to our waists, while arms, necks, chests, hands and faces were bleeding profusely from frequent contact with thorns and the jagged ends of broken branches. Our appearances were not prepossessing. The Colonel was the first to speak: "That —— —— vaquero," he sputtered, "said we couldn't get through this way for a week. Seems ter me we look like we'd gotten through somethin' already, —— —— him."

Though the Cocupa Sierras are a barren range of mountains, rising to a height of over three thousand feet without any soil save crumbling reddish-yellow rock, along the welcome trail at their base we noted willows and green grass. This growth is due to the proximity of the Hardy, which, in places, even crowds close up against the mountain spurs. Very shortly we found deserted Indian *remadas* or arbors and then shacks, some of which were the most substantial Indian dwellings I had seen upon the peninsula.

At one o'clock, thoroughly exhausted, we camped near a group of these shacks and enjoyed a three hours' siesta. Then we pressed on again. Our trail at once developed into a wagon road, but we quickly lost interest in roadways. While resting we had noted a yellowish haze hanging over the mountain tops to our left and heard the pelicans complaining loudly along the river. The Colonel had even remarked on our fortune in being off the desert, since it was doubtless in the throes of a dangerous sand storm. Now, in five minutes' time, a terrific gale came sweeping over the sierras driving down a yellowish sandy mist which totally hid the sun and placed us in obscurity. Breaking from the road, our animals stood cowering in the brush. Only with the stimulus of spurs and heavy curb-bits could we force our riding mules to breast the storm. Meanwhile, a yelling, half naked Indian, his long locks whipping his bare neck and brown shoulders, unexpectedly appeared in a meadow before us. Bending low over his half-crazed mustang, he wildly dashed after a stampeding herd of terrified horses. Joining their shrill cries to the general alarm, the water birds, that had been circling high above the river, closed their wings and dropped downward like great white stones.

The air became icy. With this the situation grew beyond my comprehension. The sudden change had been too complete. The very air, discolored, heavy, grating, had become possessed with strange, uncanny moanings as though Nature were rousing herself to some weird, unwonted action. Tingling with cold, whipped by the wind, cloaked in depressing yellow gloom, moving in the midst of a setting appalling beyond that of any storm or earthquake I had ever experienced, I could only blankly wonder what further play of the elements we were about to witness. I had not long to wait. Suddenly the world seemed a-quiver. Then the heavens resounded with a whirling, deafening crash of thunder. Even as the last reverberations died away, jolting and rumbling into the far distance, a blaze of brilliant white light flared weirdly down through the cloaking obscurity. Another instant and a drenching torrent of rain swirled upon us as though the very clouds had ripped asunder.

For two hours the violence of the storm in no wise abated. During that time we did not advance a league. With difficulty we kept our mules on the highway and rode against the burros, urging them from their shelters in the brush. We lost sight of one another. We could not hear each other's voices. Finally, passing through bars in a brush fence, I arrived at three shacks built of upright posts and thatched with *tule*. Within were gathered a crowd of long-haired, hideously painted Cocupa Indians. Dismounting, I sought the protection of the largest shack for my camera and saddle-bags. In five minutes the Colonel joined me. In half an hour the rain ceased, the clouds vanished and we saw the setting sun sink behind the Cocupa Sierras.

As the only one of our new acquaintances who possessed any knowledge of Spanish accepted the storm without comment we stifled our curiosity, and upon the cessation of the downpour, calmly pitched our tents, a few rods from the shacks, made a fire and began to dry our blankets and clothing. In consequence of a severe kick from a burro the Colonel was suffering painfully.

In thinking over the strange storm I decided that it was possibly a combination of a sand and thunder storm; that the fierce current of the former had come over the sierras laden with yellow sand and had been, in crossing, deflected upward to a chilling altitude from which it had swung downward in the van of a thunder storm. This is but a surmise.

While gathering firewood I saw another sight peculiar to the Hardy country, a toad as large as a "cottontail" rabbit! As I neglected to follow the Colonel's advice and "rope" the batrachian, it disappeared during the night. His further suggestion, "Since you haint got its pictur, don't talk about that critter in the States. Folks there'd say you wuz an infernal liar," shall therefore receive due respect and I will leave the toad for some scientist to find and classify.

Tuesday forenoon we traveled northward and northwesterly, exploring the country of the Cocupas. We found a great number of Indian shacks, half of which were deserted, the occupants having gone either to the southwest for piñons or northward to work for the whites along the Border. All of these shacks were built in fields enclosed by brush fences. Although the soil—alluvial bottom land along the Hardy— seemed as fertile as the most productive acres in the valleys of the Sacramento or Mississippi, only small portions of the fields were under cultivation. Except for occasional patches of melons or corn, we saw no growing crops. As the Colonel remarked, "With fishin' handy an' corn a-plenty, why should they plant more'n they need?"

Although the Indians we had seen Monday evening were clothed with the overalls and calicos of civilization, these that we now saw evidently had forgotten the admonition of

Pattie and his trappers, for the children and the old men and women displayed the most limited wardrobes. A khaki coat—frequently with two or three gaudy buttons—a breech-clout and a smile sufficed for the grandfathers while their helpmates wore a narrow girdle supporting three or four short, triangular flaps of rags—and entirely dispensed with coat and smile. The little children made the most of the smile. It was all they had! But no, I am doing an injustice to the sartorial adornments of these youngsters, for nearly all of them wore bead necklaces so arranged as to fall in three successive loops, the lowest one reaching almost to their plump, brown little stomachs. Although to my great delight, we met several slender, erect, copper-hued braves as fierce looking and as handsome as any Indian warrior of the story books, the greater number were dark, thick-set, heavy featured people, duplicates of other Cocupas whom I had met about Calexico and Yuma a year or two before. All wore their hair long. Several of the older and apparently leading men kept their locks drawn about the crown of the head like a turban.

To my extreme regret, men, women and children protested so vigorously against the use of my camera that a few old people and some retreating figures were the only "snaps" I could secure. We came across one couple reputed to be over a hundred years old. Their reddish-brown skin hung in folds, their flesh had worn away until the lower thigh bones were visible; their eyes were sunken. The brave was totally blind. And yet, on our arrival at their shack, the old fellow tottered forward, protectingly, before his mate, while she, poor, shrivelled, doubled up ancient, turned her dim eyes tenderly upon him, ready to guide his faltering steps.

Although innumerable water fowl congregate along the Hardy and Colorado and some few "mule" deer and wild hogs live in the cane-breaks of the delta, the Cocupas are practically without fire-arms. They are well enough supplied, however, with two kinds of bows. With the smaller they kill birds and rabbits, while their long bows will send a shaft through a "mule" deer. Tuesday morning I engaged in an archery contest with a Cocupa. We each discharged three arrows at a board two feet square set upright one hundred paces from us. Using a small bow, he scored two hits; my own record I refrain from recording!

Finally, after seeing forty-seven different Indians, and having learned that few of the tribe* were at Pozo Vicente, the rancheria a half a league farther up the river, we purchased two dozen plump ears of green corn and turned away to the southwest with the intent of finding a salt lake to which the Indians had frequently referred. In this corn transaction we ascertained that the Cocupas are "sound money" people, counting the Mexican peso as half a dollar!

We traveled steadily, gradually leaving the lowlands and climbing into the Cocupa Sierras, where we found an old trail of which the Indians had advised us. Following this we wound through a mountain pass and down upon the Cocupa Desert beyond. In the late twilight we halted, abruptly. A long narrow body of water barred our farther advance. We had found Laguna Maquata, the Laguna Salada, or Salt Lake, of which the Indians had spoken.

After dismounting we perceived to our amazement that we had chanced upon the best camping ground either of us had ever seen on any desert. Numerous bunches of *galleta* or desert grass awaited our hungry stock, a small, inviting pool of clear water marked the passage of the thunder storm, the sand was firm and clean while the air had that rare sweetness only known to those who have wandered upon the desert immediately after a fall of rain.

* Note D: Appendix.

"When you rekolect," muttered the Colonel, staring about in pleased surprise, "that after '96 all this country seen no rain for seven year, you'll allow we're in dead luck."

While my worthy comrade picketed the animals, I prepared a supper of steaming hot corn on the cob, potatoes boiled with their jackets on, broiled "jerked" venison, flapjacks and wild honey. His work finished, the Colonel threw himself down on his blankets, observing, with interest the progress of my culinary operations. Presently he chuckled, softly. "Out with it, pardner," I ventured, by way of encouragement.

"I wuz jest a-thinkin'," he began, "oncst in the seventies when I wuz with a cattle outfit in Wyoming, we hearn tell of a whoop up dance that wuz comin' off at Cheyenne. Us fellers wuz great hands at dancin'—even usto learn the squaws to polkey. So we figgered on goin' in a bunch, an' when one of the new boys, a shy young feller, said he wuz no hands with ladies and wouldn't go, we told him ter git a starch collar an' come along pronto. So all hands went, but at the dance the shy un set 'round too skeered to pound the floor. Then I fixed it with a young school marm I knew, and took him up an' give him a knock down. Well, a-try'n to waltz he trod all over her, shameful, an' never said a word sociable like, but jes looked so glum you'd a-thought he'd lost his best horse. So she up an' says, 'Mr. Harvey,' says she 'what's you thinkin' about?' At furst he didn't answer. Then he sees how sympathetic like she looks, an' he busts right out, 'Oh, mam,' says he, 'I do feel so solemcully like in here. I miss my "chaps," "taps" and "latigo straps"!' "*

The Colonel paused a moment, then continued, "When I

* These three—*chapparejos,* or leather riding breeches, *tapaderas,* or leather stirrup covers, and *latigo* straps, the straps with which a saddle "cinch" is tied to the iron rings of the saddle—are essentials to the frontier cowman.

see you in January, you looked thin and wuz way off on your feed. At the table I passed you the onions and you said you didn't eat onions. The other day on the desert you wuz munchin' away on a raw onion like it was an apple. Jest now I was a-thinkin' that when you get back to the States a-dressin' up, a-sleepin' indoors on a bed an' a-goin' to an orfice, you'll think on life along the trail an' pretty soon you'll get mighty solemcully for *you'll* miss your 'chaps'——"

The sentence was left unfinished. For an instant the old trooper raised one hand warningly, the next he rolled over behind the fire. Out from the distance came the faint jolting of a loping horse. "Some one's on our trail," muttered the Colonel, ominously.

The prospect didn't please me. Why should any one be trailing us? Presently we could hear the hoof beats of a considerable cavalcade; at this the Colonel growled savagely and reaching over among his blankets drew out his Leuger from its holster. Already we could make out a gray horse with darker animals following in single file. They were not a hundred yards distant.

"*Buenos noches*," roared the Colonel, rising to his feet.

Instantly the approaching line swung off to the right, then halted. I shouted a "good evening," first in Spanish, then English. There was no response. "Cocupas," grunted the Colonel, slipping his revolver into its holster. "But we'd better bring in our stock." Within five minutes they were tied immediately about us. Meantime, fifty steps to our right, flickered up a tiny flame. "Huh," said my companion, "three bucks, with long huntin' bows, two squaws an' two kids. Jest a piñon party. I'm goin' to turn in."

Five minutes later an erect, middle-aged brave appeared before us. His proportions were superb; his features clear cut and strikingly handsome. Unarmed and practically unclothed, his peaceful intent was further evidenced by the gift of a melon and by his attending companion, a small, wide-eyed boy. I gave them each a flap-jack which they ate with relish. They were soon followed by a buxom squaw leading a pretty little girl. Later, a dark, sturdy, sinister-looking young buck drifted in upon us. Squatting close about the fire, they enjoyed such supper as I gave them. A few lumps of sugar made the little people happy. However, not a word of English or Spanish could we get from any of our visitors. Presently we cut the melon. In shape it resembled a water melon, in taste the "nutmeg" variety of the canteloupe. The Colonel grimly declined a slice, but as soon as the Indians began nibbling theirs, I fell to.

We must have made a queer scene there on the edge of the great desert! The stolid, bright-eyed, copper-hued Indians crouching by the fire, my grizzled frontier companion lying on his blankets, his revolver close at hand, our shadowy stock munching at the grass about us, the clear sky high above with the pale moon and glittering stars. Suddenly, our visitors arose. Then, without a word having been said, they slipped away in single file. The Colonel, long accustomed to and little interested in Indians, fell asleep at once. With me it was different. I had enjoyed the visit—and I felt a trifle nervous over the close proximity of our neighbors.

Finally, at eleven o'clock, after building up the fire and opening my blankets, I examined my six-shooter, preparatory to sleep. The cylinder refused to turn. The storm had wet and rusted the mechanism. Reaching over to my saddle, I jerked my carbine from its sheath and throwing up the muzzle before me, jammed a cartridge into the chamber. The effect was instantaneous—and unexpected. At the sharp click of the lever, there was a wild commotion among the bunches of *galleta* grass toward which the muzzle chanced to be directed and a dark figure threw itself into a depression of the sand beyond. The rest of the night I had insomnia. Anyway, I didn't sleep.

In the early morning the dark young buck paid us a brief visit, leaving without a word. As he walked away, I saw a revolver projecting from his hip pocket. Commenting on this, I made brief mention to the Colonel of the evening's occurrence, "and that was the chap, I expect," I said, in conclusion. To me the experience now seemed interesting and I spoke without thought of the disregard of an early frontiersman for Indian life when his outfit is concerned.

Instantly my warrior companion whipped out his deadly Leuger and with repeated curses, drew it down upon the Indian. "The dirty coyot'," he muttered, coolly, "he'll never try to cut out stock again!"

I threw myself forward, just in the nick of time. "For God's sake, Colonel, let him go," I cried.

CHAPTER XXIV

THE END OF THE TRAIL

WITH much flourishing of their long bows the Indians were under way five minutes later, the buxom squaw in the lead. She was on foot. Well mounted and strung out in single file, the others followed close in her wake. Immediately at her heels, plodded an old gray mare, bearing a large net-work sack bulging out with camp supplies. On top of this load was perched the pretty little girl. The boy rode a wild young burro. The fine looking brave possessed the only saddle and bridle in his outfit, the others riding with blanket and hakemore. As my volcanic companion still rumbled defiance, I did not regret the departure of the Indians.

After allowing them an hour's start we followed in their tracks—presumably they would lead to fresh water and no other trail was in evidence. The body of water which had seemed to bar our advance the preceding evening we found to be merely the lower end of the Laguna Salada and easily fordable. As our course for the day was northwest and west we had every opportunity to observe this most strange lake. It reaches out into the barren desert for eight or nine leagues with a width of from one hundred to several hundred metres. According to Indian report, it gains depth, width and saltiness from the overflows of the Hardy; when there has been no rain storm and no recent overflow, it is almost drinkable; at other times, lured to its shores by thirst, men have died miserable deaths.

Shortly after fording the Laguna Salada I caught sight of a pair of nice looking young porkers rooting along the shore. Though presumably property of the Indians, they looked so inviting, that I readily found in recent events, acceptable justification for extreme action. Accordingly, my mind pleasingly filled with toothsome visions of roast pig, I hastily dismounted, carbine in hand. But alas! my companion interrupted me, even as I was drawing a bead. "Say, them aint wild hogs!" he exclaimed, excitably. "Them must belong to the Cocupas. You haint got any right or call to kill them shoats." And this, in all earnestness, from the man who a few hours earlier was about to shoot down an Indian, without a tremor! Utterly bewildered, I desisted and we moved on. Gradually, slowly, out of a confused maze of thoughts I began to appreciate the Colonel's frontier code of ethics. "Allus kill a rattlesnake an' a thievin' Indian," it would run, "but don't never hanker arter live stock that aint yourn. No, not even arter an Indian's hog."

We found the desert near the Laguna so barren and salty that I rather doubt whether it would be passable in summer except immediately after a shower. Even as it was my mule Pedro gave out early in the afternoon and I had to mount Chappo, a large, stalwart Socorro burro, which we had rescued from the Kaliwas near Valle Trinidad. At six o'clock in the evening we arrived at the base of a lofty range of rocky sierras which marked the farther side of the desert. Here, in the mouth of an arroyo, we made camp; but no sooner were we comfortably settled than we heard the shrill cries of Indian children at play, from which we rightly concluded that we were in the vicinity of some encampment. The Colonel, therefore, brought in the stock while I prepared supper. Soon a number of mounted Cocupas passed us. One, a man of forty, addressed me in broken Spanish. Over twenty of his people, he explained, were camped nearby. In a day or two a larger party would join them after which they would ascend the sierras for piñons and deer. Meantime, would I give him meat, tobacco, coffee and sugar? Wholly dissatisfied with the small gift which I graciously handed over, the buck fell into a somber study. Presently, with deep guile, he again addressed me: His wife was a wonderful cook, he explained. Why should a stalwart white hunter cook? The wife should do the white hunter's cooking for two weeks, and in return the white hunter should pay him ten dollars for her services. The Colonel, coming into camp at this moment and understanding the buck's proposition, roared with laughter, whereupon the Indian rode away in high dudgeon.

Early the following morning we were in the saddle. Without any preliminary dilly-dallying we rode plump into the Indian encampment and with a proper and judicious distribution of tobacco began to make inquiries concerning the nearest white man's road. As one of the bucks responded by waving a hand toward the south and southwest and then successively pointing to the rising sun and to the west where it would set, we interpreted this sign play as meaning that a southwesterly course would bring us to a road by nightfall. Following this theory we ascended the face of the sierras by an indistinct and fearfully abrupt Indian trail. As we arose above the plain a magnificent view unfolded below us: at our feet the broad gray desert with its long shimmering salt lake, farther to the north and east the yellowish Cocupa Sierras and the parti-colored Sierra del Pinto; over beyond these the delta of the Colorado and the Hardy.

High up among great cliffs and mid barren surroundings we clambered, suffering the meantime intensely from the unrestrained rays of the fiery sun. Soon the Colonel's mule gave out, then Chappo became sullen. Not only did we have

to walk but our mules were so determined to move no further that all our reserves of energy were required to urge
them on. Five hours of this sort finally brought us to the
crest of the sierra, an elevation of at least a mile in an ascent
no more than seven times that distance. During this climb
we had each drunk over a gallon (eleven three-quarter-pint
cups) of water! On a short allowance I do not think that
either of us could have managed for in the dry intense heat
of a Baja California summer, heavy exercise, except in the
timber country, produces such violent perspiration that frequent and copious draughts of water are absolutely essential.

On the crest we found a region of white granite picachos,
scrub oaks and piñon trees where criss-crossing trails advised us of the recent presence of cattle. When we had
advanced perhaps a mile into this country, a heavy storm of
rain suddenly burst over us. Quickly the air grew chilly,
and amidst crash on crash of thunder and vivid flashes of
lightning, a shower of hail stones, the size of pigeon eggs,
beat upon us. For twenty minutes the storm raged wildly,
completely soaking us and our outfits. To add to our
vexation every cow path became a hurrying stream so in-
distinguishable from its neighbor that, after losing time following various water courses, we had to admit that we had
lost our trail. The balance of that day and the ensuing
forenoon were spent in vain search north, south and west
for some pass through the cliffs and brush. I would not
want to say how many picachos we climbed in determined
effort to locate our bearings. Finally, we worked into the
open timber country to the southwest and in the late afternoon made camp on the edge of a beautiful fresh water pond
which we assumed to be Laguna Hanson.

A wagon road was near at hand and upon this we set
forth the ensuing day, northward bound. For thirty-five
miles we traveled through a delightful pine forest where the

nights were frosty and the morning air sharp and bracing; then we descended to the lower altitude of scrub oaks, brush, warm weather and dust. After passing a succession of jewel diggings, ranchos and gold mines we found ourselves face to face with the American border town of Campo. Swinging off to the west, we passed through Tecarte Valley and hugging the Line closely for two days, rode into the little town of Tia Juana on the 6th of September, 1906.

Twenty-five days had elapsed since our departure from Socorro; twenty-two of them had been spent in the saddle, a driving—and most appropriate—finish for the seven months of my explorations.* The Colonel estimated the distance covered in the twenty-two days at five hundred miles, an altogether respectable figure; my own notes show forty less. But the time of year, the untrod wilderness, the changing temperatures and the varying altitudes had been the most trying elements of the experience. Inured to hardships though we were, we both realized that we had been traveling. The mules seemed to have a similar view. The burros, however, came through in marvelous form.

Tia Juana! Nine and a half months earlier, as the mellow light of the dying day, the shortest lived day in all the year, flickered along the horizon, I had made camp near this forlorn little border pueblo for the first night of my wanderings on the peninsula. As my journey began at Tia Juana, there let it end.

As I write these closing lines there comes over me a flood of recollections—of gorgeous sunrises and sunsets, of evenings about the camp fire with copperhued brave or swarthy Mexican telling of days that are gone, of nights on the lone deserts with the glittering stars and white moon close overhead. Once more with Señor Dick I am riding southward along the King's Highway. Again I see the

* Note E: Appendix.

lordly big-horn and hear the sharp crack of the carbine. Again the Laird and I read Kipling and Balzac while without the tent storms the Madame. Once more I gaze over the desolate wastes of the Llanos de Ojo Liebre while Castro in hollow tones presages impending doom. This gloomy picture fades and before me now are the lovely valleys of San Ignacio and Comondú. Again I hear the soft melodies of the sweet voiced muchachas of Mulege. Again I am resting in the orange groves by the regal Mission of San Xavier. Once more is Praemundi calling and I half rise, ready to mount, as I hear his crisp, *"Señor, listo caminando."*

But what wild memory is this that now seizes me? Ah, the intrepid Colonel with his ingenuous profaneness! What are you saying, comrade of the wilds? What? Your prophesy! Well—mayhap, now in office confines, mayhap I do long for the trail, mayhap I do feel "solemcully like." Yes, you are right I do "miss— my chaps, taps and latigo straps." Perhaps, yes, God willing, I'll come again.

[FINIS]

APPENDIX

1. NOTES.

Note A, Chapter IV. Lower California is the least known and most unsettled section of all Mexico. Over seven hundred miles in length, it varies from thirty-five to one hundred and forty miles in breadth. Its total population is not in excess of thirty thousand. Take out the dozen largest towns and less than five thousand persons remain; they are scattered over nearly forty million acres of territory. More than three-fourths of this great area is mountainous. For the benefit of those desirous of further information concerning conditions in Lower California, reference is here made to the author's *"Mother of California"* (1908, Paul Elder & Co., Publishers, New York and San Francisco. Price, $2.00), from which, through the courtesy of Paul Elder & Co., the following chapter is here reproduced.

"PHYSICAL LOWER CALIFORNIA.

"Geographically, Lower California is a long, jagged peninsula, lashed on its western and southern shores by the booming waves of the Pacific Ocean, and separated from the mainland of Mexico by the restless Colorado River and by the opalescent waters of the Sea of Cortez, or, as that body is termed with less grace but greater frequency, the Gulf of California. With a general trend from northwest to southeast, this strange territory attains a maximum length of some two hundred and fifty leagues, although its breadth in places is a scant ten and nowhere exceeds fifty leagues. In round numbers the area of Lower California exceeds thirty-eight million acres, and of these, seventeen and a quarter million are north of the twenty-eighth parallel of latitude. In calling the gulf the Adriatic of the West and in likening the Peninsula to their beloved Italy, the Jesuits made an excellent general comparison, both topographically and climatically. Lower California is a hundred miles the longer, however, while the Italian peninsula has the greater breadth.

Also, the latter enjoys more moisture and has more level land.

"From the American boundary on the north to Cape San Lucas, shouldering high above cactus-clad plains, small oases and parched deserts, there extends throughout the California Peninsula a mighty range of grim mountains, sloping away to the west, breaking off to the east in abrupt, awe-inspiring cliffs. Of these sierras, five thousand feet is but an average height, and he who explores their lofty ridges is rewarded by views of majestic grandeur which some day will be heralded among men. Rich in boulders, cliffs, minerals and cacti, the entire Peninsula is strangely devoid of trees and springs, except about the timber plateaus of Laguna Hanson, San Pedro Mártir Sierra and in the Laguna Sierras above San José del Cabo. Few passes bisect the main range. In one section of these sierras mesas are the rule, in another lofty peaks are outlined sharply against the sky. Truncated cones are frequent. San Pedro Mártir Sierra, in many reports and without valid ground therefor, termed 'Calamahue Mountain,' attains an altitude of 10,126 feet and is the highest peak in Lower California; certain of its unscaled heights should appeal to the daring of the more intrepid members of the Sierra, Mazama, Alpine or kindred mountain-climbing associations. Throughout the main peninsula range the soil is usually shallow; frequently there are massive, beetling shoulders of rock, devoid of any earth; again and again long white scars mark where sudden torrents of prehistoric or modern times have torn aside the thin covering and exposed a granite heart; and yet within sight of this poverty of soil there is found at times an arroyo bottom where a spring bubbles out beneath the shadow of a palm and waters marvelously rich acres of sandy loam.

"Sections of this sierra have local names. The mountains back from San José del Cabo are known as the Laguna— and also as the San Lazaro—Mountains, those immediately south of La Paz are called the Cacachilas; the grim ridges and peaks back of Loreto were known, even among the ancient padres, as the Sierra Giganta; the sierras, southwest of San Ignacio and separating the llanos of Ojo de Liebre and Magdalena, are called, indiscriminately, the Sierra Pintada and the Santa Clara Sierras; San Pedro Mártir Sierra is a range by itself, extending for fifty miles northwest and

southeast and having a plateau width of nigh ten miles: the
timber-covered mountains northwest of Santa Catarina
Mission are spoken of, locally, as the Laguna Hanson
Mountains, and north of them lie a group of sharp peaks
referred to as 'The Picachos'; immediately west of the
mouth of the Colorado River lies a weird range of barren,
sand-swept mountains called the Sierra del Pinto, and a few
miles northwest of the Pintos lie the Cocupa Sierras.

"Part and parcel of these sierras are their deep and tortuous arroyos, immense, long and winding gorges slashed
deep into the sierras and frequently containing springs or
water-holes and spots of alluvial soil.

"The sierras and the arroyos tell of their prehistoric life.
The vast stretches of lava formation, the sea-shells on the
lofty ridges and peaks, the mud volcanoes at the headwaters
of the Hardy River, the spark of life that still throbs rebelliously within the lofty Tres Virgenes towering above San
Ignacio, the not infrequent *temblors,* the mighty chasms,
rent asunder by the awful convulsions of nature; these all
bespeak the volcanic origin of the land. Geologists class the
sierra back-bone of the Peninsula as a continuation of the
mountain ranges in eastern San Bernardino and Riverside
Counties and in central San Diego County in the State of
California. They parallel the range with submarine sierras,
evidenced by a series of islands and rocks fifty leagues off
the western shore of the Peninsula and separated therefrom
by great depths of water. These scientists say, further, that
the region about and immediately above San José del Cabo
is the remnant of a formerly existing tropical peninsula that
extended southward along the Mexican coast, taking in the
Tres Marias and other islands and separated from the balance of the present California Peninsula by a channel passing westerly from the Bay of La Paz to the Pacific Ocean.
They proceed with their theory and make another prehistoric island of the territory between the Cape Region and
the twenty-ninth parallel of latitude north. Certainly, along
the line of each of these supposed channels the sierras dip
downward and the Peninsula is extremely narrow.

"Examined from a modern topographical standpoint,
Lower California consists of four natural subdivisions, viz.:
the Cape Region, embracing the Cape San Lucas section and
extending northward slightly above the latitude of La Paz

to, say, 24° 20′ north; Central Lower California, extending northward from the Cape Region to the twenty-eighth parallel north; the "Waist," the narrow, rugged region from the twenty-eighth to the thirtieth parallel of north latitude, and La Frontera, including the territory from the thirtieth parallel to the international boundary (lying just north of the thirty-second parallel of north latitude and defined, by the Treaty of Guadalupe Hidalgo, as a straight line running from the junction of the Gila and Colorado Rivers to a point one marine league south of the port of San Diego as located by a survey made in 1782). Climatically, and from their flora and fauna, Central Lower California and the Waist are intermediary between the Cape Region, which is semi-tropical, and La Frontera, which is not unlike Sonora and the southern part of the State of California.

"The large sections of the Peninsula which are not sierra regions are usually either wide deserts or hot barren llanos, or plains. Guadalupe Valley, above Ensenada, in La Frontera, is an exception, being vastly similar to the great farming valleys so frequent in the State of California. Scattered here and there about La Frontera are excellent tracts of farming land, such as the valleys of San Telmo and Rosario, and along the Hardy and the Colorado Rivers there are thousands of acres of fertile and level land, which by reclamation would become extremely productive. The land of the Colorado Desert also is alluvial and produces heavily after irrigation, as does that about San Quintin. The desert back of the Cocupa Sierras and bordering on the Laguna Salada and the San Felipe Desert, further south, are excellent grazing districts, but the title of 'desert' well describes them.

"The Waist is practically devoid of level lands, excepting mesas or llanos, floored with lava. In the neighborhood of Los Flores, however, there are some rather large valleys.

"In Central Lower California are found the most extensive llanos on the Peninsula, those of Ojo de Liebre and Magdalena; they border on the Pacific Ocean and contain hundreds of thousands of acres of level or rolling land. Could these be cleared of cacti and reached by water, they would make good agricultural land, unless alkali materialized.

"The Cape Region is the most productive portion of the Peninsula, the San José Valley and the country about San

José del Cabo and Todos Santos being beautiful garden spots.

"But while La Frontera has greater known level tracts of land, suitable for farming purposes, than have the three southern sub-divisions, throughout the sierras, in the latter there are immense arroyos, floored with fertile soil and watered by small streams; these arroyo spots are unsurpassed for their productiveness and support the greater part of the population of the Peninsula. The good soil in these three sections of the country is usually of an ashy volcanic loam.

"The Colorado and the Hardy are the only rivers that touch Lower California. The so-called 'rivers' of Tia Juana, San Vicente, Santo Domingo, Rosario, Mulege, Comondú, Purísima, Todos Santos, San José, etc., are small streams except in time of exceptional storm or of cloudburst. Of these last named 'rivers' the Purísima carries the largest volume of water; accurately speaking, it is a long chain of broad water-holes, scooped deep in the rocky bottom of a great arroyo where rain- and spring-water alike gather. The San José and Todos Santos streams are in the Cape Region; the Purísima, Comondú and Mulege streams in Central Lower California; and the Rosario, Santo Domingo, San Vicente and Tia Juana, together with the Hardy and the Colorado Rivers, are in La Frontera. The Waist boasts no streams.

"The Hardy River and the Colorado River are in classes by themselves. Books have been written concerning the Colorado: its romance has been published, its tragedy is being enacted. For generations its tidal bore caused men to marvel and to fear to approach its mouth, and yet, in September, 1906, burro deer, coyotes and a man waded across the river just above its junction with the Hardy, passing, in their journey, the carcass of a whale left stranded high and dry! Formerly, when the snow began to melt in the high mountains where it headed and spring rains fell, the Colorado poured down into the Sea of Cortez with a mighy torrent, and then, before the powerful tides of that sea, its waters were forced back, only to return as a tidal bore close in the wake of the retreating tide. Doubtless the river will return to this course now that it has been brought back to its bed again. In this play of ocean and sea the Hardy, too, had its part, over-

flowing into the desert by the Laguna Salada when the
Colorado overflowed, and then draining back into the
Colorado at its leisure.   After its overflow the Hardy is
from fifty to a hundred yards in width and, its snaky course
considered, doubtless fifty leagues in length.   Its headwaters are among a group of some sixty mud volcanoes,
situated about eight leagues south of the international
boundary and an equal distance west of the Colorado
River.   These 'volcanoes' have been described as 'circular
holes containing boiling mud and exhaling a naphtha-like
odor.   Many of them are encrusted with mud forming
cones three to four feet high, from the apex of which proceed mingled vapors of water, sal amoniac and sulphur.'
Between the brackishness of its source and the incoming
tide, the Hardy is a murky, salty stream.

"North of the Hardy River there is a considerable
laguna, or lake, and several smaller ones.   Laguna Salada
(sometimes termed Laguna Maquata) is a long, narrow,
brackish lake southwest of the main ridge of the Cocupa
Sierras; reinforced by the overflows of the Hardy, at other
times this lake dwindles down into two sloughs.   Eight or
nine leagues further southwest, surrounded by pines and at
an altitude of over five thousand feet, lies Laguna Hanson,
a crystal gem of water.   At the meadow of La Grulla on
the heights of San Pedro Mártir Sierra there is a very
small pond.   All of these bodies of water are in La Frontera.   In the Waist of the Peninsula there are two small
lagunas, one known as Lake Chapala while the other has
no known name.   In the Cape Region there is a laguna in
the sierras above San José del Cabo.   These lagunas are
nothing more than ponds.

"With a coast line so indented that its full length is over
six hundred leagues in actual measurement, the Peninsula
is richly endowed with harbors and bays.   Fleets might
search the seas for more magnificent retreats than Magdalena Bay on the Pacific and Playa Los Angeles on the Gulf.
The first of these is described in the publications of the
United States Hydrographic Office as 'one of the most spacious and safe harbors in the world, (it) is about fifteen
miles long, northwest and southeast, and twelve miles wide.'
The actual length of this great sheet of water, however, is
nearer forty than fifteen miles, but points making out from
the mainland and from Santa Margarita, a long narrow

island crowded in shorewards, divide it into two bays of which the northerly one is termed Magdalena and the southerly Almaca, or Almejas, Bay. Among the old-time whalers these bays were known as Weather and Lee Bays. Numerous large lagoons branch out from Magdalena Bay. Although there is a small settlement on Margarita Island, the only really excellent water is brought from the Rancho of Matancita, on the mainland, leagues distant. Through the courtesy of Mexico, the United States is permitted to send her men-of-war to Magdalena Bay for target practice, and the booming cannon of the great white ships awaken, periodically, the echoes about the lonely harbor. Playa Los Angeles is a superb sheet of water, covering an area of nigh twenty-five miles. Protected on the east and the northeast by no less than fifteen islands and islets, it is a tranquil, land-locked harbor where whales are wont to bring forth their young, undisturbed by clanging bells, escaping steam or the splash of anchors. The majestic curve of its shore lines and its inviting stretches of sandy beach call forth the admiration of the few strangers who chance to behold them. The Bay of Sebastian Viscaino on the west coast is full sixty miles in width and over fifty in its inland reach. Puerto San Bartolomé, also on the Pacific, and Pichilingue, Puerto Escondido and Santa Rosalia on the Gulf are magnificent, well-protected harbors, while the entire coast line is notched with small bays and open roadsteads at least a dozen of which are noteworthy, though they remain practically unvisited.

"The islands adjacent to the coast are as numerous as its indentations. Indeed, their aggregate area has been estimated at one-fifteenth that of the Peninsula. Few of them are inhabited, however, save by sea-fowl, rabbits and goats, sheep or deer. The more important are Cedros, Natividad, Guadalupe, and Margarita Islands off the west coast, and Ceralbo, Espiritu Santo, San Josef, Santa Catarina, Carmen, San Lorenzo, Angel de la Guardia, and Montagu in the Gulf. Of these Angel de la Guardia, forty miles in length and with an extreme width of ten miles, is the largest; Cedros, twenty-nine miles in length and with an extreme width of nine miles, is second; the others named are from six to seventeen miles in length. The majority of all these islands are mountainous; Guadalupe boasts a peak with an elevation of 4,523 feet, the heights of Cedros approach 4,000 feet, while a range nigh to that elevation runs the length of Angel de la Guardia. Though of volcanic origin many of these islands have more or less vegetation, several of them have been noted guano fields; Guadalupe and Cedros possess considerable timber; Angel de la Guardia is absolutely barren.

"There is excuse enough for barrenness in Lower California, however, for there rain is capricious: sometimes it may fall in every season of the year, sometimes it may forget to fall at all. In this strange country rain is an event and even happens without clouds. Snow is somewhat regular in the northern sierras, dew comes with the midnight in the Waist of the Peninsula, and fogs are not infrequent along the western coast above the Cape Region. It may be safely said that the Cape Region and the country bordering on the Sea of Cortez receive their rainfall from the tropical summer rains originating in the Gulf of Mexico, the heaviest and surest rainfall being precipitated along the sierra backbone. It may also be said that the west coast of La Frontera, or that portion of it above San Quintin, is subject to most uncertain winter rains, the tail end of storms which originate in the far North. Throughout the country the rain-water disappears almost as soon as the rain is over.

"Of springs, Lower California has a strangely limited number. The majority of them are found in the sides or heads of the sierra arroyos. Some of these, such as Agua Dulce and Youbai in the Waist of the Peninsula, the springs of Comondú and Purísima in Central Lower California and the spring at San Bartolo in the Cape Region pour out immense bodies of water. The absence of springs on the great deserts and llanos is so complete that deaths by thirst have been numerous, and yet it is quite probable that artesian water might be found by boring either on the llanos above San Quintin, or along the more extensive stretches in Central Lower California near the Pacific Coast. Water has been readily found on these llanos by sinking wells of from forty to one hundred feet in depth, but no one seems to have been possessed of requisite energy to try for the liberal government reward offered to him who first obtains an artesian flow. There is a fine bubbling soda spring at the old Mission of Calamyget, arsenic and borax springs have been found, and *aguas calientes,* or hot springs, are not infrequent. Peculiar to the country, however, and the most frequent watering-places in Lower California, are the *tinajas,* or natural cisterns. These are water-holes found in the rock-bottoms of arroyos where rain collects. In some of these tinajas there are thousands of gallons of water, and in them small fish and water-terrapin are found. These tinajas are the salvation of those who travel about the Peninsula.

"Considering its immense coast line, Lower California is not a land of many or severe winds. Off the northeastern portion of the Cape Region there occurs, at intervals of several years, a local hurricane known as *El Cordonaso.* While this hurricane has an ill reputation, it is of amusing interest from the tradition surrounding its name. According to the residents, Oliver Cromwell ravaged the east coast of the Peninsula during the seventeenth century as a buccaneer, and so severe were his depredations that the hurricane was named for him. Even residents of education are thoroughly satisfied that the doughty Oliver visited the land during his time! Heavy winds occur periodically along the twenty-eighth parallel, and in the winter cold winds sweep across the northern portion of the Sea of Cortez and acquire added iciness from the snowy heights of San Pedro Mártir. On the Gulf northwesterly winds prevail from October to May and southeasterly winds from May to October. The prevailing winds throughout the Peninsula are from the northwest and the southwest. The magnetic variation of the compass in Lower California reaches from six to fourteen degrees.

"The air of Lower California is dry and pure and the atmosphere, except on the fog-swept western coast, is marvelously clear. Southward from the thirty-first parallel one may easily read in the white light of the full moon, and in the Cape Region the Southern Cross adorns the heavens. South of the mouth of the Hardy River and off Ojo de Liebre treacherous mirages in many and varied designs deceive the vision and vex the traveler. Perhaps the very narrowness of the Peninsula gives to its atmosphere a touch of the bracing air of the sea, or perhaps the dryness of the land gives the air an intense purity: whatever the cause, the result is that there is probably no more healthful climate in the world than that of Lower California. This was the verdict of the Jesuit missionaries who were in touch with the "uttermost parts of the earth"; this was the verdict of the New York Volunteers who occupied the country during the Mexican War and whose officers likened the climate to that of Persia or Arabia, reporting in a year but two deaths from natural causes among fifteen hundred people; this has been the verdict of those who have resided in or explored the land. Certainly it is a country where disease is infrequent and wounds heal readily, where extreme age is no rarity and physicians are practically unknown. Probably from a standpoint of health the most favored sections are along the line of the high sierras and throughout the Waist of the Peninsula.

"The mean temperature of Lower California is not known. The coldest region is along the line of the San Pedro Mártir Sierra, Valle Trinidad, the country about Santa Catalina Mission and through the Laguna Hanson range in La Frontera. Throughout this high plateau region there is an abundance of ice during the winter months and the nights are always cold. The Colorado and San Felipe Deserts in La Frontera and the llanos back from Magdalena Bay experience as great heat as any sections of the country, but it is not a moist heat. For balmy air the Cape Region and the east coast of the Waist are unsurpassed.

"In so summery a clime the least rainfall is sufficient to deck the land with a profusion of wild flowers and only an absolute drought destroys the abundant good grass, varieties of which haunt even the deserts. But the most frequent form of vegetation throughout Lower California is the cactus. It has its blooming time, too, for in the spring it sends forth blossoms of the deepest and most gorgeous hues. The mesquit and the attractive palo verde hover near the arroyos, the former attaining to immense girth in Central Lower California and in the Waist Region. In La Frontera pines are practically unknown until the Cape Region with its piñons and scrub-oaks is reached. The cacti flourish everywhere. The useful viznaga, the vicious cholla, the ocotilla, or its cousin, the Palo Adan, the maguay and the tuna: these thorny growths greet the traveler as he crosses the international boundary, and he parts with them only at the Cape. The giant cardones and the prized pithaya thrive south of the thirty-first parallel, while the graceful cirio or milapa is indigenous to the Waist. In La Frontera there are few palms, but in the other sections of the country they stand guard above the springs and water-holes."

Note B, Chapter XIX. In the fall of 1907 Mexico granted to the United States the right to establish and maintain coaling stations at Magdalena Bay for a period of three years. Thereafter and on the 16th of December, 1907, sixteen ships-of-the-line, flying the Stars and Stripes, left Hampton Roads, Virginia, bound for the Pacific Ocean. After brief visits at Trinidad, Rio de Janeiro, Punta Arena and Callao, the fleet put in, on the 12th of March, 1908, at Magdalena Bay, having made a cruise unprecedented in the naval annals of the world. A month's rest was had at Magdalena Bay to permit the gunners to engage in target practice. While thus occupied these superb marksmen, aided by the clearness of the atmosphere, promptly made innumerable new records for big gun shooting.

From Hampton Roads to California the 16,000 ton *Connecticut* bore the flag of Rear Admiral Robley D. Evans, U.S.N., the commander in chief of the magnificent squadron, who thus fitly crowned a splendid career of nigh half a century in his nation's service.

Note C, Chapter XXII. In his *"Noticia de la California"* (Madrid, 1757), the old chronicler Miguel Venegas presented a crude wood-cut of the California mountain sheep, probably the earliest recorded likeness of the species. Hornaday's *"Camp-Fires on Desert and Lava"* gives recent and entertaining account of Mexican big-horn as found in Sonora. It is of interest to note that the suggestion contained in this latter work and in the *"Mother of California"* has borne fruit and that these noble animals are now protected by federal enactments. In passing, I have not seen any of the specimens collected on the Mexican mainland by Mr. Hornaday.

Note D, Chapter XXIII. In numbers the Cocupas are the most considerable Indian tribe in Baja California. So many of them, however, pass back and forth across the Colorado visting their kinsmen in Sonora that an accurate enumeration is impossible. I should consider three hundred a close estimate of the Baja California members of the tribe. The reputation of the Cocupas for peace has always been excellent and in sharp contrast to that of their neighbors, the Yumas and Yaquis.

Note E, Chapter XXIV. I had traveled some twenty-five hundred miles in the saddle besides an equal distance on the Pacific and the Gulf. Accepting local estimates, thirty-five hundred miles would be more accurate for the land journeying; the value of such estimates, however, has been commented upon in Chapter XV. Though I crossed the Peninsula eleven times, six days at the old Mission of Santa Maria and an equal time in Santa Rosalia were the longest rests made along the way. An idea of the arid nature of Lower California may be gathered from the fact that out of two hundred nights spent in the open, seventy were "dry camps."

As the reader of investigating mind may be interested therein I submit the following data not directly noted in the text, viz.: Beginning my wanderings in poor health, I experienced occasional periods of indisposition and dizziness during the first six weeks; after that I "got my second wind," concluding my adventures twenty pounds heavier than at the outset. Despite sleeping in rainstorms, numerous drenchings and sharp and sudden changes of temperature, I did not suffer from a single cold. And yet upon my visit to San Francisco in June, I was "sniffling" after the first night, sleeping indoors!

The varying, and not infrequently alkali, waters of the country seem to have no injurious effects on the system. Of foodstuffs I found broiled meats (whether fresh or dried), hardtack, flour-and-water *tortillas,* boiled rice with wild honey, stewed apricots, prunes and peaches, the most satisfying and wholesome. Of beans and cereals I shortly tired, while rice, which I rarely eat at home, was always acceptable. Not infrequently I experienced a childlike longing for candy or lump sugar. On the deserts I had little appetite, though I continually craved fresh fruits and vegetables and astonished myself by enjoying raw onions; in the sierras I greatly appreciated fatty meats and was always hungry. As I never care for tea, coffee or milk, I lived without such beverages. Moreover, I carried neither canned goods nor ham. Between antelope, bighorn and deer, native dried beef and the superabundance of ducks, doves, rabbits and quail, I ate but little bacon.

Finally, I used forty revolver and one hundred and ten carbine cartridges and nine hundred .22's. Of three cameras one, only, came through uninjured.

2. LOWER CALIFORNIA BIBLIOGRAPHY.

ANON. *Voyage of Mons. Chappe D'Auteroche to California to Observe the Transit of Venus.* London, 1778.

ANON. *Lives and Voyages of Drake, Cavendish and Dampier.* New York, 1832.

ANON. *Lives and Voyages of Early Navigators, with a History of the Buccaneers.* New York, 1835.

ANON. *Historical Outline of Lower California.* San Francisco, 186—.

ANON. *Lower California, Its Geography and Characteristics.* New York, 1868.

ANON. *A Real American.* "Bentley's Miscellany," Vol. LI, p. 210.

ANON. *Christian Work in the "Barren Peninsula."* "The Month," Vol. XVII, p. 454, 1872.

BAEGERT, JAKOB. *Nachrichten von der Amerikanischen Halbinsel Californien.* Mannheim, 1772. (English rendition, in part, by Dr. Charles Rau, published in Smithsonian Report, Washington, D.C., 1863.)

BANCROFT, H. H. *North American States,* Vols. I. and II, found in Bancroft's Works, Vols. X and XI (containing Bibliography to which reference is here made). San Francisco, 1884.

BARTLETT, JOHN R. *Personal Narrative of Explorations and Incidents Connected with United States and Mexican Boundary Commission.* New York, 1854.

BEECHEY, CAPT. F. W. *Narrative of a Voyage to the Pacific in the "Blossom," in 1825-8.* Philadelphia, 1832.

BELCHER, CAPT. SIR EDWARD. *Narrative of a Voyage Around the World During the Years 1836-42.* London, 1843.

BOWERS, DE MOSS. *An Island of Mystery.* "The Wide World Magazine." 1909.

BROWNE, J. ROSS. *A Sketch of the Settlement and Exploration of Lower California.* San Francisco, 1869.

BROWNE, J. ROSS. *Explorations in Lower California.* "Harper's New Monthly Magazine," October-December, 1868.

BUFFUM, LIEUT. E. GOULD. *Six Months in the Gold Fields in Upper and Lower California.* Philadelphia, 1850.

BURNEY, JAMES. *Chronological History of the Discoveries in the South Seas.* London, 1803-17.

BUSTAMENTE, C. M. *Historia de la Compañia de Jesus en Nueva-España.* Mexico, 1841-2.

BUTLER, BENJ. F. *In the Matter of the Lower California Company.* New York, 1873.

CABEZA DE VACA, ALVAREZ NUÑEZ. *Journey of, 1528-36.* English edition by Fanny Bandelier. New York, 1905.

CASTENADA. *The Journey of Coronado, 1540-2.* English edition by George Parker Winship. New York, 1904.

CLAVIJERO, FRANCESCO XAVIER. *Storia de la California.* (Spanish edition, Mexico, 1852.) Venice, 1789.

CLINCH, BRYAN J. *California and Its Missions.* San Francisco, 1904.

COSTANO, MIGUEL. *Historical Journal of the Expeditions to the North of California, 1768-70.* Translated from the Spanish. London, 1790.

DAMPIER, WILLIAM. *A New Voyage Around the World.* London, 1692.

DAVIDSON, PROF. GEORGE. *Submerged Valleys of California.* "Proceedings of the California Academy of Sciences," 3d Series, Geology I, p. 99, etc., 1897-1904.

DAVIS, RICHARD HARDING. *Real Soldiers of Fortune.* New York, 1907.

DE KAY, DRAKE. *In Relation to the Occurrences at Magdalena Bay, Lower California, Mexico.* San Francisco, 1871.

DELLENBAUGH, F. S. *Romance of the Colorado River.* New York, 1902.

DIAZ, DEL CASTILLO, BERNAL. *True History of the Conquest of Mexico.* English edition, London, 1800.

DIGNET, M. LIÓN. *La Basse Californie.* Annales de Géographie, Vol. IX. (1900), p. 243. Paris.

DOUBLEDAY, C. W. *Reminiscences of Filibuster War.* New York and London, 1886.

DOYLE, JOHN T. *Pious Fund of California.* "Overland Monthly," Vol. XVI, p. 239.

DUFLOT, DE MOFRAS. *Exploration du Territoire des l'Oregin, des Californies et de la Mer Vermeille* (containing Bibliography to which reference is here made.) Paris, 1844.

DUHAUT-CILLY, AUGUST. *Voyage Autour du Monde.* Paris, 1843-5.

DU PETIT, THOUARS. *Voyage Autour du Monde sur la Fregaté "La Venus."* Paris, 1840-4.

EISEN, GUSTAV. *Explorations in the Cape Region of Baja California.* "Bulletin of the American Geographical Society," Vol. XXIX, No. 3, p. 271, 1897. *Explorations in the Central Part of Baja California.* "Bulletin of the American Geographical Society," Vol. XXXII, No. 5, p. 397, 1900.

EL FLORECIMIENTO DE MEXICO. "Edición Ilustrada," 2 de Abril, de 1900, Mexico.

ELLICOTT, JOHN M. *Should We Possess Lower California?* "Overland Monthly," Vol. X, 2nd Series, 1890.

ELLISON, O. C. *In the Sea of Pearls.* "Sunset Magazine," December, 1905.

EMORY, WILLIAM H. *Report on the United States of Mexican Boundary Survey; U. S. Department of the Interior.* Washington, 1857-9.

ENCYCLOPAEDIA BRITANNICA. *California; subtitle, "Lower California."* Edinburgh, 1877.

ENGLEHARDT, FR. ZEPHYRIN. *Missions and Missionaries of California.* San Francisco, 1908.

EVANS, ADMIRAL ROBLEY D. *An Admiral's Log.* New York, 1909.

EVANS, TALIESAN. *South of the Boundary Line.* "Overland Monthly," Vol. II, August, 1873.

FACIO, M. SANCHEZ. *The Truth About Lower California.* San Francisco, 1889.

FERREL, BARTOLOMÉ. *Voyage of Cabrillo, 1542.* (English translation contained in Report upon U. S. Geographical Surveys west of 100th Meridian, Vol. VII, Archæology, pp. 299-314.) Washington, 1877.

FINDLAY, A. G. *Directory for the Navigation of the Pacific Ocean.* London, 1851.

FOLSOM, GEORGE. *The Despatches of Hernando Cortez.* London, 1843.

FORBES, ALEXANDER. *A History of Upper and Lower California.* London, 1839.

FREEMAN, LEWIS R. *A New Sportsman's Paradise.* "Western Field," San Francisco, 1904. *The Mountain Sheep in North America.* "Pacific Monthly," March, 1909.

GARCES. *On the Trail of a Spanish Pioneer, 1775-6.* (Edited by Elliott Coues.) New York, 1900.

GÓMARA, FRANCISCO LOPEZ DE. *Historia del Illustriss et Valorosus Capitano Don Hernando Cortez.* Rome, 1556.

GREENHOW, ROBERT. *Memoir of the N. W. Coast of North America.* Washington, 1840.

GRINDELL, E. P. *The Lost Explorers.* "The Wide World," August, 1907.

GRUNSKY, C. E. *The Lower Colorado River and the Salton Basin.* "Translations of the American Society of Civil Engineers," Vol. LVIII, p. 1, 1907.

HAKLUYT, RICHARD. *The Principal Navigations, Voyages and Discoveries of the English Nation.* London, 1589.

HAKLUYT, RICHARD. *The Principal Navigations, Voyages, Traffiques and Discoveries of the English Nation.* London, 1600.

HARDY, LIEUT. R. W. *Travels in the Interior of Mexico 1825, 1826, 1827 and 1828.* London, 1829.

HARRIS, CHARLES M. *A Cruise after Sea Elephants.* "Pacific Monthly," April, 1909.

HELLER, EDMUND. *A List of Mammals Collected by Edmund Heller in the San Pedro Mártir and Laguna Hanson Mountains, etc.* "Publication No. 79, Field Columbian Museum," June, 1903.

HITTELL, JOHN S. *History of the City of San Francisco.* San Francisco, 1878.

HORNADAY, WILLIAM T. *Camp Fires on Desert and Lava.* New York, 1908.

HUMBOLDT, ALEXANDER VON. *Essays on New Spain.* London, 1811-22.

IVES, LIEUT. J. C. *Exploration of the Colorado River.* Washington, 1861.

JAMES, GEORGE WHARTON. *The Colorado Desert.* Boston, 1906.

JOHNSON, W. F. *Four Centuries of the Panama Canal.* New York, 1907.

KATE, LE DOCTEUR H. TEN. *Matériaux pour Servir a l'Anthropologie de la Presqu'lle Californienne.* Paris, 1884. *Reizen en Onderzolkingen in Noord-Amerika.* Leiden, 1885.

LETTRES EDIFICANTES ET CURIEUSES, ECRITES DES MISSIONS ETRANGÈRES. Paris, 1716.

LAPEROUSE, JEAN FRANCOIS. *A Voyage Around the World.* Edinburgh, 1798.

LASSEPUS, ULISSES URBANO. *De la Colonización de la Baja California.* Mexico, 1859.

LE CONTE, JOHN L. *Account of Some Volcanic Springs in the Desert of the Colorado.* "Silliman's American Journal of Science," Second Series, Vol. IX, p. 1, May, 1855.

LEESE, JACOB P. *Historical Outline of Lower California.* New York, 1865.

LOS ANGELES TIMES. Mexican Number, December 19, 1903.

LUMMIS, C. F. *The Diary of Fr. Junipero Serra.* Edited in "Out West," 1902.

MACDOUGAL, DANIEL T. *Delta of the Rio Colorado.* "Bulletin of the American Geographical Society," Vol. XXXVII, No. 1, 1906. *The Desert Basin of the Colorado Delta.* "Bulletin of the American Geographical Society," Vol. XXXIX, No. 12, 1907.

MEXICO—SECRETARIO DE FOMENTO. *Exposición que hace El Secretario de Fomento sobre la Colonización de la Baja California.* Mexico, 1887.

MILLER, R. J. *Around the World with the Battleships.* Chicago, 1909.

MORRELL, CAPT. BENJAMIN. *Narrative of Four Voyages to the South Seas.* New York, 1832.

NORDHOFF, CHARLES. *Peninsular California.* New York, 1888.

NORTH, ARTHUR WALBRIDGE. *The Mother of California, Being an Historical and Geographical Sketch of the Little Known Land of Baja California.* San Francisco and New York, 1908.

NORTH, ARTHUR W. *Francesca of Mexicali.* "Sunset Magazine," September, 1905. *The Mother of California.* "Sunset Magazine," November 1906-January, 1907. *The Uncharted Sierra of San Pedro Mártir.* "Bulletin of the American Geographical

Society," Vol. XXXIX, No. 9, September, 1907. *Map of the Sierra of San Pedro Mártir.* "Bulletin of the American Geographical Society," Vol. XXXIX, No. 12, December, 1907. *Hunting the Bighorn.* "Sunset Magazine," October, 1907. *Resources of Lower California.* "Bulletin of the International Bureau of American Republics," Vol. XXV, No. 6, December, 1907. *Magdalena Bay.* "Sunset Magazine," March, 1908. *The Native Tribes of Lower California.* "American Anthropologist," new series. Vol. X, No. 2, April-June, 1908.

ORTEGA, JOSÉ DE. *Historia del Nayaret, Sinaloa, y ambes Californies.* Barcelona, 1754. Mexico, 1887.

OTONDO Y ANTILLON, ISIDORO. *Nouvelle Descente des Espagnols de l'Isle de Californienne.* Paris, 1685.

OTONDO Y ANTILLON, ISIDORO. *Some Discoveries Made in the Island of California in the Year 1683, contained in "A Relation of the Invasion and Conquest of the Floridas."* London, 1686.

PALOU, FRANCISCO. *Relación Historia, Etc.* Mexico, 1787.

PALOU, FRANCISCO. *Noticias de la Nueva California.* 1874.

PATTIE, JAMES O. *Personal Narrative of James O. Pattie of Kentucky.* (Cincinnati, 1833.) Reprint, Cleveland, 1905.

POLK, PRESIDENT JAMES K. *Extracts from Private Journal, 1847-8.* (Vide, American History Told by Contemporaries. 14th Paper, Vol. IV, edited by Albert B. Hart. New York, 1903.

POLK, JAMES K. Messages. (Vide, *Messages and Papers of the Presidents.*) Washington, 1900.

POWELL, J. W. *Seventeenth Annual Report of the Bureau of American Ethnology to the Smithsonian Institution.* Washington, 1898.

PRESCOTT, W. H. *History of the Conquest of Mexico.* New York, 1843.

RAMUSIO, GIOVANNI BATTISTA. *Terzo Volume delle Navigationi.* Venice, 1556.

Relación del Viaje hecho por las Galetas Sutil y Mexicana en el Año, 1792. Introdución por M. F. De Navarette. Madrid, 1802.

REEVE, J. K. *The Peninsula of Lower California.* "Lippincott's," Vol. LIII, p. 71, 1894.

REVERE, LIEUT. J. W. *A Tour of Duty in California.* Boston, 1849.

ROOSEVELT, PRESIDENT THEODORE. *Messages to Congress 1907.* Washington, 1907.

RYAN, W. REDMOND. *Personal Adventures in Upper and Lower California, 1848-9.* London, 1850.

SALES, LUIS. (F. L. S.) *Noticias de la Provincia de California en tres Cartas.* Valencia, 1794.

SALVATIERRA, JUAN MARIA. *Cartas.* (Vide, *Doc. Hist. Mexico,* Serie 2, Tom. I, pp. 103-57.) Mexico.

SALVATIERRA, JUAN MARÍA. *Relaciónes, California, Estab. y Prog. de las Missiones de la Antigua California.* (Vide, Doc. His., Serie 5, Tom. V, Ms. Mexico, 1791-2.)

SLADE, C. B. *Hunting Sheep and Antelope in Lower California.* "Outing," Vol. XXXIX, No. 5, February, 1902.

SOUTHWORTH, JOHN R. *Baja California, Illustrado.* San Francisco, 1899.

STEWART, W. F. *Last of the Filibusters.* Sacramento, 1856.

TAYLOR, PRESIDENT ZACHARY. *Messages and Papers of the Presidents.* Washington, 1900.

U. S. HYDROGRAPHIC OFFICE, Bureau of Navigation. *West Coast of Mexico.* Washington, 1880.

U. S. DEPARTMENT OF STATE. *Proceedings of the International (Water) Boundary Commission of the United States and Mexico.* Washington, 1903.

U. S. CONGRESS HOUSE DOCUMENTS, Vol. III, No. 1, *Foreign Relations, 1902, App. 2, Pious Fund of the Californias, 57th Congress, 2nd Session, 1902-3.* Washington, 1903.

VAN DYKE, T. S. *Sport on the Lower Colorado.* "Western Field," February, 1905.

VENEGAS, MIGUEL. *Noticia de la California.* Madrid, 1757. (English edition, entitled *Natural and Civil History of California.* London, 1759.)

WALKER, GENERAL WILLIAM. *The War of Nicaragua.* New York, 1860.

WELLS, W. V. *Walker's Expedition to Nicaragua.* New York, 1855.

INDEX